FORTUNE TELLERS

FORTUNE TELLERS

THE STORY OF AMERICA'S FIRST ECONOMIC FORECASTERS

Walter A. Friedman

PRINCETON UNIVERSITY PRESS

PRINCETON AND OXFORD

press.princeton.edu

Jacket art: (From left) Walter Babson, Irving Fisher, John Moody, Charles J. Bullock,
and Warren Persons. "James H. Brookmire's Barometer" (below, right) and
"Cycle Chart of Business and Banking" (bottom). Courtesy of Babson College Archives,
Yale University Manuscripts & Archives, *American Magazine* (September 1922),
Harvard University Archives, Brookmire Economic Chart Co., 1913.

Library of Congress Cataloging-in-Publication Data
Friedman, Walter A., 1962–
Fortune tellers : the story of America's first economic forecasters / Walter A. Friedman.
pages cm
Summary: "The period leading up to the Great Depression witnessed the rise of the
economic forecasters, pioneers who sought to use the tools of science to predict the future,
with the aim of profiting from their forecasts. This book chronicles the lives and careers of
the men who defined this first wave of economic fortune tellers, men such as Roger Babson,
Irving Fisher, John Moody, C. J. Bullock, and Warren Persons. They competed to sell their
distinctive methods of prediction to investors and businesses, and thrived in the boom years
that followed World War I. Yet, almost to a man, they failed to predict the devastating crash
of 1929. Walter Friedman paints vivid portraits of entrepreneurs who shared a belief that the
rational world of numbers and reason could tame—or at least foresee—the irrational
gyrations of the market. Despite their failures, this first generation of economic forecasters
helped to make the prediction of economic trends a central economic activity, and shed light
on the mechanics of financial markets by providing a range of statistics and information
about individual firms. They also raised questions that are still relevant today. What is
science and what is merely guesswork in forecasting? What motivates people to buy
forecasts? Does the act of forecasting set in motion unforeseen events that can counteract
the forecast made? Masterful and compelling, Fortune Tellers highlights the risk and
uncertainty that are inherent to capitalism itself"— Provided by publisher.
Includes bibliographical references and index.
ISBN 978-0-691-15911-9 (hardback)
1. Economic forecasting—United States—History. 2. Business forecasting—United
States—History. 3. Economists—United States—Biography. I. Title.
HC102.5.A2F76 2014
330.082′273—dc23   2013031457

British Library Cataloging-in-Publication Data is available

This book has been composed in Garamond Premier Pro

Printed on acid-free paper. ∞

Printed in the United States of America

1 3 5 7 9 10 8 6 4 2

For you, Susan Burgin

CONTENTS

||||||||||||||||||||||||||||||||

PREFACE
||||||||||||||||||||||||||

This book is about early attempts to develop ways to predict the economic future and to sell those predictions to managers, brokers, and individual investors. The modern forecasting field, which emerged in the early twentieth century, had many points of origin in the previous century: in the credit rating agencies, in the financial press, and in the blossoming fields of science—including meteorology, thermodynamics, and physics. The possibilities of scientific discovery and invention generated unbounded optimism among Victorian-era Americans. Scientific discoveries of all sorts, from the invention of the internal combustion engine to the insights of Darwin and Freud, seemed to promise a new and illuminating age just out of reach.

But forecasting also had deeper roots in the inherent wish of human beings to find certainty in life by knowing the future: What will I be when I grow up? Where will I live? What kind of work will I do? Will it be fulfilling? Will I marry? What will happen to my parents and other family members? To my country, to my job? To the economy in which I live? Forecasting addresses not just business issues but the deep-seated human wish to divine the future. It is the story of the near universal compulsion to avoid ambiguity and doubt and the refusal of the realities of life to satisfy that impulse.

Economic forecasting arose when it did because while the effort to introduce rationality—in the form of the scientific method—was emerging, the insatiable human longing for predictability persisted in the industrializing economy. Indeed, the early twentieth century saw a curious enlistment of science in a range of efforts to temper the uncertainty of the future. Reform movements, including good, bad, and ugly ones (like labor laws, Prohibition, and eugenics), envisioned a future improved through the application of science. So, too, forecasting attracted a spectrum of visionaries. Here were "seers," such as the popular prophet Roger Babson, Wall Street entrepreneurs, like John Moody, and genuine academic scientists, such as Irving Fisher of Yale and Charles Jesse Bullock and Warren Persons of Harvard.

Customers of the new forecasting services often took these statistics-based predictions on faith. They wanted forecasts, John Moody noted, not discourses on the methods that produced them. Readers did not seek out detailed information on the accuracy of economic predictions, as long as forecasters proved to be right at least a portion of the time. The desire for any information that would illuminate the future was overwhelming, and subscribers to forecasting newsletters were willing to suspend reasoned judgment to gain comfort. This blend of rationality and anxiety, measurement and intuition, optimism and fear is the broad frame of the story and, not incidentally, why forecasters who were repeatedly proved mistaken, as all ultimately must be given enough time, still commanded attention and fee-paying clients.

The importance of prediction in society is revealed by the many words used to describe it: to "divine," "augur," "foretell," and "prophesize" are but a few. To "prognosticate" is to predict from signs or symptoms, including in medicine. "Scrying," a fantastic but largely forgotten word, means trying to tell the future from gazing at a crystal ball or mirror.

To "forecast" is often differentiated from these, for it generally means to anticipate or predict a future condition or event through the analysis of data or through rational study.[1] To forecast is to make a prediction using tools not easily employed by the general public but requiring expertise. Especially after the growth of meteorology, "forecast" was routinely used in the late nineteenth century (as today) in conjunction with weather prediction. "The work of forecasting weather, and in particular of giving timely warning of destructive gales, is the first and most obvious practical application of meteorological science," wrote H. N. Dickson in *Meteorology* (1893).[2]

"Forecast" began to be commonly used for economic prediction in the early twentieth century. Today, modern economies are saturated with the word—in discussions of the stock market, gross domestic product, interest rates, housing prices, and innumerable other subjects. Within the term itself is the combination of scientific aspiration and an indication of older traditions. Both parts of the word, "fore" and "cast," carry significance. "Fore-" means simply "in front" or "beforehand" or "in advance." But the second part of the word is more interesting. "To cast," usually meaning to throw, is an important word, with a remarkable sixty-nine definitions in the *Oxford English Dictionary*. Among its various definitions is "To reckon, calculate, estimate," and this meaning appeared in Chaucer: "Of 25 yeer his age I caste." A similar definition is "to calculate astrologically, as to cast a figure, horoscope, nativity, etc.," and "to interpret (a dream)." In this sense, forecasting means to calculate the future before it happens. There is also another definition of "cast," though, which is "to put 'into shape' or into order; to dispose, arrange," as in a 1589 reference, "The sermon is not yet cast." Combining these two ideas, forecasting is at once the effort to discern the future before it happens; but it is also the ability to alter the very thing that one predicts. Embedded within the word is the ambivalent meaning of, in the case of economic forecasting, both predicting the economic future and shaping it. It was in both these areas—predicting and shaping—that the early twentieth-century forecasters sought to apply the tools of statistics and economics to solve the ancient problem of future uncertainty.

FORTUNE
TELLERS

INTRODUCTION
||||||||||||||||||||||||||||||||||||||||||||

In 1899, astrologer Evangeline Adams moved her business from Boston to New York's Upper East Side. Adams later wrote that her horoscope had directed her move, but Manhattan also had a greater concentration of her most lucrative and reliable clients: businessmen and investors in securities. When her hotel burned down shortly after her arrival, someone (possibly Adams herself, given her genius for self-promotion) informed the newspapers that she had predicted it the previous day, and she became a celebrity.

Over the next thirty years, many New Yorkers sought Adams's advice on market trends, anxious for any insight—however absurd its foundations—that might help them evade the ravages of economic turbulence. In addition to stock market tips, she offered advice on general business trends. She originated the Adams Philosophy, which she described as "a compound of truths of all truths, applied in the light of an intelligent optimism to the requirements of Western everyday life." A financial newsletter she began publishing in 1927 further broadened her reach, and she became a household name when she "correctly" predicted the stock market crash of 1929. By 1930 she was giving radio broadcasts on WABC and writing a regular newspaper column in the *Washington Post*. Most of the thousands of letters she received each day asked for advice about investing; prior to the Depression, most had asked about love. She died a wealthy woman in 1932.[1]

Even in her own time, many regarded Evangeline Adams as a fraud and scam artist.[2] Her success, however, points to a profound anxiety about the future. Capitalism, after all, is a uniquely future-oriented economic system in which people make innovations, apply for patents, watch interest rates, and in other ways "bet on the future."[3] The owners of capital deploy their resources—that is, they make investments—so as to maximize their future earnings. The early twentieth century was an unusually perilous time to make such investments, however. Entrepreneurs and big business had transformed

America from a predominantly agricultural society to an industrial one, and the pace of change seemed only to increase.

Amid all the wondrous new inventions of the age—steam-powered locomotives, electric-powered factories and lighting, automobiles, synthetic fibers (like rayon, which emerged in the nineteenth century), and so on—the unquenchable human longing for predictability and certainty persisted. Adams's story reflects an intense curiosity—and anxiety—over what the future held for the nation's increasingly industrial, integrated, and volatile economy.

More troubling than the pace of change was the degree of economic turmoil. Not only was the American economy being transformed at high speed, but periods of rapid growth and prosperity were interspersed with economic crises and depressions that destroyed fortunes, families, firms, and lives. Financial crisis was followed by severe economic hardship in 1837, 1857, 1873, 1893, 1907, and 1920—to say nothing of the events of 1929 and the Great Depression. Many attributed these downturns to speculation and to schemes by leading business titans and politicians. By the early twentieth century that type of thinking began to change. Entrepreneurs and academics began to define patterns of periodic fluctuations in production, employment, and other economic activity as the "business cycle." In 1915 Harvard Business School professor Melvin Copeland wrote, "It is now generally agreed by students of the subject that the ups and downs of business prosperity are due to deep-seated influences, and business men are more and more giving up the long persisting notion that changes in business conditions are caused primarily by tariff acts, political happenings, or court decisions."[4]

The unpredictability of the business cycle, however, was both a political and an economic problem. For businesspeople, downturns meant lower profits, decreased returns on investments, inventory gluts, and idle factories. For labor, the troughs of the business cycle could mean disaster. Few industrial workers had enough savings to last more than a couple of weeks, and unemployment quickly led to hunger, homelessness, and privation. The landmark clashes of late nineteenth- and early twentieth-century labor history tended to occur in periods of hardship. After 1917, the new Soviet Union loomed as a reminder that socialist revolution was a real alternative to capitalism if the economy became untenable as a result of violent swings.

For all of these reasons, the late nineteenth and early twentieth centuries saw a surge of interest in speculation about the uncertain future. Evangeline Adams and the promotion of astrology was one manifestation of this phenomenon. The rising popularity of works of futuristic science fiction, such as Edward Bellamy's *Looking Backward* (1887) and H. G. Wells's *The Time Machine* (1895) and *The War of the Worlds* (1898), was another demonstration of public interest in the future.

Academics and intellectuals shared similar concerns. Walter Lippmann, one of the period's preeminent public thinkers, argued in *Drift and Mastery: An Attempt to Diagnose the Current Unrest* (1914) that many of the era's problems stemmed from the incompatibility of old institutions and practices with a dramatically changed social and economic context.[5] In *Risk, Uncertainty, and Profit* (1921), the University of Chicago economist Frank H. Knight described an economy in which businesspeople constantly sought ways to gain control over their changing world. "At the bottom of the uncertainty problem in economics is the forward-looking character of the economic process itself," he observed. Plans for production, to give just one example, required predictions from the outset. "The producer ... must *estimate* (1) the future demand which he is striving to satisfy and (2) the future results of his operations in attempting to satisfy that demand."[6] Knight wrote that businesspeople tried their best to reduce the amount of risk in society by purchasing insurance, by forming trust companies, and by improving their bookkeeping and other methods of management. Despite these measures, many aspects of business and life remained uncertain, including when the next economic crisis would hit.

FORECASTERS

This is a book about a group of entrepreneurs who, like Evangeline Adams, identified a business opportunity in the anxiety about the economic future that pervaded the early twentieth century. It is a story, in part, about how fortune telling was professionalized. Unlike Adams, whose insights into the future rested on her purported ability to read the stars, the entrepreneurs profiled here were statisticians and economists who based their predictions on their claim to systematic scientific insight. This book describes the first generation of economic forecasters and the methods they created to predict the future of the economy.

The forecasting field was initially developed by entrepreneurs like Roger Babson and John Moody following the Panic of 1907, as businesspeople were forcefully reminded, yet again, of the ups and downs of the economy. By World War I, there were only about ten forecasting agencies operating in the United States. Professional economists, like Irving Fisher and Warren Persons, advanced the field after the war, joining the growing ranks of forecasters. By 1925, Fisher wrote, "We now have nearly fourscore forecasting agencies to help the business man."[7]

These forecasters emphasized what today we would call the "real economy"—upcoming changes to production, employment, trade, and services—rather than trends in the stock market. They usually distributed their predictions in weekly bulletins that carried relevant business news and economic indexes. Along with their predictions, forecasters often included charts and graphs that showed economic change over time and pointed to the future. These had various names, such as Babson's Composite Plot and the Harvard Economic Service's Index of General Business Conditions.

Forecasters also devoted time to sales and marketing. Successful forecasting agencies developed ways to publish, distribute, and advertise their predictions. Some forecasters built sales forces to travel from office to office in lower Manhattan or in Boston and Chicago. Others sent their representatives to Rotary Clubs and churches in smaller cities and towns to give lectures. Nearly all forecasters advertised in the *New York Times*, the *Wall Street Journal*, the *Commercial and Financial Chronicle*, and the *Chicago Tribune*. Some forecasters packaged snippets of their forecasts to be sold through news syndicates and to appear in daily newspapers such as the *Alton (Illinois) Evening Telegraph*, the *Salt Lake Tribune*, and the *Montana Standard* of Butte.

While entrepreneurs and academics developed the industry, the American government also became deeply involved. Herbert Hoover, in particular, proved to be a big advocate of forecasting. He pushed the Department of Commerce, which he headed from 1921 to 1928, to increase the amount of economic data that it collected and published. He made it a priority of government to study the nature of business cycles and to bring business executives to Washington, D.C., to improve their ability to spot upcoming trends.

Together, these actors—entrepreneurs, academics, and politicians—helped raise the stature of economic forecasting and embed the practice in every corner of business and government. They sought to create a distinction between the "respectable" profession of scientific forecasting, on the one hand, and the practices of fortune telling and speculation, on the other. In this effort they enjoyed wide institutional backing. Courts of law routinely supported those who made predictions based on dispassionate scientific rules rather than those who, say, enlisted the help of the stars.[8] Many U.S. jurisdictions established statutes prohibiting the practice of "occult arts" in fortune telling. In a typical prosecution dating from 1918, a woman was arrested in New York and charged under the state Code of Criminal Procedure (section 899-3); she was found to be a "disorderly person" who was *pretending* to tell fortunes."[9] Despite her fame, Evangeline Adams lived under constant threat of such legal action.

Forecasters' reliance on science and statistics as methods for accessing the future aligns their story with conventional narratives of modernity. The German sociologist Max Weber, for instance, argued that a key component of the modern worldview was a marked "disenchantment of the world," as scientific rationality displaced older, magical, and "irrational" ways of understanding. Indeed, the forecasters profiled in this book certainly saw themselves as systematic empiricists and logicians who promised to rescue the science of prediction from quacks and psychics. They sought, in the words of historian Jackson Lears, to "stabilize the sorcery of the market."[10]

The relationship between the forecasting industry and modernity was an ambivalent one, though. On the one hand, the early forecasters helped build key institutions (including Moody's Investors Service and the National Bureau of Economic Research) and popularize new statistical tools, like leading indicators and indexes of industrial production. On the other hand, though all forecasters dressed their predictions in the garb of rationality (with graphs, numbers, and equations), their predictive accuracy was no more certain than a crystal ball. Moreover, despite efforts of forecasters to distance themselves from astrologers and popular conjurers, the emergence of scientific forecasting went hand in hand with rising popular interest in all manner of prediction. The general public, anxious for insights into an uncertain future, consumed forecasts indiscriminately.

PREDECESSORS

For all their novelty, the forecasters of the early twentieth century did not emerge out of nowhere. The preceding two or three centuries, and particularly the nineteenth, were a period of activity and progress for a wide variety of predictive endeavors. Economic forecasting drew on a prehistory of three overlapping though distinct streams: changes in climate-related prediction, advances in quantitative business techniques and information gathering, and developments in economic theory.

Nineteenth-century innovations in meteorology were powerfully suggestive for the first generation of economic forecasters, though the meteorologists drew on different bodies of empirical data and theoretical techniques. Natural philosophers of the Renaissance and earlier investigated atmospheric phenomena, but the science of meteorology did not systematically engage with the subject of prediction until the mid-nineteenth century. It was only then, with the development of a long-distance telegraph network, that empirical observations about the winds could arrive in advance of the winds themselves.[11] In 1849, the United States initiated the first state-sponsored network of climate observatories under the Smithsonian Institute, followed within a decade by similar efforts in France, Belgium, and Britain. The methods of the nineteenth-century weather forecasters were largely superseded after the turn of the century by the work of Norwegian scientist Vilhelm Bjerknes, who developed equations for the hydro- and thermodynamics of the atmosphere.[12] Regardless of its lasting scientific value, however, nineteenth-century weather forecasting became a fruitful site for debates on the relationship and value of deductive and inductive approaches to the study of complex systems or, as contemporaries called it, the practices of speculation versus observation.[13] One contribution to this burgeoning science, John Tice's *Elements of Meteorology* (1875), inspired Samuel Benner's *Prophecies of Ups and Downs in Prices* (1878), which, in turn, shaped Roger Babson's approach to economic prediction. Moreover, many forecasters, including Babson and James H. Brookmire, borrowed terms from meteorology, calling their charts "business barometers."[14]

Business and economic forecasting owed more obvious debts to nineteenth-century advances in the quantity and quality of business information and statistics. Commercial and banking houses had compiled charts of commodity prices and exchange rates for centuries, allowing merchants to practice a simple time-series analysis to stay abreast of the rate of change. From the mid-nineteenth century, commercial publications—most notably London's *The Economist* (from 1843) and New York's *Commercial and Financial Chronicle* (from 1865)—published regular updates on prices and other financial data. Parliamentary efforts beginning in 1797 to comprehend the rise and fall in the reserves of the Bank of England led to innovation in index numbers and in some of the first moving averages.[15] In the United States, business statistics grew significantly in the late nineteenth century. The American Railway Association published a monthly bulletin that included freight car haulings and idle car figures. Import and export statistics were printed in the *Monthly Summary of Commerce and Finance*; bank statistics, in *Bradstreet's* and *The Commercial and Financial Chronicle*.[16] John Moody drew heavily on the work of John M. Bradstreet and other business-information analysts in forming his approach to forecasting.

Early twentieth-century forecasters also built on the work of economists, including those who described themselves as political arithmeticians. Under Oliver Cromwell, William Petty (1623–87) offered the first rigorous assessment of a country's national income and wealth, looking beyond stores of gold and silver to consider both stocks of wealth and the flows issuing from them. In 1660, with the restoration of the House of Stuart, cloth merchant John Graunt offered Charles II analyses of national birth and death statistics.[17] In the nineteenth century, the English economist William Stanley Jevons (1835–82) enlisted mathematical techniques in one of the earliest statistical analyses of the business cycle. His paper titled "Commercial Crises and Sun-Spots" (1878) linked economic fluctuations to harvest and meteorological conditions.[18] In his 1892 Yale dissertation, economist and forecaster Irving Fisher described Jevons as a major influence.[19]

CAPITALISM AND COMFORT

The forecasters profiled in this book developed their businesses in this rich and vibrant context of efforts to predict the future. In doing so, they drew on meteorological, commercial, or economic traditions—and most often some combination of them. But they also created something new. Roger Babson, Irving Fisher, John Moody, C. J. Bullock, Warren Persons, and their contemporaries were the first to envision the possibility that economic forecasting could be a field, or even a profession; that the systematic study of a vast range of statistical data could yield insight into future business conditions; and that a market existed in business and government for weekly economic forecasts. The first generation of forecasters found ready audiences for their predictions. Executives at large firms like United States Rubber, National Biscuit, and American Tobacco were eager to gather all sorts of statistical information from outside analysts, as well as from their accountants and finance departments, as they coordinated the work of their sales, manufacturing, and purchasing departments.[20]

Brokers and financiers also purchased forecasting newsletters. In the nineteenth century, most firms had financed their operations through retained earnings, but increasing numbers now did so by borrowing from banks or issuing corporate bonds and other financial instruments. New brokerages seemed to open almost daily in New York City after the turn of the century, remarked one observer, to raise capital for new enterprises or fund the expansion of existing ones. In 1913, for instance, roughly $1.5 billion of American bonds were issued, almost all of which passed through U.S. bond houses.[21]

Finally, forecasters also found a growing market for their predictions among individual investors. At the start of the twentieth century, only 500,000 Americans owned stocks; by the end of the 1920s, that figure had increased twenty times to 10 million. That works out to less than 1 percent of the adult population in 1900 versus 12 percent in 1929.[22] The rise in stock ownership was a result of increasing wealth and strong marketing campaigns, including the World War I Liberty Bond drive, that advocated securities ownership.

Forecasters promised to help people make money and profits in an economic system that seemed especially chaotic and unpredictable—and at the same time seemed to offer great potential returns. They reassured investors, bankers, and managers in large part because they promised that the trends of prosperity and depression were decipherable.

More broadly, forecasters offered comfort to those who feared that capitalism, as an economic system, was too dangerous and volatile. Forecasts, after all, were more than predictions of the future. They were assumptions about what the economy was and how the economy worked. By pointing out trends in data and creating charts and models, forecasters made capitalism seem natural, logical, and, most of all, predictable.[23]

Such reassurances were significant during a time when the idea of a democratic capitalist economy was under great threat in many regions of the world. Some social scientists thought that democratic capitalism was merely a temporary form of government that would give way to something better—either a utopian socialist state or a technocracy.[24] The realities of the early twentieth century were far more brutal. World War I was especially bloody, with some nine million casualties. Europe was left with an array of political systems:

thirteen republics and thirteen kingdoms, many of which were constitutional monarchies. And the war's aftermath continued to be a period of violent revolution and civil war, most notably in Russia. Other countries, including Germany, Poland, France, and Italy, had active communist parties. In the 1920s and 1930s several European countries took far-right turns to fascism, including Italy, Spain, and Germany. By the late 1930s, dictators ruled much of Europe.[25]

Comparing Biographies

Rather than relating the emergence of forecasting in a chronological format, *Fortune Tellers* adopts a more biographical approach. Each chapter tells the story of one influential forecaster. Chapters 1–3 focus on, in turn, Roger Babson, Irving Fisher, and John Moody. Each of these forecasters represented a different way to make predictions and to make sense of the economy. Chapter 4 looks at the team of Charles J. Bullock and Warren Persons, who led the Harvard Economic Service, and their effort to build economic "observatories" around the world.

Chapter 5 takes up the work of economist Wesley Mitchell and his role in Herbert Hoover's Business Cycle Committee at the Department of Commerce. This chapter details the role of the state in promoting and enabling the forecasting industry. As commerce secretary, Hoover sought to provide objective and precise data to improve the ability of business managers and business analysts to make forecasts. This, he believed, would lead business-people to employ countercyclical strategies to lessen the extremes of the business cycle.

This book crosses the traditional boundaries between the history of economic thought and cultural history. The scholarly contributions of Irving Fisher, for instance, are described alongside the commercial exploits of Roger Babson, who believed that Newtonian forces determined the movements of the economy (what comes up must come down). An entirely different history of forecasting could be told that emphasized the work of business cycle analysts or economists, such as Joseph Kitchin or Holbrook Working, in improving analytical and conceptual approaches to forecasting in this period.[26]

Fortune Tellers, by contrast, leaves aside the narrative of progress in economic science. It focuses instead on the lives of the entrepreneurs who advertised, marketed, and promoted their predictions to the general public. For example, Roger Babson, Irving Fisher, and John Moody were all popular authors and columnists who wrote on a range of topics, including health and religion. Fisher, not unlike his English contemporary John Maynard Keynes of Cambridge, was an avid investor; and both of the Harvard scholars examined here (Charles Bullock and Warren Persons) had careers on Wall Street as well as in Harvard Yard. This mixture of commerce and academia is not incidental: one interest informed the other, and together they reveal a portrait of a society preoccupied with the problems of uncertainty and money-making.

The individuals profiled in this book were chosen in part because of their contemporary significance—Roger Babson, for example, boasted the greatest circulation for his forecasting newsletter—but also because they each understood the logic of capitalism differently. Each one looked at a growing amount of information on the U.S. economy on prices, manufacturing output, crop production, interest rates, and other statistics. Each came up with different ways to harness these data to pierce the mysteries of the future, whether by looking at historical trends, analogies, and expectations or by other methods.

Each of the forecasters, too, had a different view of science—the intellectual and practical approach that would help eliminate uncertainty from the economy. For Roger Babson, "science" meant investigating the application of the theories of Sir Isaac Newton, especially Newton's third law of motion, to economic phenomena. For Irving Fisher, it meant the pristine world of mathematics and its power to reveal causal relationships. For John Moody, "science" meant transparency and the nearly limitless gathering of business information about industries and markets. For C. J. Bullock and Warren Persons, at Harvard, the scientific method meant observation, especially the careful monitoring of change over time in critical economic sectors, such as securities prices, production figures, and interest rates.

The enlistment of scientific order, of all types, helped forecasters create their models and their visions of the economy. But it also led some of them, at times, to embrace social engineering schemes, including Prohibition and eugenics, that had large followings at the time. Sherwood Anderson's 1919 novel, *Winesburg, Ohio*, captured the darker aspects of this part of American society in this period. He depicted a town in which people, during a time when ideas were rapidly changing, became obsessed with a single truth, holding onto it until it dominated and disoriented them. Anderson described his obsessive characters as "grotesques," a harsh term, but one that captures the dangers that could result from single-minded determination and zeal for control amid a world in flux.[27]

The story of modern economic forecasting begins with Roger Babson, who, more than anyone else, helped invent this complex figure, the "forecaster."

CHAPTER 1

Roger W. Babson: The Rule of Past Patterns

||||||||||||||||||||||||||||||||||||||||||||||||||||||||||||||||||||||||||||||||||||

oger Ward Babson (1875–1967) was an unlikely founder of today's economic forecasting services. Academic economists tend to dismiss his
contributions to the field. John Kenneth Galbraith ridiculed Babson's forecasting methods as "hocus-pocus" and "mysticism," and even contemporaries
regarded him as a confirmed eccentric.[1] George W. Coleman, a longtime
business associate, described Babson in 1929 as "a unique personality, complex and baffling to a high degree," possessed of a "restless, driving energy."[2]

Babson actively promoted dubious social engineering schemes ranging
from the prohibition of alcohol to bizarre dietary reforms and eugenics. He
was a serial entrepreneur, starting or acquiring businesses for manufacturing
commodities as diverse as fire-alarm boxes, paper towels, sprinkler systems,
and gravel. A longtime sufferer from tuberculosis, he redesigned his own home
and office to maximize the flow of fresh air. Babson's lifelong admiration for
Isaac Newton culminated in his acquisition of the world's second largest collection of Newtonia (behind only Cambridge University) and the founding
in 1948 of the Gravity Research Foundation, an organization dedicated to
researching the pull of gravity—with the hope of one day overcoming it. The
study of gravity, Babson thought, would help scientists find a way for man to
fly without using an airplane and to create a perpetual motion machine.[3]

Yet Babson's outsized personality contributed to his achievements as an
economic forecaster. His eccentricities—like the folksy, avuncular voice with
which he dispensed both business predictions and chestnuts of financial
wisdom—had the effect of humanizing his forecasts. *Babson's Reports*, the
weekly newsletter Babson and his staff produced from his hometown in the
Boston suburbs, was among the first to use systematic statistical analysis of

economic data to predict future economic conditions. In it, Babson published statistics on production and manufacturing achievements, bank clearings, stock-exchange transactions, business failures, immigration rates, import and export levels, and gold prices, among other miscellaneous information. Starting in 1911, Babson combined several different types of time-series data into a compelling graph of economic activity, called the Babsonchart, which he relied on to predict the direction of national business activity. Taken together, Babson's graphs and commentary offered his readers a new conception of "the economy" as a complex but unified system that operated according to its own internal logic and hence could be predicted by means of sustained, systematic study.

Most ordinary Americans at the turn of the twentieth century did not subscribe to the notion that prices, currencies, employment rates, and other variables were part of an interrelated, national economy. The economic booms and busts of the previous century were typically ascribed not to any sort of regular business cycle but to fate, the weather, political schemes, divine Providence, or unexpected shocks like new tariffs or earthquakes.[4]

Roger Babson, drawing in part on nineteenth-century writing on commercial cycles, saw things differently. Week after week, his newsletter explained to its readers that economic events were neither random nor uncertain but governed by forces that could be understood through careful study. He began issuing regular forecasts after the Panic of 1907. By 1910 he was one of the *New York Times*'s featured commentators on economic affairs. Babson sought to increase the participation of small-time American investors in the marketplace. He built a large sales force to market his newsletter in cities and towns and sent representatives to give talks on the mechanics of the business cycle at regional churches and chambers of commerce.

Academic economists justifiably regard much of Babson's science as suspect. But to leave it at this is to misunderstand his contribution. Babson did not so much push forward the frontiers of economic theory as identify an appetite. At the turn of the twentieth century, Americans harbored an insatiable demand for information that could shed light on future economic conditions. Perhaps more than any of his competitors, Babson met this demand, and he made himself rich in the process. He offered prognostications on everything from prices to employment to sales. After Babson, the forecaster was an instantly recognizable figure in American business.

GETTING STARTED

Babson's entrepreneurial upbringing equipped him with a nose for opportunity that would later bring him to economic forecasting. Babson's father sold dry goods in the seaport town of Gloucester, Massachusetts, which, at the time of Roger's birth in 1875, had a population of fourteen thousand. Roger traveled with his father by horse and buggy to local towns to sell items and collect bills. His father was a shrewd but conscientious man who kept regular hours, was prompt in paying and collecting bills, and imparted business advice, especially on the importance of sound investment for the future—the area in which Babson built his career. "He explained to me that the world's greatest invention was six per-cent compound interest, which goes on twenty-four hours a day, seven days a week, and fifty-two weeks a year," recalled Babson in his 1935 autobiography.[5]

In his mid- and late teens, hardship and tragedy forced Babson to become self-sufficient. In 1890, when Babson was fifteen, his father suffered a nervous breakdown and retired from active business. To help out, Roger worked installing electric doorbells and took a part-time job on a highway construction team. In 1893 Roger's thirteen-year-old sister Edith drowned in a local pond. Babson's father tried to revive her but failed. Roger was away when it happened; he had traveled to see the Chicago World's Fair and only managed to return to Gloucester after the funeral. The death "cast a shadow" over his family that "never wholly passed," he later wrote.[6] He would name his first and only child after her.

After finishing Gloucester High School in 1894, Babson followed his father's advice and attended the Massachusetts Institute of Technology (MIT), then located in Boston's Back Bay. Now the nation's leading institution for science and engineering and located in Cambridge, at the turn of the twentieth century "Boston Tech" was primarily a trade school.[7] In 1935, Babson recalled that he had "hated the place and all the courses." The institution, he felt, was stodgy, unimaginative, and devoid of vision. The faculty included "the ablest men in their respective fields ..., yet these professors and instructors apparently entirely overlooked the great industries which were to develop in the twenty years following my graduation." No one at the school, he charged, was perceptive enough in the late 1890s to see in the horseless carriage—then mostly a novelty—the great automobile industry that would develop after the turn of the century or anticipate the demand for the phonograph that the Edison and Victor companies were then marketing. His professors also failed to foresee the importance of the "moving-picture machine," radio, or air travel, despite the advances in all three technologies during his time as an undergraduate. Instead, he continued, MIT taught railroading, electrical engineering, chemistry, and other "fully-developed subjects."[8] While Babson's recollection is self-promotional, it nonetheless captures his sense of restlessness at the institution.

Despite his impatience with hidebound academics, Babson discovered at MIT several of the intellectuals who would influence his later forecasting. The main professor to exert a lasting influence on Babson was George F. Swain, a civil engineer who served on state commissions to inspect railway bridges. Swain was, by accounts of former students at MIT and later at Harvard (where he moved in 1909), a brilliant and rigorous thinker. Swain is best known for his book *How to Study* (1917) and for his articles on statistics and on manufacturing.[9] Along with encouraging Babson's interest in the fields of engineering and statistics, Swain trained him to use a laboratory-oriented collaborative approach to research, a skill Babson employed when he founded Babson Statistical Organization. Babson's forecasts were produced by teams of statisticians, working together on large tables reminiscent of the MIT laboratory.[10]

Swain also introduced Babson to the works of Isaac Newton (1642–1727), the great English mathematician, astronomer, and alchemist, who became, for Babson, the embodiment of scientific wisdom.[11] Throughout his career, Babson would try to associate his own economic writings with Newton's scientific insights, especially those about gravity. Though these associations were superficial in nature, Babson's admiration was sincere. He and his wife spent a fortune acquiring books once owned by Newton and other Newtonia. In 1953 Babson acquired a graft from the apple tree under which Newton supposedly discovered gravity when the apple hit his head. The tree stands today on the Babson College campus in Wellesley, Massachusetts, where it is surrounded by a metal gate and decorated by a plaque.[12]

SELLING BONDS

After graduating, Babson found work at the financial firm E. H. Gay, which had offices in Boston and New York. Babson began his career in the bond industry, the largest sector of the investment business around the turn of the century. In 1913, more than $1.5 billion in bonds were marketed in the United States. Bonds were the chief source of funding for states and municipalities for public works, for the railroads, and for many industrial corporations.[13] Bond houses were increasing in number in New York City, Boston, and elsewhere to raise capital for new enterprises or fund the expansion of existing ones.

Babson's first job was to sort and index a pile of bond circulars his employer had collected for months. Babson then briefly went into the bond-selling business for himself in New York but without much success.[14] In 1901 he began working for a former partner of Gay's, Charles Cummings, who specialized in selling public-utility bonds. The company was involved in financing the Syracuse Lighting Company, the Utica Gas & Electric Company, and a large dam on a waterway in upstate New York.[15] These were significant projects that had the potential to provide essential services for these regions, but they also presented scheming entrepreneurs with the opportunity for speculation and fraud.

The securities business taught Babson two lessons he would carry with him for the rest of his career in the forecasting trade. The first was a cynicism toward the financial world, particularly that centered in Wall Street. Babson believed that the vast majority of companies in the transportation and electric industries were organized to sell securities rather than transport people or generate power. He also became aware of the extent to which aggressive salesmanship shaped the market and even determined prices.[16]

The second lesson had to do with the growing complexity of American business and of the investment industry in particular. Sorting and indexing his employer's great heap of miscellaneous bond circulars, Babson had realized the potential demand for a more systematic presentation of the growing volume of business information. In the years after 1900, the number of bond offerings was increasing dramatically and more companies were hiring clerks and occasionally statisticians to track them. In 1913, one expert noted that the attitude of Wall Street firms was changing: "One of the greatest houses on the street may still have no statistical department, except that which is carried home nights under one or two well-rounded hats; but on the other hand, a firm of national reputation and esteem has recently admitted into partnership a man whose claim to the distinction is his profound railroad scholarship."[17] The growing number of businesspeople who had attended either college or a commercial school (like Folsom's Mercantile College, where John D. Rockefeller studied bookkeeping) helped stimulate the interest in analyzing business statistics.[18] As the number of available statistics grew, so did the demand for people who could make sense of them and decide which were worthwhile and which not.

The "Man Who Would Not Die"

These lessons helped shape Babson's career, which, at the turn of the century, was just beginning. For a time, however, personal life took precedence. In 1900, Babson married Grace Knight and they bought a house in Wellesley, outside Boston.[19] Grace was the daughter of a preacher, the Reverend Richard Knight. She had briefly attended Mount Holyoke College and was working as a nurse at Massachusetts General Hospital when Babson married her. Babson's reflections, in his autobiography, about the union were not particularly romantic. "It was a mixture of human nature, sex urge, and true love, without any of these forces predominating," he wrote.[20] But she was a "good partner" who played a significant role in many of Babson's plans.

After the wedding, the two moved to a new home in Wellesley. But the marriage was soon tested. In the fall of 1901, Babson contracted what seemed to be a cold that lingered for many months. In February 1902, at the age of twenty-six, he learned that he had tuberculosis—a disease that then affected millions of Americans, including forecasters Irving Fisher and Warren Persons. Although the pathology of the disease was well-known by 1902, effective therapies were few until the discovery of the antibiotic streptomycin in 1946. Before then, consumptive patients could do little more than seek out fresh air. Patients lived, ate, and slept outside, even in the depths of winter, in the hope that cold, dry air would send the disease into remission. Sometimes the fresh air cure helped, but even after years or decades of remission, dormant tubercular lesions in the lungs or elsewhere could become active again. From the patient's perspective, a diagnosis of tuberculosis was not so much a death sentence as a sentence to a life in limbo. As medical historian Sheila Rothman wrote, "almost every aspect of consumption was marked by an uncertainty that bred apprehension and bewilderment."[21] In search of a milder climate and higher altitude, Roger and Grace Babson, like many others at the time, traveled west to Colorado Springs and eventually to California. They returned to Wellesley within two years, however, to see if Babson could recover at home in the New England winter.

Babson's disease played an important role in his choice of career. Large, dense cities were thought to be unhealthy for tuberculosis sufferers, so, on his return from the West, Babson resolved to start a business out of his suburban home. Inspired by a speech he heard by Booker T. Washington in Wellesley advising young people to specialize narrowly in a single field rather than spreading themselves too thin, Babson decided to make his contribution in the nascent field of business statistics.[22]

While working in the securities industry, Babson had seen how financial firms were giving increasing time and attention to the compilation and analysis of information. Every bank, investment house, and brokerage laboriously compiled and analyzed bond listings, and Babson saw that there was much duplication of effort. It would be far more cost-effective for firms to outsource the collection and distribution of market data to a specialized company. Babson was neither the first nor the only entrepreneur to recognize the growing demand for such publications at the time. The business information industry was quickly emerging at the time, with Henry Varnum Poor as the true pioneer of the field; he had started publishing financial information, including earnings, on railroads in the mid-nineteenth century.[23] New Jersey native John Moody had published a manual of statistics about industrial companies since 1900. The leading business periodicals were the *Wall Street Journal*, which had been founded in 1889, and the *Commercial and Financial Chronicle* (1865). But there was no single source of information on all bond offerings, so Babson decided to enter that field.

At age twenty-nine, Babson founded the Babson Statistical Organization with a total capital of $1,200 for the purchase of a typewriter, an adding machine, and office supplies.[24] Babson's first business product was the Babson Card System. It provided to subscribers descriptions on individual index cards of bonds offered by different companies. He soon started a parallel service with information about stocks.[25] These products lowered the cost that firms had traditionally paid when they gathered this information on their own. Babson directed the Babson Statistical Organization from his home, where he could attend to his health by making fresh air a priority. He designed a special winter coat, with a slot for a heating pad in the back, and slept with the windows open throughout the year. He worked outside and required the

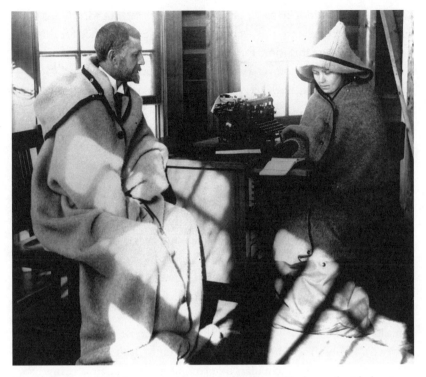

Roger Babson, c. 1912. After contracting tuberculosis, Babson liked to work with the windows open, even in cold weather, and designed coats for himself and his staff to wear. Source: Babson Collection, Babson College.

same of his assistants, mostly young women from the town. In cold weather, Babson remembered, his assistants wore robes and mittens and hit the typewriter keys with "rubber hammers."[26] Grace Babson also played an important role in her husband's business, serving as treasurer for many years.

The Babson Statistical Organization displayed the gender stratification that was typical of the early forecasting profession and the rest of the early twentieth-century financial world. Women were present, but they tended to play supporting roles. Some, like Grace Babson, or Irving Fisher's wife, Margaret Hazard Fisher, were spouses whose time or inherited wealth was pressed into the service of their partners' enterprises. Others, like the young women Babson employed as his assistants, were part of the broader feminization of the clerical workforce in the decades around 1900. Between 1900 and 1930, the proportion of women in paid clerical positions in the United States and

Canada doubled from 26 to 52 percent.[27] Babson's second wife, Nona Margaret Dougherty, fell into this second category. She had worked for the Babson Statistical Organization for a quarter century when she married her eighty-one-year-old employer a year after Grace Babson's death in 1956.[28]

For the most part, however, these women remain anonymous, with the exception of the occasional staff list or photograph. The public face of forecasting—like other realms of the investment world—was overwhelmingly male. A few women, like Hetty Green (1834–1916), demonized as the "Witch of Wall Street," made an impact on Wall Street as successful investors; a few others, like Evangeline Adams, managed to create an audience for their predictions with their unique astrological insights. It was exclusively men, however, who claimed insight into the future on the basis of science and statistics.

As his health improved, Babson began taking sales trips to Cleveland, Detroit, Chicago, St. Louis, and New York. "I made the trips myself to the banks and bond houses of Boston, and got on the mailing lists of all vendors of securities in other cities wherever located," recalled Babson in 1935. "The cooperating subscribers also gave me the use of the bond offering circulars which came in to them. Hence we became a clearing-house for the firms which employed us."[29] Babson's clients paid $12.50 per month (or about $140 per month in today's dollars) for his circulars that compiled data on new offerings.[30]

Babson's first customers were members of the financial industry, including the investment bank Kidder Peabody and a number of other Boston-area brokerage houses. Babson soon launched a wide array of publications related to the securities industry, including a separate service listing municipal bonds. He also published pocket-sized books for salesmen, *Bond Offerings*, which listed a large number of corporate bonds along with the houses trading them.[31] Finally, Babson showed an early interest in educating the public about financial investments and started a correspondence course on purchasing bonds, a move that presaged his later interest in business education.[32]

THE PANIC OF 1907

Babson's early career gave him the financial know-how and the yen for statistics that he would later draw on when he turned to forecasting. It was the Panic of 1907 that accelerated his interest in that field.

The Panic was particularly perplexing to many observers, as it seemed to come without warning. The episode is known as the Banker's Panic, in large part because of its evolution. In 1907, a group of industrialists and financiers hatched a scheme to corner the market on copper—that is, to purchase enough of the commodity's stock to be able to manipulate its price. Though this group, headed by F. August Heinze and his brother Otto, failed, they sparked a panic among investors, who sought to liquidate their shares. Runs followed on the deposits at two of the largest New York City trust companies: the Knickerbocker Trust and the Trust Company of America. Many of the city's banks failed, including the Empire City Savings Bank, the First National Bank of Brooklyn, and the Williamsburg Trust Company. The effect was calamitous. The Dow Jones Industrial Average lost 48 percent of its value from January 1906 to November 1907.[33]

In 1908, the crisis deepened. Annual pig-iron production declined 39 percent from 1907 to 1908; bank clearings fell 45 percent; and with only 3,654 miles added in 1907, new railway lines were down 40 percent over the same period.[34] Financial writer Alexander D. Noyes noted that part of the reason for the resulting alarm was that existing wisdom in financial circles, due to the strength of banks and to efficiencies in industry, held that panics were a thing of the past: "The opinion then entertained by these practical banking experts ... was that 'aggregation of banking resources' and 'coordination of industry' had, between them, created a new economic situation, where old-fashioned financial and commercial panics, such as those of 1893, 1873, and 1857, would be no longer possibilities."[35]

J. P. Morgan and other New York financiers pledged large sums of their own money to help restore confidence. Morgan gathered prominent New York bankers and other financial leaders in a meeting room in his home, keeping them there until they agreed to help. Among those assembled were George F. Baker, president of First National Bank; James Stillman, of the National City Bank of New York; and Secretary of Treasury George B. Cortelyou. Standard Oil titan John D. Rockefeller also deposited $10 million in National City Bank. This helped raise confidence and lessen the sense of crisis. But afterward, Morgan's maneuvers raised concern about the powers of New York City bankers—and eventually helped garner support for the 1913 formation of the Federal Reserve, a central banking system pledged to promote the nation's financial stability.[36]

Babson happened to be in New York during the bank runs. He was not a speculative trader—he regarded the stock market as little better than a casino—but as a seller of business information publications, he visited Wall Street regularly to peddle his publications to investment firms and private investors. Babson, accustomed to his offices in leafy suburban Wellesley, later recalled the scene as dramatic: "On that day I actually saw men turn gray."[37] But Babson's thoughts were not on the traders he saw tearing their hair out. Rather, his thoughts turned toward the "hundreds of thousands of thrifty investors throughout the country who saw their savings wiped out." In that moment, he later claimed, he resolved to devise a way to alert those frugal souls to the economic storms looming on the horizon.

The Panic inspired Babson to move from merely reporting business information to analyzing its implications for the future. Starting in 1908, Babson published his forecasts of general economic conditions in a weekly newsletter, *Babson's Reports*, which he sold for $7.50 per month. The following year, the Babson Statistical Organization began offering similar information in book form, as *Business Barometers*, a title that was updated regularly—typically every year or two, though less frequently after the mid-1930s—until 1961, six years before Babson's death.

Babson was one of the first economists to publish periodic indexes of what economists would later call the "macroeconomy."[38] Babson created a category he called "business activity," which was composed of aggregate statistics, such as crop production or new railroad mileage, rather than the financial data of individual firms.[39] He argued that most brokers paid attention only to facts related to specific companies, including statistics on their debt and earnings, but not statistics related to industrial or agricultural output.

Babson thought that company-specific information could be helpful in determining *which* securities to purchase but useless for knowing *when* to buy or sell them profitably.[40] For Babson, that was the bigger problem, as the Panic of 1907 revealed. Babson urged investors to purchase a diversified portfolio of securities that they could hold for years; but, ideally, the real challenge was purchasing at the ebb of a cycle and selling at the crest.

Babson was an early believer in the idea of the "business cycle." In a 1910 article for a social science journal Babson wrote that "all financial history" consisted of distinct cycles of four phases: a period of prosperity; followed by decline; then depression; and then improvement. The "world's trade," Babson continued, could not maintain a state of equilibrium. All of human history had experienced such swings. "Joseph with his seven fat years and his seven lean years expressed nothing more," Babson mentioned, referring to the passage in Genesis 41 when Joseph makes a prophecy for the fate of Egypt.[41] The role of the forecaster was to figure out in which phase of the cycle an economy currently resided.

Babson's Precedents

Babson's ideas about forecasting were shaped by current theories of investing advice that early market watchers had circulated in the late nineteenth and early twentieth centuries. One such guru was Charles Dow, who died in 1902 but whose ideas about investing remained popular afterward. Dow, cofounder of the *Wall Street Journal*, wrote a number of articles on the importance of trends in indexes of securities prices that could be used to predict movements. His followers cobbled these together to form the Dow Theory, an active investment management strategy that is regarded as the foundation of modern technical analysis. Dow's theories were, in particular, kept alive by William Peter Hamilton (1867–1929), who edited the *Wall Street Journal* in the 1910s and 1920s.

But Dow's adherents and Babson differed over which series were significant and how to interpret them. Dow believed that the prices of securities embodied the knowledge and expectations of all investors about their true value and hence could be used to forecast changes in the real economy. Therefore, Dow concluded, the course of economic booms and busts could be discerned by looking at the stock market, especially the Dow Jones Industrial Average (an index of twelve stocks that Dow himself had created in 1896).[42] Babson came to the opposite conclusion: the stock market was subject to the whims of speculators, while the real economy could not be fooled.

Far more important to him was the work of Samuel Turner Benner (1832–1913), a popular economic prophet who had gained a following in the late nineteenth century, when financial panics were frequent, and had developed a deep connection between financial forecasting and meteorology. In 1906, one of Babson's Wellesley neighbors had given him a copy of *Benner's Prophecies of Future Ups and Downs in Prices* dating from the 1880s. Babson liked the practical nature of Benner's work, whose central message was the importance of good timing for sound investments: "There is a time in the price of certain products and commodities, which, if taken by men at the advance, leads on to fortune; and if taken at the decline, leads to bankruptcy and ruin," wrote Benner.[43] Babson believed that Benner, "without doubt, clearly foretold the panics of 1884 and 1893, and the prosperous years intervening."[44]

Like Babson, Benner was something of an eccentric. Contemporaries often referred to him as "the Ohio farmer." In 1925, a bookshop employee remembered him, a half century before, as rural and unsophisticated, "an old fellow with his pants in his boots," who was eager to market his predictions. As with Babson, economic crisis—in this case the Panic of 1873—spurred Benner's interest in cycles of boom and bust.[45]

For Benner, commodities were the key to predicting the rise and fall of business conditions. Benner's family, formerly prosperous hog and corn farmers, had operated charcoal furnaces in the iron ore section of southern Ohio. In 1876, Benner printed a pamphlet called *Benner's Prophecies of Future Ups and Downs in Prices: What Years to Make Money on Pig Iron, Hogs, Corn, and Provisions*.[46] In it, Benner predicted the directions of average annual prices in future years: "the average price of No. 1 foundry charcoal pig-iron in the markets of our country will be higher in the year 1878 than in 1877" and "the average price of fat hogs in the markets of our country will be lower in the year 1876 than in 1875." Benner also made forecasts of business panics, writing in the 1870s, for instance, of "a commercial revulsion, and a financial crisis in the year 1891"—a crisis that did not in fact arrive until 1893.[47]

Benner was a preacher of the doctrine "As Iron Goes the Market Goes."[48] He regarded iron prices as the key to America's overall economic health and hence as predictors of periods of panic and expansion. Iron was "the most useful of all metals, in fact the bone and sinew of our civilization." It was, he continued, "the most important element of progress." Without it, the sewing machine, reaper and mower, spinning jenny, power loom, steamboat, railroad, and land and submarine telegraph all would have been impossible. "Pig-iron," he concluded, "is the barometer of trade, and as the sudden falling of the mercury denotes violent changes in the atmospherical world, so does the periodical decline in the price of pig-iron indicate panic, depression, and general stagnation in business."[49] Indeed, Benner used mystical language to describe the power of the metal, which when awoken from the "slumber" of a depression brought the whole economy up with it. "AROUSE, PIG-IRON!" Benner exclaimed in one passage of the book. "Monarch of business! Come forth from the chambers of thy slumbering silence, the dawn of a new era is at hand! Hogs, corn, and cotton fall into line, and start in motion the wheels of commerce, industry, and trade!"[50]

Benner believed that the length of the price cycle of iron, with periods of growth and decline, was fifty-four years. He called this the Cast Iron Rule and asserted that similar price cycles existed for other commodities. This rule, "when applied to pig-iron, hogs, corn and provisions, is as persistent as the attractive and repulsive forces of the magnet."[51] As his language indicates, Benner thought that economic patterns were like seasons, or like planetary movements, and needed only to be understood.

Benner's work shows the strong connections between economic forecasting and the emergent field of meteorology. He was influenced by the writings of contemporary meteorologists who traced the movements of planets and were guided by astrological assumptions. Benner's book came out a year after John H. Tice's *The Elements of Meteorology* (1875), which emphasized the role of planets in causing weather cycles—and which Benner cited as an inspiration.[52] In later years, Babson and other forecasters, like the St. Louis native James H. Brookmire, borrowed the term "barometer" when describing their economic indexes. Indeed, their whole conception of the economy was atmospheric. Forecasters could observe patterns and look for clues but could not alter future economic events. Benner also helped popularize the forecasting price chart, with a single-line graph that represented the seemingly sharp up-and-down turns in the market.[53]

Benner found an audience among investors, speculators, manufacturers, and entrepreneurs. *Benner's Prophecies of Future Ups and Downs* went through fifteen editions and continued to be published until 1905, with little variation in content. One advocate for the book was John H. Patterson, head of the National Cash Register Company, a major business leader of the late nineteenth and early twentieth centuries and the mentor of IBM's president, Thomas J. Watson. Patterson frequently consulted Benner's book and took from it two lessons: that a "business cycle" existed and that one needed to be wary of the depression that would follow prosperity. Patterson came to follow pig-iron prices closely: "He read the pig-iron quotations every day of his life and had them tabulated.... Whenever he found that the junk men were eagerly buying scrap iron, he made ready for an advance in business."[54] The well-known Wall Street financier and market bear Henry N. Smith was also said to follow Benner's advice.[55] The *Wall Street Journal* associated Benner

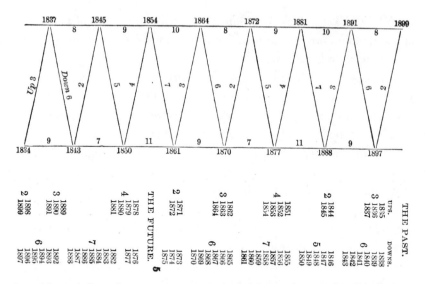

Samuel Benner's chart of pig-iron prices, 1875, revealed the past (1835–75) and the future (1876–97). The chart embodied Benner's idea of a fixed natural cycle in the average annual price of pig iron, a cycle that he also believed mapped perfectly to overall business activity. The price cycle went as follows: 3 years up; 6 down; 2 up; 5 down; 4 up; 7 down. This would then be repeated: 3 years up, 6 down, etc. Source: Samuel Benner, *Benner's Prophecies of Future Ups and Downs in Prices: What Years to Make Money on Pig Iron, Hogs, Corn, and Provisions* (Cincinnati: Published by the author, 1875).

with meatpacking magnate Philip Armour and Charles Henrotin, president of the Chicago Stock Exchange, suggesting that he advised them in making investments.[56]

Despite his illustrious supporters, a 1904 article in the *Wall Street Journal* revealed skepticism mixed with attention to Benner's prognostications. "Although Wall Street professes to be above superstition and although it poohpoohs prophecies and ridicules prophets, there is one seer who usually commands general attention in the Street," the article noted, characterizing Benner as something of a guru, a figure of interest, not entirely taken seriously. "Wall Street laughs at 'Benner's Prophecies,' but it always reads them closely."[57]

Academics later accorded Benner some respect for his pioneering efforts. In 1939, Harvard Business School historian N. S. B. Gras commented in *Business and Capitalism*, "The advisers of business … had constantly in mind the business cycle of three years or of ten years but rarely thought of the secular trend in business, though Benner who began his studies in the 1870s had the general idea and even attempted to mark off the ups and downs in a chronological table."[58] Joseph A. Schumpeter, in a footnote in his *History of Economic Analysis* (1954), noted, "[T]here were several contributions that, though they passed unnoticed, foreshadow later developments. The 'hog cycle,' e.g., was discovered by S. Benner as early as 1876."[59] The economic historian Arthur H. Cole noted, in the *Business History Review* (1961), that a comprehensive study of economic fluctuations would include "a history of increasing sophistication anent the phenomenon called the business cycle from Samuel Benner downward."[60]

The Babsonchart

Following the Panic of 1907, Babson took Benner's book to his old MIT professor George Swain. The two of them pored over this and other books on financial prediction and speculation, and Babson developed charts similar to Benner's, using new data from pig iron and corn and hogs. Swain then gave Babson the idea of including a "normal" line separating the high and low points. He also suggested to Babson that the new chart called to mind Sir Isaac Newton's work on equal-and-opposite reactions. With that, the idea of the Babsonchart was born.[61]

Babson followed several of Benner's tactics. The most important was Benner's belief that past patterns, found in statistical series, would repeat into the future. Compelling visual presentation was another technique the Wellesley oracle borrowed from the "Ohio farmer." Babson's forecasting methods came to rely on a system of graphing the ups and downs of his aggregate variables— much like Benner's schematic graph of the vacillation in iron prices.

But Babson's forecasts moved beyond Benner's Cast Iron Rule in several ways: basing his forecasts on many combined data series instead of one; getting rid of the idea that cycles were fixed in duration and timing; and producing his reports weekly rather than annually. He called the resulting graph the Babsonchart, or at times the Compositplot, publishing the first in 1911 and at regular intervals thereafter.

To create his chart, Babson followed three basic steps. First he collected a wide array of business statistics, beginning with twelve data series on manufacturing, construction, crop production, railroad haulings, and other figures indicative of industrial production. To this he added a number of miscellaneous statistics: on business failures, bank clearings, commodity prices, and stock market prices.

The second step in creating his chart was to combine these different series into a single number, a "barometer" figure, representing the health of the general economy.[62] To do this, he evaluated how each of his data series was changing: Were manufacturing levels rising or falling? What about crop production? Though Babson never spelled out his exact method of combining data, he explained that change itself—that is, the extent and direction of change—was the important factor rather than the actual numbers. The use of percent change allowed Babson to render a range of variables into similar units, rather than their real values in pounds, bushels, prices, and so forth.

The final step was the placement of the "normal line." This was the innovation recommended by his mentor, George Swain, and was intended to show whether the economy was functioning above or below its "natural" level— and hence indicating if a potential boom or depression were under way. Babson considered the idea of a normal line to be a major contribution to the analysis and forecasting of business conditions. Without it, Babson would not have been able to graphically separate areas of "action" and "reaction" or to convey a sense of economic equilibrium.[63]

In order to place the normal line correctly, Babson relied on an idiosyncratic application of Sir Isaac Newton's Third Law of Thermodynamics— that for every action there is an equal and opposite reaction. Babson believed that as science progressed, it would be discovered that Newton's laws of physics governed not just the actions of, say, a tennis ball tossed in the air and then falling to earth but every realm of the social sciences as well. Correspondingly, Babson placed the line in such a way that the plot of aggregate business activity would reveal, on a graph, an area of economic "expansion" following an equal area of "recession" fluctuating above or below a line representing normal growth.

To formulate predictions, Babson invented the Area Theory. He argued that in order to make an accurate prediction, the time of a fluctuation (either a recession or an expansion) must be multiplied by its severity in order to determine what might come next (*Time × Intensity = Area*). In a letter of October 7, 1915, Babson explained to a colleague that "[w]hen the two factors of time and intensity are multiplied to form an area, the sums of the areas above and below said line of normal growth X-Y must, over sufficiently long periods of time, be equal."[64] In other words, a sharp, short depression could

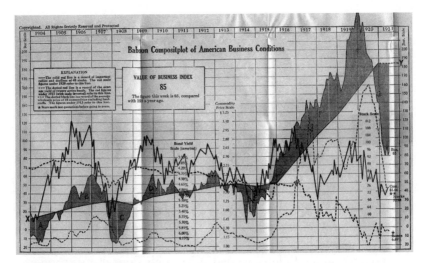

The Babsonchart, from 1921. The large shaded areas marked A, B, C, D, E, F, and G represent depressions below and expansions above the "normal" line. Babson believed that areas of expansion (B, for instance) would be equal to areas of recession (C, for instance) that followed. While the chart contained a variety of statistics, it emphasized measures of industrial production. The chart also contained a wealth of other information, including stock prices, bond prices, and commodity prices. Source: Roger W. Babson, *Business Barometers Used in the Accumulation of Money* (Wellesley Hills, MA: Babson Institute, 1921), inset.

be followed by a long, shallow expansion. The placement of the normal line was determined by adjusting it to form "equal" and "opposite" areas on the graph.[65]

Babson therefore treated the Area Theory as a universal truth. It was not an idea to be tested.[66] Babson moved the normal line in order to create equal and opposite areas; they did not arise from the data. This was an important point that many of his readers, who simply gazed at the chart, could easily have missed.

Along with the main line showing business conditions, the Babsonchart also contained graphs of stock and bond prices. These, Babson felt, gave clues to the upcoming turning points in the general economy. As he noted directly on his chart, Babson believed the high points of the stock market came in the early part of the "overexpansion area." The low points came during the early parts of the depression. Similarly, high bond prices predominated at the end of the depression area and low bond prices at the end of the overexpansion period.

Babson's forecasting method was a combination of science and scientism. The Area Theory, with its bow to Newton, was little more than a dressed-up version of the obvious observation that markets go up and down over time. Babson believed that the relationship of Newton's theory of action-reaction was related to the business cycle via the psychology of the masses and particularly the tendency of most people to follow the herd and act without rational self-control. "Business conditions depend chiefly on what men do," wrote Babson.[67] Periods of economic depression produced a discernible impact on people's minds. In an era of depression, mills were idle, there was little demand for goods, and prices were low. Reduced consumption was caused by a lower pool of wages but also by a feeling of "hard times," which induced people to save rather than to spend. As a depressed climate spread, men and women abandoned the purchase of any type of luxury good and concentrated on necessities. Failures abounded. The only firms that survived were the efficient, low-cost producers of essential products.

Conversely, a period of prosperity made businesspeople and consumers careless. Consumers overspent, buying new cars or second homes, and luxury sales increased. Using the language of action-reaction to explain economic behavior, Babson wrote, "As the natural reaction of adversity is economy, thrift, industry, and temperance, so the reaction of prosperity is to make men extravagant, wasteful, self-indulgent and careless."[68] His writing reveals a tendency to imbue economic performance with moral significance.[69]

According to Babson, exuberant booms were thus caused by wastefulness and speculation. Improved efficiency and sensible spending could lessen these fluctuations perhaps, though they would not eliminate them entirely. Hard times also served as a useful corrective to excess. This was not an uncommon position at the time. As Herbert Hoover recalled in his memoirs, a large portion of his administration, led by Andrew Mellon, the treasury secretary from 1921 to 1932, believed in the remedying qualities of "liquidation" during hard times. As Mellon's logic went, "It will purge the rottenness out of the system. High costs of living and high living will come down. People will work harder, live a more moral life. Values will be adjusted, and enterprising people will pick up the wrecks from less competent people."[70] But Babson took the emphasis on character still further. The best way to lessen the severity of cycles, Babson thought, was through the spread of Christian humility and temperance, and even through the breeding out of "unfit" Americans through eugenics, a movement Babson heartily endorsed. Babson also became heavily active in promoting business education, creating correspondence courses and eventually founding three colleges (the Babson Institute, Webber College for women, and Utopia College).

Despite its failings, the Babsonchart and the newsletter it appeared in, *Babson's Reports*, familiarized a broad readership with the idea of a national economy and its depiction in numbers and graphs. The Babsonchart brought "the economy" vividly to life for an audience accustomed to regarding prices, currencies, employment rates, output, and other variables as separate and often local phenomena rather than parts of an interrelated system. In Babson's chart, everything was exhibited: stock prices, bond yields, and a "business activity" index. Babson's chart aimed to provide businesspeople a sense, at a single glance, of the economic "weather" in ways similar to a meteorological map.

Babson compared his forecasting system to the invention of wireless telegraphy, which would, for instance, warn a ship's captain of coming storms: "Of course, the captain of an ocean liner wants to know what the weather is today, and carefully writes a description of it in his log, but primarily he is interested in what the weather will be tomorrow."[71] Together, Babson's charts and maps represented business conditions as a complex interrelated system. He often used nautical themes in his work, calling his employee newsletter *Log of the Crew* and placing a merchant ship on the Babson Institute's coat of arms.

Babson felt that businesspeople focused too narrowly on information that related to their own region—a jeweler in Cleveland, for instance, only cared about conditions in that city—and needed to consider national economic statistics as well. Moreover, businesspeople were interested only in statistics related to their specific product line. Babson proposed that merchants and manufacturers needed to recognize that "each business, even although apparently local, is dependent on the business of the entire country" and, moreover, that "each business is dependent on the condition of business in other lines."[72] A banking crisis in New York might mean a loss of credit for entrepreneurs in other parts of the country. This work helped promote a sense of a national, interconnected economy.

PREDICTION AND PERSUASION

After starting *Babson's Reports*, Babson began to sell off some of his other news services. In 1913 he sold his *Circular* of bond offerings to Arthur Elliott, who formed the National Quotation Bureau; this went on to become an important product on Wall Street, known as "pink sheets."[73] He offloaded *Moody's Manual* (acquired in 1907) to Roy W. Porter in 1914, though he remained involved in its operation. In 1913, Babson sold the Babson Card Service for the large sum of $60,000 to a new firm, the Standard Statistics Bureau (later part of Standard & Poor's).[74]

Babson then set out to grow his forecasting business. Babson wrote that his early marketing efforts entailed "remarkable selling" on his part. "Shoe leather and doorbell-ringing were … important factors."[75] In January 1910, for instance, Babson journeyed through several cities, including Buffalo, Chicago, Cleveland, New York, Pittsburgh, and St. Paul. He made a careful list of subscribers in a small pocket-sized notebook: Fidelity Trust, Cleveland Trust, First National Bank, A. G. Edwards & Co., Third National Bank, E. F. Hutton, and Lazard Bros.[76]

Babson organized a sales force and opened offices in large cities across the country. In 1912 he organized agencies to sell *Babson's Reports* in London, Paris, and Berlin. At the start of World War I in 1914, 20 percent of his clientele was in Europe.[77]

Part of Babson's selling strategy was to make important friendships. Babson promoted the service to well-known individuals, like Thomas Edison, with whom he struck up a correspondence on the subject of gravity and other topics. In 1907, he wrote the sixty-year-old inventor (who was twenty-eight years Babson's senior) that he had arranged a complimentary subscription to *Babson's Reports* and that Edison could expect to receive the Babsonchart every Tuesday. He also had "ordered a plate glass sent you which you can put on the table back of your desk in the library to keep the sheets under. Each week a new sheet will be sent you in a mailing tube and will you kindly instruct your secretary to remove the old sheet and throw the same away inserting under the glass the new sheet." With the Babsonchart filed under glass, Edison could easily compare a graph of his own personal investments to the ups and downs of Babson's graph. This was the method Babson recommended to his clients—a somewhat dubious exercise. Edison, though, replied: "Many thanks for your offer. I will run your statistics now and then … and see what I can screen out."[78]

Babson became a sought-after public speaker, and the newspapers reported his predictions as newsworthy events. He talked to audiences about trends in crop production, new construction rates, business bankruptcies, and other forms of economic activity, and offered investment advice.[79] By the time World War I broke out, Babson was a leading market guru.

Babson advertised heavily for subscribers to his newsletter, describing his company in 1910 as the largest statistical organization in the United States. He also wrote dozens of articles per year, including one for a gardening magazine intended to reach women investors, and many on business conditions for the *Saturday Evening Post*.[80] He developed a close working relationship with the *Post*'s editor, George Lorimer, and in article after article predicted the future of America's industries: leather goods, steel, paint and varnish, and maritime. In 1915, Babson earned $20,000 from Curtis Publishing for his writing (about $462,000 today).[81]

The *New York Times* inflated his importance, introducing him in July 1910 in the following way: "Roger W. Babson, lecturer on economics at Harvard, the University of Pennsylvania, the Massachusetts Institute of Technology, and the London University, is a statistician of prominence."[82] Although Babson may have given a talk at these schools, he never held a formal position at any of them.

Newspapers also helped establish Babson as a wise and somewhat moralizing expert who railed against speculation, excessive consumption of luxuries, and gambling and drinking. Babson used his ability to survive tuberculosis to reinforce his message about the value of hard work and determination. A number of publications—including the *Saturday Evening Post* and *American Magazine*—ran stories about the "man who refused to die."[83]

Babson's reputation took off in the years between the Panic of 1907 and World War I. He wrote a series of articles in 1910 for the *New York Times* in which he established himself as a specialist in economic crises—past, present, and future—and distinguished himself from the mere stock market commentator, differentiating his work, which emphasized output and industrial production, from that which dealt only in securities. In the article "Recoveries from the Famous Panics of America," Babson wrote: "I ... like to ignore stock market panics, as the ultimate growth of our Nation does not depend upon the stock market, but upon general business, and therefore it is wise for us all to broaden our horizon and consider not simply Wall Street but all of the mercantile houses on Broadway, the factories and industries up the State, and the farms throughout the entire Nation."[84] The idea that output is the best way to measure the economic health of a nation is something that most economists today believe, though of course they measure it differently than Babson.

World War I

The U.S. entry into World War I in April 1917 forced Babson to suspend his business expansion. He took leave of his statistical organization to work for the U.S. government. Ultimately the experience and contacts he gained in Washington opened his eyes to the variety of data the government was collecting, taught him the power of propaganda on a new scale, and allowed him to raise his business empire to still greater heights after the war ended.

In turn, the U.S. government gained much from statisticians and economists during the war. At the start of the conflict, the federal government lagged behind private entrepreneurs in knowing how to chart, distribute, and interpret economic data.[85] Statistics available during the war were haphazardly collected and inadequate in their coverage.[86] When President Woodrow Wilson declared war, for instance, there were at least twenty separate data-gathering bureaus in Washington—most of which were narrow in their mission and acted independently of other bureaus.

Accordingly, when war was declared, the government moved to co-opt the expertise of management experts for the war effort. Mobilization bore the unmistakable stamp of American fascination with efficient management systems. Economists and statisticians brought to Washington new ideas about creating statistical portraits of the mobilization effort and increasing the efficiency of labor. Harvard psychologist Robert Yerkes persuaded the surgeon general to administer his Alpha and Beta tests, devised to measure general intelligence, to 1.75 million army soldiers.[87] Industrial psychologist Walter Dill Scott of the Carnegie Institute of Technology helped the army select officers by means of his "mental alertness" tests, originally devised to aid personnel departments in the selection of salesmen.[88]

Among the most important efforts in the collection of data were undertaken by statistician Leonard Ayres in the Council of National Defense and by Harvard Business School's Edwin Gay, who served as chair of the Central Bureau of Planning and Statistics of the War Industries Board. Ayres, for instance, oversaw the creation of about 230 organizational charts to help create a sense of order in the chaos of Washington. Edwin Gay promoted the use of cost accounting as a way to improve the economic efficiency of organizations.[89]

After Armistice, economist Wesley Mitchell, who worked with Gay and headed the Price Bureau of the War Industries Board, underlined the war's importance for the field of economic statistics. "The war forced a rapid expansion in the scope of federal statistics and the creation of new statistical agencies," he recalled. "What is more significant, the war led to the use of statistics, not only as a record of what had happened, but also as a vital factor in planning what should be done."[90] The war experience made government officials aware of the value of accurate data to inform decision making—and especially the need for improved government methods of estimation and forecasting.[91]

Babson was part of this group of experts. Appropriately enough, given his talents at marketing and publicity, Babson first worked briefly for the Committee on Public Information under George Creel, a Denver newspaperman selected by Woodrow Wilson to mobilize public opinion about the war. The committee gained notoriety for its cruel depictions of barbaric Germans and for its efforts to suppress antiwar sentiment. Babson spent most of his time in the Poster and Pay Envelope Division of that organization, designing propaganda posters and writing patriotic messages that were tucked inside employee pay envelopes.

But his most important wartime work was for William B. Wilson, the secretary of labor, where he served as director-general of the Bureau of Information and Education. Unlike some business executives who declined compensation for their war work, Babson was not a dollar-a-year man: his salary was $5,000 per year ($75,000 today).

Like his work under Creel, his job was to sell the war to employers and wageworkers. The "immediate purpose of this service was to promote sound sentiment in industrial plants to combat unsound industrial philosophies, and to acquaint the public with the national war labor program of the Government," Babson wrote in 1919.[92] He gathered statistics and stories about the successes of mobilization. He hired speakers to give patriotic talks to workers throughout the country and made short motion pictures. He also supervised the making of inspirational artwork for factories and public buildings. The bureau operated on a large scale: the short pieces written by bureau staffers on industrial production and extraordinary achievement were sent to 150 newspapers throughout the country, with the goal of reaching 12 million readers per day; the bureau enlisted a volunteer speaking force of 400 in an effort to stimulate production, reduce turnover, and stifle protest; and the poster division distributed 700,000 to 1,000,000 posters monthly.[93] This was an extraordinary education for Babson about scale production.

Through his war work, Babson deepened his acquaintance with the newspapers, news agencies, employers, and union leaders. He had the opportunity to correspond with and meet governors, mayors, and a range of businesspeople in order to gain their support for the war. Babson also observed the strategy behind the marketing of Liberty Bonds, which included the use of dramatic posters, mass sales rallies, celebrity endorsements, and other tools of mass marketing. "The war taught us the power of propaganda," Babson recalled.[94] These lessons, combined with a renewed appreciation for the power of centrally collected statistical information, were put to use in his postwar business endeavors in forecasting.

BABSON IN THE "NEW ERA"

The period from the end of World War I until the Great Crash of 1929 was a golden age for business forecasting, and for Babson in particular. The number of stocks available to investors increased dramatically, making each individual investment decision complex. "Chewing gum or cheese; hairnets or socks; hats, shoes, underwear, shirts, collars, toothbrushes—the modern investor, small or large, can be a partner in any kind of business that suits his particular fancy," noted a contemporary commentator.[95] The fastest-growing companies were the industrial organizations, such as the oil and steel and automobile companies, which sought large pools of investors. (In 1900, AT&T had 7,000 shareholders; by 1920, it had 140,000. U.S. Steel had 54,016 in 1901 and 154,243 in 1928; in these same years, the number of shareholders at Procter and Gamble rose from 1,098 to 37,000.)[96]

As the securities market boomed, the business information industry grew along with it. Babson found he had competition in the forecasting field. John Moody's weekly business bulletin, which had started in 1909, continued to gain subscribers. The Harvard Economic Service's *Weekly Letter* began publication just after World War I. Luther Blake, at the Standard Statistics Bureau in New York, started publishing predictions in a *Daily Trade Service*. At the Cleveland Trust Company, the statistician Leonard Ayres gained a national reputation as a forecaster by editing the bank's *Business Bulletin*, a four-page publication that began in 1920.[97] That same year, Richard D. Wyckoff formed Wyckoff Analytical Staff Inc., promoting theories of forecasting based on Charles Dow's earlier work on stock market trends. In the mid-1920s,

In 1919 *Babson's Reports* moved into this new administration building, having outgrown its previous headquarters. Source: Babson Collection, Babson College.

Yale economist Irving Fisher began to publish a weekly "Business Page," which contained his predictions.

Despite the growing competition, Babson returned to Wellesley with high expectations for his forecasting business and for statistical analysis in general. "Just as the Civil War was followed by an advance in practical mechanics, the World War will, in my opinion be followed by an advance in practical economics," he wrote in 1922 to President Warren G. Harding (in one of the many letters he sent to U.S. presidents throughout his career). "As never before, business men will strive to act upon facts and figures rather than guesswork and hunch."[98]

Over the course of the 1920s, Babson built a series of interconnected businesses to serve the demand for information. In that decade, he also founded two private colleges to offer business training. Though Babson named Leroy Peavey as president of the Babson Statistical Organization in 1925, he continued to direct the company in an informal capacity for decades.[99] All of the Babson businesses were headed by the same person, the face and personality of the organization. Though he delegated much of his work, he also felt personal ownership of each enterprise. Babson, for instance, carried a key that allowed him access into any building on the grounds of his college.[100]

Babson created something of a kingdom in Babson Park, the name he gave to the part of Wellesley he owned. He built a cluster of businesses, with media outlets, a news-reporting syndicate, his first business college, and a publishing enterprise. Babson purchased an interest in the Boston, Worcester & New York Street Railway Company, which provided public transportation between Boston and points west and south. In the mid-1920s, he opened a radio station in Wellesley to broadcast religious programs and advertise Babson's products. Babson brought several family members into the financial news industry at this time, including his cousin David L. Babson, who worked on *Babson's Reports* in 1928 after graduating from Harvard College. He sold the *United States Bulletin*, which he acquired from the government after World War I, to another cousin, Paul T. Babson, renaming it the *United Business Service*.[101] Paul would later become a vital part of the Babson organization before eventually building his own substantial businesses in statistical information—and, in 1939, orchestrating the formation of Standard & Poor's. Babson coached Paul, advising him of the need to be innovative in the financial news industry rather than a bland recorder of facts. "I have always taken the position that the difficulty with Poor's was that it lacked an individuality," Roger wrote to Paul of a rival publication. This criticism could not be leveled against Roger Babson himself.[102]

In 1920, the Babson Statistical Organization had about 12,000 subscribers, bringing in revenue of about $1.35 million.[103] Some of these subscribers bought multiple specialized Babson products, including the *Speculative Bulletin*, the *Commodities Bulletin*, the *Industries Bulletin*, and the *Labor Bulletin*.[104] At that time, the organization (now with about three hundred employees) was divided into three sections: a production department, which researched and wrote the weekly reports; a marketing department, which included the salesmen and the advertising staff; and an administrative department, which was made up of accountants and bill collectors, numbering eighty altogether. Of all employees, slightly more than half were women, although the sales staff contained only men.[105] The marketing efforts were intense and systematic and involved direct mailings and the use of a sales force. There were forty-three salesmen operating in 1921, most of whom worked in the large northern and midwestern cities. None was in the South.[106]

Though Babson endeavored to market his commercial and investment service to banks, brokers, and merchants, he also sought out individual investors in rural towns throughout the country. He published pamphlets that promised great returns; one claimed, "Make your capital grow from $6,000 to $600,000!" He sent out his salesmen to give lectures on how to interpret the Babsonchart. In 1920, salesmen offered grand seminars in the cities of Boston, Buffalo, Chicago, Cincinnati, Cleveland, Kansas City, Pittsburgh, and St. Louis.[107] Babson started his own newspaper syndicate in 1923, the Publishers Financial Bureau, which included 420 papers.[108]

Some of Babson's new business ventures were not directly concerned with forecasting but were oriented toward business education and the creation of a new class of statistically savvy businesspeople. One of his largest projects was the founding of the Babson Institute, later Babson College. In 1919, the institute opened with an enrollment of twenty-seven and was located at Babson's former home on Abbott Road in Wellesley. (Babson had just purchased a new residence in the same town.) He built a large campus of 450 acres in 1923. Educating and cultivating business leaders was one of Babson's lifelong interests. "I am interested most of all in developing a new race of businessmen," he wrote in his 1935 autobiography.[109]

The institute began with a two-year intensive course in the fundamentals of business for those "who by inheritance or other circumstances are to occupy positions of authority and responsibility."[110] Citing the existence of other schools that would help people who were willing to climb up through the ranks, Babson intended his institute for those who were partway there—the sons of successful businesspeople or professionals who needed encouragement and discipline. Though the curriculum ranged widely, the subject of economic fluctuations featured prominently. An early catalogue notes that among the school's required courses was one on "Business cycles and their effect on industry, commerce and prices."[111]

Many of the teachers were businesspeople, and the institute focused on practical experience. Students worked on group projects, took field trips to manufacturing companies and other firms, and viewed industrial films. They were expected to wear business clothes, keep business hours (8:30 AM to 5:00 PM), and punch a clock. Each had a desk with a telephone, typewriter, adding machine, and Dictaphone. Students were allotted secretarial help for the typing-up of their assignments and correspondence. Among the graduates of the first class was Dan Gerber, who became the founder of Gerber baby foods. Today the college is internationally distinguished for teaching entrepreneurship. At the time, the school provided a great pool of workers to staff Babson's statistical organization.

THE FLORIDA LAND BOOM

While Babson purchased substantial real estate in Wellesley, he also bought property in other areas, especially Florida, where he built a winter home. Babson became a major real-estate holder in Florida, buying land there in 1922 and developing a new "Babson Park" about fifty miles south of Orlando. In the late 1920s, he founded a business college for women in Florida, Webber College (now Webber International University), named after his first granddaughter, Camilla Grace Webber.

One of the most important events that changed Babson's view of forecasting was the Florida land boom. It was not, of course, the country's first speculative craze in real estate. It followed, for instance, land bubbles in Chicago in the mid-1830s and Southern California in the late 1880s. But the Florida land boom was one of the greatest speculative booms up to that time in the United States.

Florida was heavily promoted as a vacation destination by ingenious developers like Carl G. Fisher (1874–1939), an automotive enthusiast and salesman who helped develop Miami Beach and lured northern investors by placing billboards in New York's Times Square promising great returns. Lots were bought from blueprints, with salesmen describing the features of the "predevelopment" property. Walter Hill, the vice president of the Retail Credit Company of Atlanta, described the hype generated for these imagined communities: "[T]he buyer gets the promoter's vision, can see the splendid curving boulevards, the yacht basin, the parks lined with leaning cocoanut trees and flaming hibiscus." Around Miami, subdivisions often sold out the first day of sale. Purchasers did not usually pay the whole amount but simply reserved the right (for thirty days) to arrange payment for a property. They then resold these rights, which, in turn, were sold over and over again.[112]

Magazines, billboards, and newspapers described real estate opportunities. Individual cities were given alluring nicknames: Miami was "Magic City"; Orlando was "City Beautiful"; and Fort Lauderdale, "Tropical Wonderland."[113]

Babson experienced firsthand Florida's boom-bust cycle in real-estate prices that occurred in the mid-1920s. "Pandemonium reigned," wrote Babson of the dramatic inflation of property prices. "There were more Rolls-Royces and Lincolns in the state of Florida in 1926 than in any other state in the country."[114] There were promotions for banana plantations, oil explorations, and fake schemes of all kinds.

A collapse in prices came in 1926 with the sudden escalation of negative press coverage of real-estate swindles, with rising railroad prices, and with the capsizing of a large boat, the 240-foot *Prinz Valdemar*, that was on its way to become a floating hotel.[115] The worst episode came in September when a severe hurricane damaged much land around the Florida panhandle. "A syndicate in which I was interested bought about seven thousand acres of ranch land fifteen miles East of Lake Wales at about fifteen dollars an acre in 1924–25," wrote Babson. "In 1926 they refused fifty dollars an acre for this same property. In 1928–29, five dollars an acre was the best bid!"[116]

The lesson of the Florida boom and bust was important for Babson, reminding him of the role of mob psychology in bringing about inflated prices and panics. Babson believed that "greed" and "fear" had caused the cycle. When northerners grew older and began visiting Florida, they occasionally bought property. Then more came, Babson explained, also wanting property and driving the price up. Those who sold decided to reinvest in Florida, pushing demand even higher. "When a man makes a profit, he cannot help telling of it," Babson observed. Soon, he reasoned, people in the North were looking to speculate in Florida real estate; this included northern realtors. Newspapers and magazines further increased interest in the "boom."[117] The Florida

Roger Babson, 1925, when he was fifty years old. This is the year he officially retired as president of Babson Statistical Organization, but he never truly left. Instead he presided over it and his other businesses, wrote for newspapers and hosted business conferences in Wellesley, and managed his investments. Source: Babson Collection, Babson College.

crash became a cautionary tale that Babson referred to when reminding investors of the hazards of economic downturn.

BABSON'S MESSAGE

In the 1920s Roger Babson confirmed his place as the country's most popular economic prophet. His many books and articles comprised a torrent of words that was not likely written by a single person. It is likely that several new hires per year were trained to write in Babson's style.

Babson's interests ranged widely over the topics of investment strategies, business cycles, health fads, eugenics, public policy, church attendance, and God. His book *Religion and Business* (1920) reads like a precursor to advertising executive Bruce Barton's *The Man Nobody Knew* (1925), which portrayed Christ as a businessman. Babson's book was also the type of vacuous, boosterish writing parodied by Sinclair Lewis in his novel *Babbitt* (1922). Babson, Barton, and Babbitt all had names that evoked boosterism, babble, and what H. L. Mencken called America's "booboisie."[118]

Roughly half of the text of *Babson's Reports* was dedicated to practical advice rather than forecasts and analysis. The advice was specific and suggested a high degree of confidence in the accuracy of the predictions. Babson did not merely note that he expected "a decline in the failure totals next year [1923]." He wrote, for instance, "Whereas this year [1922] approximately 22,000 concerns have failed, we expect to see this total reduced next year below 18,000. Whereas the liabilities of concerns failing this year will amount to about $600,000,000, the total in 1923 may not be over $400,000,000."

In the same article, he took this forecast one step further and indicated exactly what he expected the client to do with this information. "Collections should be easier. Your credit policy with concerns doing a domestic business should be more liberal during 1923," he counseled, for instance.[119] This is an important point, for it transformed Babson from merely being a forecaster to being an advisor.

Alongside his charts and graphs Babson offered simple Christian wisdom, noting that "business and religion are so intertwined it is hardly possible for business to exist without religion."[120] While he preached Christian messages of "neighborliness," he was more often evoking Old Testament warnings. He counseled consumers against "unproductive" spending, for example. The *New York Times* reported that Babson "vehemently [scolds] us all for our extravagance."[121] Babson also opposed an over-reliance on borrowing. "Avoid Debt Like Smallpox" and the "Importance of Economy" are section headings in his autobiography.[122]

Babson's Reports were distinguished by their moralizing tone and their propensity to see failures of business, and indeed the violent panics and swings in business activity, as resulting from moral weakness, greed, or lack of courage. Babson was both forecaster and "guru." He also became active in Prohibition and in an effort to increase church membership, both of which he hoped would improve morality and therefore economic efficiency.

BABSON AND THE GREAT CRASH

Babson's advertisements and billboards were everywhere in the late 1920s. Despite the pyrotechnics of the graphs, Babson's forecast method itself was appealingly simple. In the Babsonchart, prosperity was the "action" and depression the "reaction." As one analyst astutely noted, this placed Babson in the position of always swimming against the tide, "predicting doom when things looked brightest" and being "optimistic when the economy was depressed."[123]

Babson's moment of triumph came in the fall of 1929 when he became known as the primary economic forecaster to predict the famous stock market crash. The forecasting industry—including Yale's Irving Fisher, the Harvard Economic Service, John Moody, the Brookmire Economic Service, and others—largely missed it. Because of the dramatic nature of the stock market crash, their failure to predict this event made the headlines of national newspapers.

Babson made his famous prediction on the afternoon of September 5, 1929, as part of a speech at an annual business conference in Wellesley. He warned of an impending sharp drop in share prices on the New York Stock Exchange. "I shall repeat what I said at this time last year and the year before; namely, that sooner or later a crash is coming which will take in the leading stocks and cause a decline of from 60 to 80 points in the Dow-Jones Barometer," he said, at a time when the index stood at about 380. "Fair weather cannot always continue. The economic cycle is in progress today, as it was in the past.... Wise are those investors who now get out of debt and reef their sails. This does not mean selling all you have, but it does mean paying up your loans and avoiding margin speculation." Stock prices, he predicted, would go the way of land values in Florida.[124]

The statement shows Babson in classic form. It was a message of doom and gloom, delivered during a time of high optimism. The trends of the economy were beyond the control of decent individuals. They were subjected to the irrational behavior of herds of speculators and investors, the same crowd that had brought the boom and collapse to Florida.

Babson's September 5 remarks caused a commotion when they hit the news tickers in financial houses at around 2 o'clock that afternoon. A sharp sell-off began, bringing the market indexes down about 3 percent in the late afternoon in what the *New York Times* described as a "storm of selling" that became known as the "Babson break."[125]

Babson's prediction was less impressive than it seemed. Because he tended to call for "depression" in good times and "improvement" in bad times, he had begun predicting an end to prosperity as early as 1926. But the economy only continued its boom.

Unlike Babson, most other analysts were optimistic about the fall months of 1929. Babson's predictions contrasted especially with those of Fisher, who did not believe that the share prices on the stock market were overvalued. He thought, instead, that significant gains in the real economy had brought stock prices to a new and higher "plateau" that would remain and that investment trusts, which were similar to today's open-ended mutual fund firms, had reduced the risk of investing.[126]

The very next day after the "Babson break" New York Stock Exchange prices soared, making up much of the ground lost the day before. The sharp rebound following the break seemed to confirm general optimism among investors in the late 1920s and to suggest that the market was invincible. Babson was "derided up and down Wall Street," according to the *New York Times*.[127] But in the weeks after, the stock market share prices remained volatile, generally falling for the remainder of September and then rising in early October.

Though it took several more weeks, Babson's prediction eventually seemed to come true. On "Black Tuesday," October 29, 16.4 million shares were traded and the Dow Jones index fell another 12 percent from the day before, finishing at 230.[128] By November 13 the market had fallen to 199, off a re-

markable 48 percent from its early September high of 381, around the time
of Babson's September remarks.

Babson now found himself the subject of great attention. He seized his
moment of triumph and promoted his services heavily. On November 9,
1929, he ran an advertisement in the *New York Times* telling readers to
"Change to Babson's" and claiming that "Babson clients were prepared" for
the recent events and that the Babson Statistical Organization was the "Largest Statistical Community in America."[129] In Babson's newsletter of November 18, he advised that looking at the Babsonchart revealed a large area of
reaction yet to come.[130]

Babson used the opportunity to lash out at some of those who had mocked
him over the years, including several members of Congress he had known
since his wartime service. In November 1929, Babson wrote an article that
appeared on the front page of the *New York Times*, blaming Congress for
failing to sufficiently aid U.S. enterprise. "Certainly the business men of Rome
had no more on Nero when he was fiddling during that great panic of 2,000
years ago than the business men of America have on our Congress, which is
fiddling so hopelessly today," he wrote. He blamed them specifically for not
doing more to find markets for American goods overseas and sitting in Washington rather than being out on the road opening markets.[131] In reaction, one
senator called Babson "slanderous and villainous." Another, Republican William Borah of Idaho, declared, "Notice his subtle dishonesty, his manifest de-
ception, in saying the stock market has crashed because of our being here."[132]

In the days after the crash, Babson repeatedly returned to the theme of the
Florida land boom. "The motive actuating trading in Wall Street stocks is
exactly the same as the motive actuating trading in Florida land," he wrote.
"A portion of the buying is purely speculative with the idea of selling out at
a profit, and a portion is for investment." Citing the extremely low yields of
most stocks, he concluded that 90 percent of stock purchases over the past
year were, indeed, wholly speculative.

Many of Babson's salesmen and associates were on the radio in the month
after the crash. In one address, the president of the Babson Statistical Organization, Leroy Peavey, blamed the plummeting securities on competing
forecasters, like Yale's Irving Fisher and Harvard's C. J. Bullock, for encouraging speculation in the late 1920s. He also lashed out against investment
advisors who had counseled that the days of cyclical activity were over, and
on a group of salesmen and advertising men who, he claimed, "went into the

securities business out of the wreck of the Florida boom."[133] Also in November 1929, another Babson representative attributed the crash of the bull market to those who disregarded the "rules of mathematics and the laws of God."[134] Subway cars in New York carried "Be Right with Babson" placards.[135]

Babson remained bearish through the winter. On December 16, he claimed that the United States had entered into a period of depression. He interpreted the market downswing as a "reaction from excessive prosperity and extravagance."[136]

By then, Babson was a celebrity. In February 1930, the *New Yorker* profiled him as the "prophet of doom" and observed that wherever Babson went people approached him for stock tips.[137] He had become "the lion among stock-market prognosticators," commented the *Nation* in March of that year.[138] At that time, the Babson Statistical Organization had twenty-six branch offices and about 15,000 subscribers, each of whom paid about $100 to $200 per year.[139]

Babson profited from the fate of less fortunate forecasting outfits, just as he had done after the Panic of 1907, when he bought *Moody's Manual*. In 1930, he purchased Thomas Gibson's *Weekly Market Letter* for $100,000, half of what Gibson had originally asked, and gained control of the subscription list. Babson also expanded into new business ventures that year, purchasing a majority share of the American Public Welfare Company (or A.P.W. Products Company), which made paper products and distributed hygienic supplies to companies. In addition, Babson purchased the Gamewell Company, which manufactured red fire-alarm boxes seen throughout New England streets (even today), and a local insurance firm.[140]

Babson continued his downward predictions through the summer of 1930, despite some upward movement in business activity in the spring. In July 1930, Babson said that the "area of reaction" was only about 20 percent of that of the prior period and it was getting nearer the time, at 50 percent, to buy some stocks again. By September, he recommended that 20 percent of available funds be put into stocks. Clients needed to hold the rest until the action-reaction process was complete. In November, Babson observed on his chart that the "area of reaction," H-, was 40 percent of the previous area of expansion and so advised clients that they could have 40 percent of their funds in stocks.[141]

Only a year and a half after the market crash Babson suggested it was once more time to invest fully. In May 1931 he sent out a special letter, over his

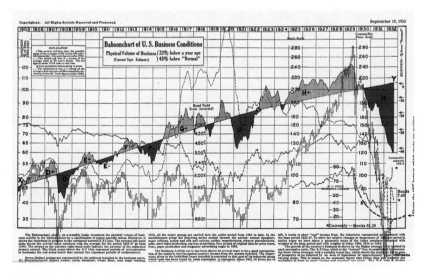

The Babsonchart from 1932, showing the two areas, H+ of prosperity and H– of recession. Babson had to adjust the "normal" line in order to make these areas balance each other. Source: Babson Collection, Babson College.

signature, which read: "Today we are again willing to risk our Organization's thirty year reputation by stating that—irrespective of what the stock market does—general business has seen its worst." The bottom of the Depression had come, he advised. Babson thought a gradual upward movement would occur but warned against depression psychology. "Right now the Babsonchart is telling us that the bottom of the business pit has been reached," Babson wrote. "This is why we are asking you to get away from the crowd of gloom spreaders who are looking backwards." He urged clients to use their remaining funds to purchase stocks.[142]

Babson continued to be optimistic through the year, but—as it turned out—he was much too early in urging his investors back into the market. Despite his public triumph in "predicting" the crash, his actual record was not as stellar. For one thing Babson had urged his clients to get out of the market in 1926, far before the boom of 1927 and 1928. This is a key point. Had Babson's clients followed his advice, they would have missed the real boom in stock market securities in the late 1920s. Babson also called the bottom of the Great Depression incorrectly. Despite confident predictions of improvement in 1931, the economy would not recover for a decade: the United States did not match its 1929 real GNP until 1939, and GNP per capita declined by 3–4 percent over that period.[143] The Dow-Jones Industrial Average would not regain its peak closing of September 3, 1929, until 1954.[144]

MOVING BEYOND FORECASTING

Nonetheless, Babson's popularity pushed him toward higher ambitions. Rather than remaining a business prophet, Babson came to see himself as a public figure in a broader sense.

Babson's work during the Great Depression came increasingly to focus on self-improvement and positive thinking. This was a market being exploited around the same time by Dale Carnegie, who began giving courses in public speaking and confidence in 1912, and whose immensely popular book of 1937, *How to Win Friends and Influence People*, urged people to gain success through smiling. Babson spoke often about self-improvement, character building, personal initiative, and responsibility. In 1932 he published *Cheer Up! Better Times Ahead!* "Just as a declension from prosperity is due to the dishonesty, inefficiency and general carelessness which develop during good times, so a return to prosperity always follows the better frame of mind which develops during a period of depression," he wrote.[145]

His greatest advice manual was never published but instead was engraved on a series of boulders in Gloucester in an area called Dogtown. Babson purchased much of this property and donated it to the City of Gloucester as a park. Among the sayings in Dogtown can be found these pithy words of advice: Keep Out of Debt, Prosperity Follows Service, Be On Time, Spiritual Power, Get a Job, Industry, and Help Mother.

In surveying the companies he operated in the mid-1930s (his forecasting service, Babson College, A.P.W. Products, and Gamewell), Babson wrote that he had profited from the waste, accidents, and "carelessness" of Americans— a big market, according to his calculations. "When the losses from foolish investments, preventable business failures, unnecessary sickness, fire and automobile accidents are all added together, we find a sum totaling about one-tenth of the total annual income of the United States," he wrote.[146] This fight against waste and inefficiency, Babson wrote, had made him wealthy. In 1932, Babson's total income was $114,000 (about $1.6 million today) and, in 1936, $190,000 (about $2.7 million today).[147]

As Roger Babson's fame increased, he became a figure resembling Henry Ford after the triumph of the Model T, a "genius ignoramus," free to speak on any subject and always able to find an audience.[148] He had long regarded Wall Street with disdain and now was free to lecture on the financial district's wretched excesses. He had a conservative approach to financial markets but not one that believed optimistically that a "free market" would solve all problems. Instead Babson believed that the capitalist economy was best observed and respected and that periodic liquidations were inevitable.[149] While Babson's approach to prescriptive economic policy was relatively hands-off, he believed the state should weigh in to control many social and political aspects of society.

In 1940 Babson ran an unsuccessful campaign for president as the candidate of the National Prohibition Party, which he believed would help improve the morality of the country and thereby affect the economy. Babson held an expansive view of the word "prohibition": not only did he wish to ban alcohol, but he was also especially keen on "prohibiting" those he considered to be unfit from voting. "[O]ur nation is like one big farmyard," Babson said. "Roaming over our land are all kinds of human animals, from wildcats and foxes, skunks and pigs, to intelligent dogs and horses. The idea that the same freedom should be given to all is absolutely ridiculous." Rather, he reasoned, people should pass an economic literacy test before gaining the right to vote.[150] Babson finished fourth, garnering 58,000 votes—just 0.12 percent of the electorate.

Babson's fear of impending doom, which served him well in the stock market crash of 1929, escalated to paranoia in the years after World War II—a time of great prosperity, when, like the 1920s, Babson saw trouble. In 1946 at the age of seventy, he founded a third school, named Utopia College. He placed the new school in Eureka, Kansas, which he reasoned was far enough away from any large American city that could be the target of a nuclear attack.[151] He encouraged investors and Babson employees to purchase land surrounding Utopia, expecting a sharp rise in real estate prices—though it was not to be. The college never prospered; it closed in 1970.

Through it all, Babson remained devoted to the theories of Isaac Newton and studies of gravity, a subject that had preoccupied him ever since the drowning of his sister Edith, a tragic event he thought about often and which he attributed to the forces that pulled her body down into the water.[152] But the idea of gravity also perfectly suited Babson's black-and-white view of the world—one of ups and downs, booms and busts, moral and immoral behavior, fit and unfit citizens, and Bostonian common sense and New York profligacy.

In 1938 he and his wife purchased the Fore-Parlor from Sir Isaac Newton's St. Martin Street residence in England for £450 (about $132,000 in today's dollars). The room was placed in the new Babson Institute Library. In 1949 he founded the Gravity Research Foundation, which supported efforts to find a "gravity insulating" device and established an annual contest that offered a cash prize to the best two-thousand-word essay on the subject. The contest has attracted notable scientists (Stephen Hawking won in 1971) as well as cranks. In the late 1950s, Babson was busy collecting birds in an effort to understand how they flew. He claimed to recall Thomas A. Edison saying to him, while pointing to a bird in the air, "That bird can do what no man can do—namely fly with its own power. I wish, Babson, that you would take a greater interest in birds."[153]

Babson died in 1967, at age ninety-one, leaving an estate of $9.2 million (equivalent to $60 million today).[154] His business empire lived on, however, producing publications until the 1980s.

Babson's legacy extended beyond the success of his business, however. Despite his obsessions with Isaac Newton, proper ventilation, Prohibition, and sententious platitudes, his belief in the importance of industrial output remains an important contribution to the way economic growth is understood today. True, the cockeyed Newtonian logic behind the "action-reaction" model, the kitchen-sink method of combining data series, and the arbitrary placement of the "normal line" inspired a number of critics to write harsh reviews. But in the years prior to the formulation of GNP, Babson's index was one of the most widely used indicators of economic performance and volatility. In 1924, the nation's premier expert on business cycles, economist Wesley C. Mitchell, noted that "the Babsonchart offered the most reliable help of any [business index] for the years 1903–1919" in dating the months when business cycles turned up or down.[155]

Perhaps most important, Babson helped create the figure of the "economic forecaster" in popular culture and in business circles. He popularized the idea of the business prophet, who spotted trends in the economy that were beyond the control of individuals or policies.

CHAPTER 2

Irving Fisher: The Economy as a Mathematical Model

||||||||||||||||||||||||||||||||||||||||||||||||||||||||||||||||||||||||||||||||||||||||||||||||||||||||||

Irving Fisher (1867–1947), Babson's opponent in 1929, was a prominent forecaster in the early twentieth century, frequently listed in contemporary surveys of leading forecasters in the 1920s.[1] He was also a towering figure in the field of economics, partly because he was among the first to bring high-level mathematics to the discipline and helped form the basis of modern macroeconomics.[2] As a sign of his stature, in 1924 the *Wall Street Journal* introduced John Maynard Keynes to its readership as "England's Irving Fisher."[3] His work on the quantity theory of money, debt deflation, and theories of interest and capital remains influential down to the present day. The economist Ragnar Frisch, co-winner of the first Nobel Prize in Economic Science in 1969, wrote that Fisher's work was "anywhere from a decade to two generations ahead of his time."[4] In 2005 Nobel Laureate and Yale professor James Tobin commented, "Much of standard neoclassical theory today is Fisherian in origin, style, spirit and substance."[5]

Fisher could hardly present a greater contrast to Roger Babson's mail-order pieties and pseudoscience. Babson existed only on the fringes of academia and his work was often assailed in scholarly journals. "Babson is a nice gentleman," Fisher once remarked. "He receives great publicity and has a large following, but he has no academic standing."[6]

But the two men had far more in common than their public personas suggest. Some of the similarities were pure coincidence: both were shaken by the death of a sibling early in life, and a diagnosis of tuberculosis in early adulthood left the two men aware of the precariousness of life and health. Both had a father die when they were young, and both assumed the burden of providing for their mother and siblings. Other parallels indicate shared concerns and ambitions. Babson and Fisher had wide-ranging interests in all sorts of social and nutritional fads, including eugenics, Prohibition, and all-vegetable diets. Fisher's best-selling book was not a work of economics but a diet-and-health guide, *How to Live* (1915).[7] Among Fisher's favorite causes were calendar reform and the invented language Esperanto.

Both had a fascination with mapmaking, the charting of the natural and geopolitical terrain as well as the economic climate. Babson built the world's largest relief map of the United States and designed a building to house the map on his college campus in Wellesley. Fisher published *World Maps and Globes* (1944) in which he revealed a new flat projection of the globe that presented countries in their relative size accurately.[8] Also like Babson, Fisher was an inventor. He made a fortune through the sale to the Rand Kardex Company of his Index Visible, a device Fisher patented in 1912 for sorting and storing index cards and a precursor to the Rolodex. Fisher also developed a prize-winning tent to aid in the treatment of tuberculosis and a three-legged stool for traveling. Both men were excellent self-promoters who lectured widely and published many books. Both courted world leaders and offered advice, often unsolicited.

They were also, of course, interested in forecasting for much of their adult lives. Like several economists of his time, Fisher saw that an orientation toward the future was at the core of business, entrepreneurship, and capitalism more broadly. "The sagacious business man ... is constantly forecasting," Fisher wrote in *The Rate of Interest* (1907).[9] His exposition of the nature of capital and income highlighted the role of future expectations in determining present value—that is, assigning a price to a business, an investment, or other forms of ongoing cash flow. But unlike most of his fellow economists, Fisher's interest in the future extended to the making and selling of predictions. His first national economic forecasts came out in 1911 and 1912 as scholarly articles in the *American Economic Review*. By the mid-1920s, he sought a mass audience for his predictions. For much of that decade Fisher sold a weekly "business page" that ran in newspapers across the country.

Fisher's forecasting methods rested on a far more sophisticated understanding of the economy than did those of Roger Babson. The Wellesley oracle relied on a rudimentary definition of industrial production—what he called "business activity." Fisher, by contrast, believed that money and its related variables—prices, credit, and interest rates—were the key to predicting the economic future.[10]

Fisher argued that monetary instability, and its effect on prices and interest rates, was a cause of boom-and-bust cycles. Fisher's forecasts were based on his belief that *changes* in the price level (rather than the actual price level) signaled upcoming fluctuations in real output and employment. As Fisher wrote, "Any pronounced or prolonged fall in the price level usually foreshadows depression, while any pronounced or prolonged rise in the price level usually foreshadows improved conditions, from the business man's point of view."[11] Fisher perceived that such changes to the price level would cause real interest rates to differ from nominal ones and lead to economic ups and downs.

Unlike Babson, who analyzed historic trends and consulted a chart, Fisher made an economic model that emphasized causation: What brought economic volatility and how could it be predicted? Fisher intended to form a forecasting method based on a "scientific truth" rather than a purely historical one. "A scientific truth is in the conditional form: '*if A is true, then B is true*'; while an historical fact is in the unconditional form, '*A is true*' or '*B is true*,'" he explained. "My impression is that few, if any, economic students ever grasp this fundamental distinction who have not had some considerable training in the physical sciences."[12] Historians collected facts; scientists looked for a causal connection between them.

Sophisticated economic knowledge, however, did not necessarily bring predictive accuracy. Outside the world of professional economics, Fisher is best remembered for making light of Roger Babson's forecast of the stock market crash of 1929.[13] Anyone who followed Fisher's investment advice between October 1929 and the following three or four years lost everything, as Fisher himself did. But Fisher was a more astute observer than most if not all of his contemporaries, including the few who guessed correctly about the future of the stock market at that pivotal moment.[14]

FROM PREACHER'S SON TO MATHEMATICAL ECONOMIST

Irving Fisher was born in 1867 in the Catskill region of upstate New York, the son of Ella Westcott and George Whitefield Fisher. His father, a minister, was named after the eighteenth-century Anglican preacher of the Great Enlightenment. Fisher's birthplace of Saugerties was a town of modest population,

around ten thousand, but had fourteen churches.[15] The Fishers lived the itin-
erant, financially precarious life common to many preachers' families. Shortly
after Irving's birth, the family moved to New Haven, Connecticut, where the
father attended Yale, and then to Peace Dale, a mill town on the Rhode Island coast, where the senior Fisher served as a pastor for thirteen years, from
1868 to 1881. Irving was the third child of four, but only two of these children (Irving and his younger brother, Herbert) survived to adulthood.[16] In
1883 the family moved to Cameron, Missouri, where the father briefly had a
parish. His parents and younger brother then moved to New Jersey to live
with a relative after George Whitefield Fisher fell ill. Irving remained behind
to attend high school at the well-regarded Smith Academy in St. Louis.[17]

In 1884, the seventeen-year-old Fisher followed in his father's footsteps
and enrolled in Yale College. But in his first week he received the tragic news
that his father had died from tuberculosis. "He was all that was noble and
virtuous," Fisher wrote of his father to a friend. "The example he set will ever
have a hallowing influence on my life."[18] His father's death forced Irving to
become the chief breadwinner for his mother and younger sibling, who then
moved to New Haven. Fisher remained in school and helped raise money by
tutoring students. In 1890, for instance, he spent the summer in Minnesota
tutoring the sons of James J. Hill, president of the Great Northern Railroad.[19]
Despite these additional burdens, Fisher blossomed at Yale, winning prizes in
Latin, Greek, and algebra, as well as the school's mathematics prize. For the
Junior Exhibition, a public-speaking prize, he finished second only to future
politician and secretary of state Henry Stimson.[20] Like Stimson, Fisher was a
member of the secret society Skull and Bones. He was also on the school's
rowing team. In 1888, he was the class valedictorian.[21] He was awarded a
scholarship for graduate study and remained at Yale for another three years
to complete his Ph.D.

One of the most influential professors in Fisher's university life was Josiah
Willard Gibbs, a chemist and mathematician, who instructed him in mathematical theory, thermodynamics, and algebra. Gibbs was an important role
model whom Fisher viewed as interested in "truth seeking for its own sake."
Gibbs taught Fisher the scientific method, sparked an interest in physics, and
promoted the idea that science should be more mathematical.[22]

From the perspective of contemporaries, the nineteenth century had been
a continual march of scientific progress. Significant technological inventions
had transformed fields ranging from communications to construction to med-

A proud Irving Fisher upon graduation from Yale in 1888. Fisher stayed at the university for nearly a half century, entering Yale during the presidency of Chester Arthur and leaving during that of FDR. Source: Yale University, Manuscripts & Archives, Image no. 3443, box 23.f.838.

icine. In the 1820s came the introduction of Portland cement and the electromagnet; in the 1830s, the daguerreotype and the telegraph; in the 1840s, anesthesia and antisepsis; in the 1850s, Isaac Singer's sewing machine and the internal combustion engine; in the 1860s, dynamite and plastics; in the 1870s, barbed wire and the electric lightbulb; in the 1880s, the machine gun and the first practical automobile; and, in the 1890s, x-rays and great advances in vaccinations. "Science," understood not solely as a discrete field of inquiry but as a systematic, disciplined approach to knowledge, appeared to offer unlimited improvement. Like many of his contemporaries, Fisher viewed the scientific method as a pathway to a better world. Even humanists, social scientists, and psychologists, notably William James, worked to make their fields more scientific.[23]

Fisher also gravitated toward professors whose work engaged broader social issues. A second major influence was the well-known sociologist, evolutionist, and anti-imperialist William Graham Sumner, who taught Fisher political economy and politics. Sumner had gained a huge following at Yale, and a wide popular audience, for his advocacy of laissez-faire, free markets, and the gold standard. Sumner helped popularize an optimistic strain of evolutionary thinking that drew on the work of the English philosopher Herbert Spencer—namely, that natural forces of evolution would, if left alone, work to improve society.[24] Fisher later wrote, "While I was still studying for a mathematical career, I took courses under Sumner, not because I ever expected to enter economics but because I wanted to meet such a personality before leaving Yale."[25]

It was Sumner who advised Fisher to combine his interests in pure mathematics and political economy and write a doctoral dissertation in the field of mathematical economics—a new field that Fisher had not yet heard about. His dissertation, "Mathematical Investigations in the Theory of Value and Prices," was completed in 1891 and published the following year in the *Transactions of the Connecticut Academy*.[26] In it, Fisher provided an elegant mathematical statement of the theory of marginal utility and marginal cost in an effort to understand how prices are determined and how they change. Its many themes, including utility, expectations, and value, later informed his forecasting work. The Harvard economist Joseph Schumpeter called Fisher's dissertation "one of the greatest performances of nascent econometrics."[27] Paul A. Samuelson, who in 1970 became the first American economist to win the Nobel Prize in Economic Science, described it as "the greatest doctoral dissertation in economics ever written."[28]

Fisher drew upon the work of European mathematical economists Rudolf Auspitz and Richard Lieben, who published *Untersuchungen über die Theorie des Preises* (*Investigations in the Theory of Price*) (1889), an analysis of the purchasing decisions of an individual who chooses between several commodities. Fisher cited their work and reviewed a French translation of their book in 1915.[29]

Fisher also credited the English economist William Stanley Jevons, who had developed his own forecasting method based on sunspots and their effect on crops, with introducing him to the idea of marginal utility. This idea held that the value of a good or service is determined by the utility an individual gains (or loses) by an increase (or decrease) in the consumption of that commodity and, further, that the first unit of consumption of a good or service yields more utility than the second and subsequent units.[30]

The idea of marginal utility was a radical departure from the theory of value proposed by classical economists, who assumed that the value of a good was determined by the amount of labor embodied in its production. Instead, by arguing that the value of a commodity gradually diminished the more of it an individual already owned, marginal utility theory emphasized the role of consumer demand in determining prices. Thus consumers spent money on a particular item until the point at which they would get a higher amount of satisfaction spending a dollar elsewhere. Products did not have an inherent value, therefore consumers assigned value to a good depending on its relation to a basket of other goods. The more food an individual ate, the smaller the appetite for yet more; the more shoes and hats a consumer owned, the less utility he or she would find in additional ones.[31]

Fisher's contribution was to discover a more precise definition of utility, which he did by comparing the utility of one product with that of another. Fisher explained: "If an individual ... consumes 100 loaves of bread in a year the utility of the last infinitesimal, or to fix our ideas, the utility of the last *loaf* is (presumably) greater than what it would be if he consumed 150 loaves." Continuing with the bread example, "What is their *ratio*?" Fisher asked. "It is found by contrasting the utilities of the 100th and 150th loaves with a third utility ... of oil (say)."[32] He concluded that a consumer would purchase a specific product up to the point at which the additional benefit (or marginal utility) that this product rendered per unit of expense (price) exactly equaled the marginal utility per unit of expense of every other product purchased by that same individual. "*A consumer will so arrange his consumption that the marginal utility per dollar's worth of each commodity shall be the same*," Fisher wrote. "Price, production, and consumption, are determined by *the equality of marginal utility and marginal cost of production*," he concluded later in the book.[33]

Fisher explored his theory of price and value through a series of complex mathematical equations that involved calculus, geometry, and algebra. He used engineering-related terms, such as "equilibrium," "stability," and "friction," to describe economic activity, showing the influence of Gibbs.[34]

Fisher also designed a hydrostatic machine to illustrate the economic " 'exchanges' of a great city" that revealed the ways that the values of individual goods were related to one another.[35] When Fisher adjusted one of the levers, water flowed to affect the general price level of the range of goods. The device resembled a modern-day foosball table but with various cisterns of different shapes and heights representing individual consumers and producers. Water flowed through tubes to the "individuals," and the height of water represented the price level. A series of levers along the side of the machine altered the flow of water, thus changing the price level not only for an individual but

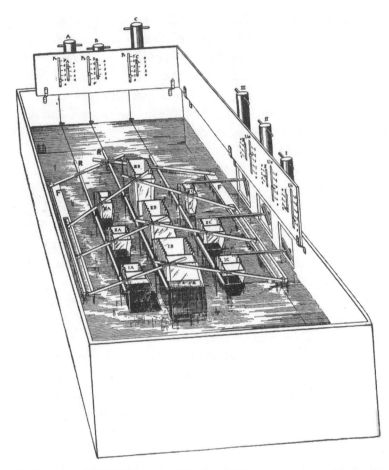

An illustration from Fisher's dissertation, "Mathematical Investigations in the Theory of Value and Prices." Fisher used the machine to demonstrate principles in his classroom. The device showed how changes to the demand or supply of a commodity—accomplished by changing the level of water through adjusting a valve or lever—altered the price and demand for other commodities as well. As water settled into its new level, the machine demonstrated the theory of equilibrium. In some ways, the machine was a grandparent of computer-driven economic forecasting models that prospered in the years after World War II. But Fisher's device was intended for illustrative purposes rather than to make calculations. Source: Irving Fisher, "Mathematical Investigations in the Theory of Value and Prices," *Transactions of the Connecticut Academy* 9 (July 1892): 38.

throughout the entire economy. The machine revealed the way in which prices, supply, and consumer demand interrelated. For example, if the price of a good fell (and the level of water rose), more consumers would purchase it, and a new equilibrium would emerge.[36]

The machine presented an entirely different way to represent economic activity than did Babson's static chart. It lacked the dimension of time and did not record historical trends. Instead it showed a seemingly timeless relationship between price levels and the volume of money in an economy.

Fisher's venture into mathematical economics would help create a whole new approach to forecasting—and economics broadly. He went against the grain of work done by his American contemporaries. Among the rising luminaries of the economics profession were Richard T. Ely, John Bates Clark, and E. R. A. Seligman, each of whom had received graduate education in Germany and was influenced by the German Historical School, which emphasized historical and institutional approaches in an effort to critique the classical economics of Adam Smith and his followers. Very few economists in the 1880s were equipped with significant mathematical training.[37] Clark of Columbia, as well as Frank Taussig of Harvard and Ely of Wisconsin, used a great deal of data in their writings but did not rely on advanced mathematics. Fisher left no doubt as to his disdain for his colleagues' methods, proclaiming his confidence in the use of "patient mathematical analysis," as he put it, to pierce through "hazy notions" that permeated much economic thought.[38]

RISING FORTUNES

In 1893 Fisher's life improved dramatically, both in terms of personal happiness and financial security. At the age of twenty-six he married Margaret Hazard, the daughter of Rowland Hazard, a wealthy businessman. Margaret's father had founded the Solvay Process Company, which manufactured soda ash, a water softener, used in the production of glass and soap.[39] The Hazard family had deep roots in Peace Dale, Rhode Island. They had operated a woolen mill there for more than a century and owned a number of impressive buildings in the town. The Hazards had also organized the Peace Dale Congregational Church, where Irving's father had been minister.

The wedding was enough of an event to be mentioned in the *New York Times*, which reported that over two thousand invitations had been sent out for the Fisher-Hazard wedding. The paper also remarked on the extravagance of the affair. Three ministers were hired to conduct different parts of the service, and an elaborate lunch was held in one of the family's buildings, Hazard Memorial Hall, a massive stone structure.[40]

After the June wedding, the Fishers went on a fourteen-month tour of Europe. While honeymooning, Irving met leading British and European economists: Alfred Marshall in Cambridge, Francis Ysidro Edgeworth in Oxford, Maffeo Pantaleoni in Rome, Carl Menger in Vienna, and, in Switzerland, Léon Walras, the economist most associated with equilibrium theory. The list of contacts revealed remarkable ambition for a young economist. Many of these scholars had a particular interest in mathematical economics and the marginal utility theory. This was Fisher's crowd, and he kept in touch with many of them for years.[41]

During the couple's honeymoon trip, Margaret's father had an enormous home built for them as a wedding present. The house, at 460 Prospect Street, New Haven, was elaborate in design. Downstairs was a music room, dining room, library, and wide entrance hall. The second floor had five bedrooms and two baths. The third had rooms for servants as well as children—the Fishers eventually had three. The house, referred to as Cleftstone and 460, became the center of Fisher's social and professional life.[42] Fisher's newfound wealth enabled him to hire a research staff and expand his range of activities much beyond that of the typical Yale professor. He set up offices in the lower level of the house for graduate students and colleagues to work on his many projects. Fisher loved technology and purchased cars, radios, and all sorts of new gadgets. He equipped his staff with telephones, Dictaphones, and typewriters.

By August 1894, when the Fishers returned from Europe and his office at the house was fully operational, the country was reeling from a financial panic that had started in 1893. The depression that followed would not fully lift for five years and was arguably the worst the country had yet experienced. The estimated unemployment rate exceeded 10 percent for over half a decade, and 15,200 firms declared bankruptcy in 1893 alone, with liabilities that topped $357 million. A brief upswing in 1895 was followed by a second trough that continued through 1896–97.[43] Fisher's next venture sought to find explanations for the increasing volatility in American financial markets.

Capital and Income

During the period 1895–98, Fisher was a prolific evangelist for mathematical economics, writing textbooks on mathematics that would aid his fellow economists: *Elements of Geometry* (with A. W. Phillips, 1896) and *A Brief Introduction to the Infinitesimal Calculus* (1897).[44] He also published a number of articles in academic journals that gave more rigorous definitions to common economic terms such as "interest" and "income" and pushed his colleagues to make economics a true mathematical science, as opposed to the political-economy or institutional approach.[45]

The mathematical study of money, interest rates, and prices became the focus of Fisher's concerns. The subject of money was indeed the most pressing issue of the mid-1890s and, especially, of the 1896 election, which pitted Democrat William Jennings Bryan, who opposed the continuance of the gold standard and agitated for the coinage of silver, against the Republican sound-money candidate William McKinley. Fisher chose to support sound money but also decided he needed to study the nature of the money supply in greater depth. This work convinced him that policies that would help people plan for the future would also help improve the stability of economies overall.

In these writings, Fisher revealed a budding interest in the role the future played in economic and business life. He showed an awareness—perhaps gained through observation of his in-laws' business concerns—of how advantageous it was to businesspeople and investors to be able to make accurate predictions. In his 1896 article "Appreciation and Interest," Fisher noted that in planning budgets and making production schedules, businesspeople were constantly forecasting future price levels, whether they realized it or not. He wrote that "business foresight" was a distinguishing part of business, and he noted a growing appetite among businessmen for statistical data to anticipate market trends.[46] The interest rate, or the cost of borrowing money, was also an essential future-looking element of capitalism. "The truth is that the rate of interest is not a narrow phenomenon applying only to a few business contracts, but permeates all economic relations," Fisher wrote in a dramatic statement in *The Rate of Interest* (1907). "It is the link which binds man to the future and by which he makes all his far-reaching decisions."[47] Fisher's method of forecasting rested upon these notions.

Fisher fleshed out his ideas about the forward-looking nature of capitalism in three landmark articles in the *Economic Journal*, a leading British periodical: "What Is Capital?" (1896), "Senses of 'Capital' " (1897), and "The Role of Capital in Economic Theory" (1897).[48] In these articles, Fisher worked through existing definitions of terms like "wealth," "income," "property," and "services," in each case trying to find a more precise description. He did the same for the term "capital," testing out and eventually rejecting definitions from Adam Smith, John Stuart Mill, Karl Marx, Léon Walras, and other economists. "According to Adam Smith, capital should produce a revenue," Fisher wrote. But, as Fisher pointed out, this definition did not go far enough. The distinction between a merchant ship and a private yacht was easy enough: one was obviously a productive asset, the other a luxury item. Other assets, however, were far more difficult to classify: "But what shall we say of an excursion steamer which carries freight as well; or of a doctor's gig when used for a pleasure drive, but also for visiting a patient, or of a luxurious carriage, employed by the merchant to carry him to his place of business?"[49]

Examples such as these showed that the definition of capital itself needed rethinking. The problem with existing definitions, Fisher believed, was their failure to take into account the dimension of time. Wealth "presents a double aspect in reference to *time*," wrote Fisher. "It forms a *stock* of wealth, and it forms a *flow* of wealth. The former is, I venture to maintain, capital, the latter, income and outgo, production and consumption. Stock relates to a *point* of time, flow to a *stretch* of time." To give an example: "Food in the pantry at any instant is capital, the monthly flow of food through the pantry is income. Machinery existing is capital, its annual replacement or increase is income."[50] Just as he had done in his dissertation, Fisher likened the economy to flowing water: "Capital" was like a lake and "income" like a river pouring into it or flowing out from it.

The proper valuation of capital, thought Fisher (again, continuing his longstanding interest in value and price), was also forward-looking, being the anticipated income of future years. The concepts of "stock" and "flow" had been recognized previously in accounting—for example, in the distinction between an asset and an investment. Fisher's contribution was to formalize and name the two concepts. This was a major contribution; both concepts are still used today as fundamental ideas in economics. The focus on *time* was also a contribution to his thinking about forecasting, for as Fisher distinguished between capital and income, he also distinguished between current value and expectations.[51]

This helped Fisher develop, quite early in his career, a view of capitalism that emphasized the role of high-technology firms that made investments in patents, innovation, and research—activities that would generate future streams of income. Fisher directed his own investments toward these technologically advanced firms and patented his own inventions. A future-oriented definition of capital and income led Fisher to offer a novel estimate of the wealth of the country, one based on future income rather than current capabilities—and one he fleshed out in his forecasting career.

How to Live

With his marriage, newfound wealth, and long list of first-rate academic publications, Fisher was doing extremely well. But in the fall of 1898, at the age of thirty-one, he was struck with tuberculosis, the disease that had killed his father. Here again, uncertainty entered his life, as it had during his early years at Yale. Fisher took an extended leave of absence from the school. Seeking fresh air, he first went to a sanatorium in the Adirondacks for about six months before traveling to the health resorts of Colorado Springs—as Roger Babson would do three years later when he contracted the disease.[52] Fisher spent about a year in the mountainous town, which was a mecca for tuberculosis sufferers.

It took Fisher six years to recover from the disease: three spent in search of improved climates in upstate New York and the western United States and three back in New Haven working at half speed. Tuberculosis affected Fisher's life and work in several ways. He believed that a relapse of his tuberculosis could occur at any time and that he might not live to finish long-term projects, so he turned exclusively to short-term ones that he could complete in periods not exceeding twelve months.[53]

The struggle with the disease also expanded his range of interests. Fisher wrote that the experience "greatly changed [my] point of view from that of an academic student of supply and demand as a mathematical problem, to that of a partaker in public movements for the betterment of mankind."[54] Ironically, tuberculosis may have made him drive himself harder.

After his tuberculosis scare, his health became almost an obsession. Fisher abandoned alcohol, coffee, tea, and chocolate and seldom ate meat. By the

Colorado Springs in 1901, showing the business district, with the mining exchange on the left and the Antlers Hotel at the back. Pike's Peak looms in the distance. This Rocky Mountain town was the temporary home of several key figures in the book when they sought treatment for tuberculosis: Irving Fisher (1899–1900), Roger Babson (1902), and Harvard's Warren Persons (1910–16). It was also the home of Robert Rhea, who helped popularize the Dow Theory, and of Alfred Cowles, the wealthy philanthropist who funded some of the earliest endeavors in econometrics. In the 1930s, because of Cowles, Colorado Springs was briefly one of the world's leading centers for econometrics when the early meetings of the Cowles Commission and the Econometric Society were held there. Courtesy of Special Collections, Pike's Peak Library District, Image number 001-3341.

late 1900s he was one of the nation's leading advocates of Prohibition. He also turned to his knack for inventing. He created a portable tent that allowed those suffering from tuberculosis who wanted to benefit from the curative effects of sleeping outside to control the amount of fresh air coming into the tent. It won a prize from the New York Medical Association.[55]

In addition to corresponding with prominent health experts—ranging from nutritionists Horace Fletcher and John Harvey Kellogg to political reformers such as Theodore Roosevelt—Fisher himself became a health expert.[56] In the 1910s he earned widespread newspaper coverage as a promoter of health reform, attracting more attention in this field than through his economic research. His opinions were reported frequently in the newspapers, including the *New York Times*.

In 1915 he published *How to Live: Rules for Healthful Living Based on Modern Science* (written in collaboration with Dr. Eugene Lyman Fisk). Chapters included advice on healthy diets and habits, comfortable clothing, the benefits of outdoor living, and the poisonous attributes of alcohol and tobacco. "We are beginning to cut loose from this false tradition and are working toward the establishment of more wholesome ideas," the text declared. Fisher and his coauthor argued that Americans should aspire to the physical form achieved in ancient Greece, as evidenced in "imperishable marble."[57]

Those who disregarded the message of the book, the authors suggested, would soon find themselves at a disadvantage, for as Americans adopted rules for healthy living, the unfit would increasingly find it hard to locate prospects for marriage. Young Americans, the book argued, had a duty to be knowledgeable about matters of reproduction; they needed to acquire the discipline to avoid behavior that could lead to venereal disease and other outcomes of immorality. "The thoroughly healthy person is full of optimism" and contributed to the future of society.[58]

The book resonated with a generation of Americans uneasy with the effects of industrialization and urbanization on their health but enamored of science and the idea of progress. "We in America inherit, through centuries of European tradition, the medieval indifference to the human body, often amounting to contempt," the book began. Fisher promoted the book at large corporations, such as U.S. Steel, American Rolling Mill, and Sherwin Williams, urging executives to buy it for their employees. *How to Live* went through twenty-one editions between 1915 and 1945 and sold nearly half a million copies.[59]

Fisher's various interests made him a remarkable personality. Wesley Mitchell's wife, Lucy Sprague, a pioneer in educational reform, recalled visiting Fisher's office space on the lower floor of his home at 460. "It occupied practically the whole big basement," she wrote. "His versatile mind had many projects going on down there simultaneously, from health projects and circular files to economic investigations." Then, at dinner, she wrote, "I got still another impression of Mr. Fisher. While I ate right through my succession of delicious courses, he dined on a vegetable and a raw egg."[60]

At Yale, Fisher conducted dietary experiments with student athletes in ways that no university today would allow. These included one test that compared athletes who chewed their food thoroughly against those who did not and one that pitted the endurance of meat eaters against vegetarians. He gained enough authority as a nutrition expert for the makers of the cereal Grape-Nuts to include his endorsement in a 1907 advertisement. It mentioned Fisher's experiments on Yale students "to determine the effects of the thorough mastication of food." Fisher, the ad claimed, found that their endurance was increased 50 percent, although they took no more exercise than before and had reduced their consumption of "flesh foods" by five-sixths.[61] Fisher also chaired a nationwide Committee of One Hundred on National Health that wrote reports and built a network of experts and public figures to agitate for "increased federal regulation of public health"—specifically, a cabinet-level department of health.[62]

Fisher's interests in health and economics were not as far apart as they might seem. He argued that the health of a nation's citizens was an essential part of its material wealth—a position that today's economists also share. Health, according to Fisher, deserved as much attention from economists as import and export totals. In 1908, Fisher estimated that the net annual economic cost of tuberculosis was $550 million (about $254 billion today).

Fisher was relentless in his effort to find order and predictability in a chaotic and unpredictable world. He approached health and economics in similar ways, through methods that emphasized the application of statistics and mathematics to problem solving. He surveyed diets in sanatoriums in the United States and Europe, for instance, in an effort to see which was best for sufferers of tuberculosis.[63]

Fisher's unbounded and unfiltered faith in the applicability of the scientific method to public health led him, by the first decade of the twentieth century, to unsettling positions. He became, for instance, a leading figure of the eugenics movement. Eugenics, as Fisher defined it, was "the vital subject of improving the inherent type and capacities of individuals of the future."[64] Fisher was hardly alone in his embrace of this cruel and misguided endeavor. The eugenics movement included highly respected scientists, such as fellow economist John Maynard Keynes, as well as complete quacks.

Fisher's interest in eugenics was not slight or passing but lasted most of his life and occupied much of his time—in giving speeches, writing articles, and serving on committees. In 1913, with Harold A. Ley, Fisher founded the Life Extension Institute, an organization whose stated aim was "to reduce life-waste and to guard and strengthen the vitality and vigor of our race." He was quoted for his studies of national vitality in his friend Madison Grant's *The Passing of the Great Race* (1916)—the influential book that raised alarm about the supposed decline of the Nordic race. Fisher was further concerned by the deaths of American soldiers during World War I, but especially so because he believed the fallen included those of superior stock; the unfit had stayed behind.[65]

Fisher was an advisor to the Long Island–based Eugenics Record Office and, in 1922, one of the founders of the American Eugenics Society. His preferences were clearly for state intervention in the screening of immigrants and other methods of preventing "race deterioration."[66]

Fisher never thought about the future as just an observer but as a planner and policymaker. He was a strong advocate of the 1924 law aimed at restricting immigration from southern and eastern Europe. For Fisher, the potential of the scientific method was unlimited, whether to bring about a stable currency, to enact health reform, or even to restrict the lives and welfare of those he deemed undesirable.

A zealous advocate of new scientific approaches to all sorts of problems, Fisher had difficulty separating medical science and pseudoscience. In at least one instance, this had tragic consequences for his family—his wife, Margaret Hazard, and their two daughters, Margaret and Caroline, and son, Irving Norton. In the late 1910s, Fisher's daughter Margaret exhibited symptoms suggestive of schizophrenia, a disorder that had only recently been identified and was little understood. Fisher searched desperately for a cure. He eventually turned to Dr. Henry Andrews Cotton, a psychiatrist and medical director of the New Jersey State Hospital in Trenton from 1907 to 1930. Cotton was thought by some to be among the vanguard for treating the mentally ill. He believed that mental illness was due to bacterial infections and he often "treated" patients by removing their teeth, which he thought to be a source of infection. If that did not work, Cotton removed sections of internal organs, especially the colon. In 1919 Cotton performed such an operation on Margaret Fisher; she died shortly afterward. Fisher was not the only one who sought out Cotton's treatment, of course, but the horrific episode conveys his willingness to embrace new scientific discovery without hesitation.[67] Nor did the episode, as devastating as it was, shake his efforts to find experimental cures for health problems.

Predicting Crises

While Fisher was devoting time to health and nutrition, he also fleshed out his theories on the relationship between price levels and the money supply. The result of his efforts, the Equation of Exchange, was one of his greatest contributions to economics and furthered his interest in forecasting. For Fisher, relationships between movements of price levels, interest rates, and deposits offered clues to future periods of prosperity or depression.

The Panic of 1907 had convinced Fisher that extreme economic fluctuations were the result of monetary changes. When too much money existed in the economy, inflation and booms resulted; with too little came deflation and depression.[68] He advanced his theories on the causes of inflation and deflation, and their effects, in *The Purchasing Power of Money, Its Determination and Relation to Credit, Interest, and Crises* (1911) and in *Why Is the Dollar Shrinking?* (1914).[69]

Fisher believed that the inability to predict future price levels was the central issue facing capitalist economies and he sought to attack the problem analytically. He began by taking up the old Quantity Theory of Money, which argued that prices varied proportionally to the amount of money in an economy. Fisher noted that as far back as 200 CE people had observed that the value of money in an economy depended on how much of it was in circulation. In the late nineteenth century, economist Simon Newcomb had concluded, with greater precision, that the level of prices depended on the quantity of money in circulation, its "efficiency" (the number of times per year it was exchanged for goods), and the value of goods purchased.[70]

Fisher formulated his own version of the quantity theory in his Equation of Exchange. Fisher used the equation $MV = PT$ to claim that the level of prices varied directly with the quantity of money in circulation, provided that the velocity of money and the volume of trade did not change.[71] Written out, the equation stated that the quantity of money in circulation (M) multiplied by the average number of times per year a dollar is exchanged for goods (V, the "velocity") is equal to the volume of trade (T) multiplied by the price of goods. In other words, "The currency paid for goods is the equivalent of the value of the goods bought."[72] Fisher provided an example:

> Suppose, for instance, that a person buys 10 pounds of sugar at 7 cents per pound. This is an exchange transaction, in which 10 pounds of sugar have been regarded

as equivalent to 70 cents, and this fact may be expressed thus: 70 cents = 10 pounds of sugar multiplied by 7 cents a pound. Every other sale and purchase may be expressed similarly, and by adding them all together we get the equation of exchange *for a certain period in a given community*.[73]

This example showed only a portion of a nation's exchange, Fisher wrote, because in fact the same money could be used several times to purchase goods in the course of a year. The average number of times a dollar was "turned over" per year was the velocity of the currency.[74]

Unlike the work of Roger Babson, theoretical economics offered a tool for seeing the economic future that did not rely on merely studying past patterns. For Fisher, the Equation of Exchange provided a way to make sense of the dynamic activity of the economy in its entirety—and was a major step forward. It explained what happened to prices and total production, overall, when the amount of money in circulation changed. It was not an argument about individual prices but the overall price level.[75] The Equation of Exchange provided Fisher with a solid theoretical foundation to move into forecasting the future of the economy as whole.

But Fisher did not stop at theory. He wondered whether the Equation of Exchange actually mapped to reality over time and began a massive research project to gather data on the money in circulation, the price level, and total output. He sought through this data to calculate the nation's velocity of money. He gathered reams of statistics, including data from the Director of the Mint and Comptroller of the Currency, from the Department of Commerce and Labor, and from the Bureau of Labor.[76]

A staff of workers in Fisher's home offices concluded that for 1909, the money in circulation (M) was equal to about $1.6 billion and had a velocity of circulation, or turnover rate, of twenty-one times per year—the number of times each dollar was spent in one year. The total value of currency spent in 1909 in the United States therefore equaled, according to Fisher, $387 billion. "The size of this aggregate will probably astonish most readers," he wrote.[77]

While its seeming simplicity may suggest that the Equation of Exchange was a modest achievement, it was in fact a major breakthrough, providing economists a way to conceptualize, in algebraic terms, the workings of the overall economy. This equation promised to provide a way to calculate how changes in the supply of money could affect ups and downs in prices.

The weight symbolizing a purse, represents M, the money in circulation in the United States (i. e. all money outside of the U. S. Treasury and the banks). It is usually between one and two billions.

The leverage of this purse, or its distance from the fulcrum, represents V, the velocity of circulation of money. Money usually turns over about twenty times a year.

The weight symbolizing a bank book, represents M', the bank deposits against which checks are drawn (usually from three to eight billions).

The leverage of this bank book represents V', the velocity of circulation ("activity") of these deposits. The deposits are usually turned over from forty to fifty times a year.

The weight symbolizing a grocer's tray, represents T, the volume of trade expressed in "units," each "unit" being the quantity which could be purchased for $1 in 1909.

The leverage of this tray represents P, the index number of prices measured as a percentage of the prices of 1909.

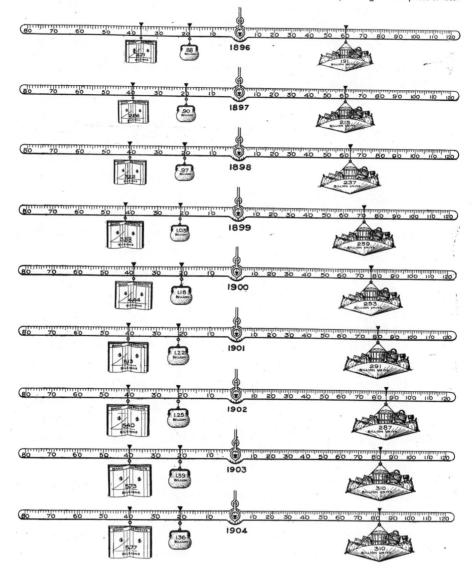

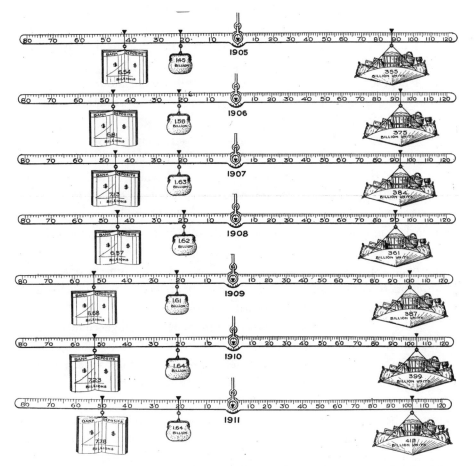

Irving Fisher's diagram of the Equation of Exchange for use in forecasting, 1912. Though Fisher did not produce a forecasting chart, he did create a diagram to illustrate the Equation of Exchange (MV + M′V′ = PT), which he depicted showing a mechanical balance. The left side of the balance symbolized the left side of the equation, with a small weight standing for M, the money in circulation, and a larger bank book standing for M′, deposits subject to check. The distance to the left of the fulcrum of the weight represented the velocity of circulation (V) and the distance of the bank book, the velocity of circulation of bank deposits (V′). The volume of trade (T) was represented by a tray on the right, with the index of prices (P) at which these goods were sold represented by the distance of the tray to the right. The diagram showed the changes in the values for all the components of the Equation of Exchange from 1896 to 1911. This chart was printed as a foldout insert into the *American Economic Review*, and readers were invited to use the diagram to predict whether a crisis was looming. Fisher wrote, "By folding the diagram in various ways, it is easy to place the balance for 1912 immediately under that for 1896 or any other particular year, and thus make a direct comparison for each of the six magnitudes. Any other two years can also be directly compared with each other in a similar manner." To predict the future, one needed to look especially at the changes in the bank deposits, which, if rising rapidly, indicated a coming crisis. Source: Irving Fisher, "'The Equation of Exchange,' 1896–1910," *American Economic Review* 1:2 (June 1911): 299.

In the 1910s Fisher expanded the equation to include bank deposits and their velocity (expressed in the following equation: $MV + M'V' = PT$; M' is bank deposits and V' is their velocity), noting that more and more people were using checks to purchase goods. This proved to be another breakthrough for his forecasting efforts.

Looking at the history of financial panics, Fisher concluded that just as a rise in the price level signaled an expansion of trade, a rapid increase in the velocity of bank deposits signaled an impending downturn. He discovered that, historically, a high turnover in bank deposits was reached in 1899, 1901, 1906, and 1909—each a year of prosperity followed by one of downturn. His findings seemed to corroborate the theory of the French economist Pierre des Essars, who also found a relationship between the feverish spending of deposits and the arrival of a crisis.[78] Fisher advised businesspeople and investors to keep a close watch on the velocity of check deposits, warning them that this figure tended to rise before a downturn.[79]

Fisher also offered explanations as to how monetary changes could bring expansion or recession. In explaining the relationship between changes in the price level and changes in the volume of trade, Fisher placed special emphasis on interest rates and credit availability: When the price level rose, he argued, interest rates (or the costs of borrowing money) were slow to respond; hence real interest rates fell. Spurred by these artificially low interest rates, businessmen invested excessively. Rising interest rates eventually acted as a check upon this, however. When interest rates finally began to rise again, borrowing slowed or ceased entirely, the value of bonds declined, loans could not be renewed on the old terms, and some companies found themselves unable to make their payments. Banks called in their loans and the money supply became contracted, causing prices to fall and the process to start over.[80]

Many contemporary economists recognized Fisher's work with the Equation of Exchange as pathbreaking. W. G. Langworthy Taylor at the University of Nebraska, reading Fisher's findings, remarked on the significance of the statistical verification of the Equation of Exchange to him and other mathematically minded economists. In 1912 he wrote in the *Annals of the American Academy of Political and Social Science* that the "announcement … burst in upon the 'dismal science' with the freshness of the news that men have begun to fly."[81]

The design was a masterful illustration of a monetary view of the economy. Fisher's work with the Equation of Exchange and his detailed studies of nominal and real interest rates were helpful in the 1913 formation of the Federal Reserve Act, which created a central bank for the first time since 1836, when the Second Bank of the United States was denied a new charter under Andrew Jackson's administration. Fisher became a friend and advocate of Benjamin Strong, the head of the New York Federal Reserve and applauded the efforts to secure a stable price level.

FORESIGHT

Almost immediately after formulating the Equation of Exchange, Fisher began using it to produce forecasts. With the publication of these predictions, Fisher, a world-class economist in theories of capital and interest, joined Roger Babson and the crowd of pundits. He looked at the changing level of prices and at the general trends in business innovation in making his estimate. Fisher published two articles in the *American Economics Review* based on updated figures for his Equation of Exchange. In June 1912, he noted an upward trend of the price level from 1910 to 1911 and accurately predicted a "slight rise in prices" and a "slight general expansion" in the total volume of trade.[82]

In June 1913, Fisher wrote that the aggregate price level for 1912 had risen about 3 percent over 1911 and that the volume of trade had expanded about 9 percent. But he was alarmed at what he saw as a "great expansion of bank deposits, and [a] great increase in their velocity of circulation," and he predicted "that we are approaching a crisis, and that this is more likely to begin earlier abroad than at home."[83] Indeed, by the time this was published, the country had already spent six months in a recession marked by a decline in production and real income that would not fully end until the arrival of war orders from Europe in 1915.[84]

The leading forecasters of the early twentieth century—Babson, James Brookmire, John Moody, and the Harvard statistician Warren Persons—all welcomed Fisher's Equation of Exchange. In 1911 Babson wrote that Fisher's equation "shows accurately and concretely what factors affect the general price level."[85] In 1913 Brookmire commented, "In his 'Equation' Fisher has with approximate accuracy discovered the velocity of circulation of money, the first time in history that this achievement has been accomplished."[86] In 1916 Persons of the Harvard Economic Service, who became Fisher's greatest academic rival in the field of professional forecasting, also praised Fisher's equation but complained that the velocities Fisher calculated "must be estimated from inadequate data and hence are subject to a large possible error."[87] As Brookmire and Persons recognized in their surveys of the field, the mathematical prodigy of Yale's Economics Department had helped increase the prestige of the forecasting industry.

Fisher, however, criticized other forecasters for not linking prices and employment or output. They seldom mentioned prices as a cause of instability and did not appreciate the difference between *changes* in the price level and the actual level of prices, he noted. In order to inform the public and to provide himself and others with the tools to forecast, Fisher spent an enormous amount of time studying index numbers and providing statistics on the purchasing power of a dollar. His staff at his home offices gathered data from government agencies, including the Treasury, from business and trade associations, and from foreign governments.[88]

Fisher sought a wide audience for his work. He thought it would be helpful to managers, who needed to assess upcoming periods of prosperity or recessions when formulating their purchasing or sales strategies. His advice was also aimed at investors who could monitor monetary and economic indicators to know when to switch between stocks and bonds, and when to quit the market altogether. The idea was to purchase in a rising market and sell in a falling one.[89]

After the 1920–21 recession Fisher began to think more about how the government could use his insights to fight unemployment and encourage growth in total output. By then the United States already had a central bank and the ability to influence the level of economic activity by encouraging money creation and lending. Fisher believed that unstable prices had great effect on output. Fascinated by this connection, he began to focus on booms and busts and the role of money in economic stability. He decided that improved money management at the level of government and by firms would mean more moderate fluctuations in economic performance and concluded that his best chance to influence policy was through writing for newspapers. That way, he could educate, at once, the leading decision makers as well as the public.

THE IVORY TOWER ENTREPRENEUR

In the early and mid-1920s, eyeing the resounding popularity of *Babson's Reports* and other forecasting services, Fisher moved to stake his claim in the field. His first task as a forecaster was to make his Equation of Exchange more useful as a predictive tool by improving his indexes of price movements. The difficulty in creating an index that would capture overall price movements arose because not all prices moved up and down uniformly. Instead, the price of various commodities moved at different rates and often in different directions. Fisher showed that the prices of a range of goods between 1913 and 1918, for instance, varied a great deal. Whereas the price of wool rose in those years by 282 percent, that of rubber rose only 68 percent. Wrote Fisher: "If we look at prices as starting at any time from the same point, they seem to scatter or disperse like the fragments of a bursting shell."[90] But, he explained, there was a center of gravity to the shell fragments and a parallel average to the scattering prices. This was the index number of the general price level.

In 1922 Fisher published an exhaustive study of this subject, *The Making of Index Numbers: A Study of Their Varieties, Tests, and Reliability*, in which he developed his ideal index, a form of geometric average that would reveal the central tendencies of a group of numbers. Fisher considered many questions about creating indexes to show changes in purchasing power: What time period should be measured? Should the price figures of all commodities and products be given equal weight—that is, should movements in the price of automobiles be as important as movements in the price of sugar? In trying to create an index of the general price level, Fisher could not gather data for every imaginable commodity on the marketplace but had to choose a representative subset. He wrote, "We want to find ... an index number constructed from a relatively small number of commodities which shall measure, as accurately as possible, the movement not only of this small number *included*, but also those *excluded*."[91] Once calculated, his index numbers showed the "*average percentage change* of prices from one point in time to another."[92]

Shortly after publishing the book, Fisher founded a new business, the Index Number Institute, which would make money by selling his price indexes and his economic opinions to newspapers. From 1923 to the early 1930s, the institute and its research staff issued weekly index numbers of wholesale commodity prices and of purchasing power. The second index number, of purchasing power, was simply the inverse of the commodity price index numbers but was important in pointing out, in a clear format, how the worth of the dollar changed.

Fisher was evangelical about the importance of disseminating economic knowledge. As he recalled later:

> The index of the dollar's purchasing power gave to several million people every Monday morning the opportunity to read of the weekly change in the dollar. It was apparently as a result of this that the phrases, "the purchasing power of the dollar," "the pre-war dollar," "the dollar of 1913," "the dollar of 1926," and other expressions, implying a consciousness that the dollar changes, came into general use; whereas previously all indexes were thought of as representing price movements of commodities—[the role of] money being forgotten.[93]

The Index Number Institute staff undertook a colossal amount of work. They gathered price data on numerous commodities from across a wide geographical region, examined them, and often produced detailed commentaries on price fluctuations. In subsequent decades, governments would gather price data and publish the price and production indexes, but Fisher and his staff undertook their task without financial support from government or philanthropic institutions.[94]

Fisher gained publicity for his new business, and he further differentiated his forecasting methods from those of less mathematically sophisticated rivals by giving frequent talks to the public and by writing editorials in newspapers.[95] He noted that most forecasters (like Babson and Brookmire) were mere analysts of historical trends who inductively identified patterns in the past and projected them into the future. By contrast, Fisher asserted, his equations and indexes were models that, by taking into account the *causes* of business fluctuations, could predict more precisely and more accurately.

Buoyed by his success in getting his indexes in newspapers, Fisher expanded the services of the Index Number Institute in the mid-1920s. He began writing a weekly series of editorials, known as Irving Fisher's Business Page, on business matters that would accompany his commodity price index and his consumer price index. This became the main forum for his forecasts. His first column appeared on Monday, January 25, 1926, in the *New York World* and elsewhere. It was titled "What Do Index Numbers Tell? Here You Can Learn about Them." Fisher promised to enlighten readers on the mysteries of the price level and the problems of fluctuating purchasing power.[96]

A prosperous and content Irving Fisher aboard the *Mauretania*, 1927. Source: Yale University, Manuscripts & Archives, Image no. 830, box 41.f.548.

FISHER'S BUSINESS PAGE

Forecasting was only one of Fisher's array of business enterprises. He was also an inventor, and one of his patented devices earned him a fortune that enabled him to enter the world of high-stakes Wall Street investing. His Index Visible held rows of overlapping index cards in such a way that they could be conveniently flipped through and sorted, allowing clerical workers to locate information stored on the cards with significantly greater speed than with a traditional filing system. Margaret and Irving Fisher invested $145,000 in the company, which they quickly recouped. Fisher started a business to manufacture the device in a factory in New Haven. As the company grew, Fisher opened a sales office in midtown Manhattan.[97] In 1925 the Rand Kardex Company, a firm that produced office supplies and business machines near Buffalo, New York, purchased the rights to the device for $660,000 (about $7.8 million today). Fisher became a director of the company, which later merged with the Remington Typewriter Company.[98] Fisher wrote to a childhood friend, "We are all making a lot of money!"[99]

The success at Rand Kardex also led Fisher to increase his staff at the Index Number Institute. The president of the organization, beginning in 1927, was

Karl Karsten (1891–1968), an economist from Indiana and former Kardex Company executive who had gained recognition by publishing *Charts and Graphs: An Introduction to Graphic Methods in the Analysis of Statistics* (1923).[100] Karsten, who made charts for Fisher, had entered the field of forecasting in 1926 when he published a highly critical review of the methods of the Harvard Economic Service, possibly at Fisher's urging.[101]

Karsten was a highly entrepreneurial figure, who fueled Fisher's business interests. He was also head of his own chart-making service in New Haven, Karsten Forekastograf, which he continued to operate after he became president of Fisher's company. The two organizations shared some staff and were, according to Karsten, closely interwoven.[102]

Karsten also took over the Index Number Institute's sales campaign. Unlike agencies that sold forecasts directly to subscribers through newsletters, Fisher placed his economic writings and statistics in the pages of newspapers. Daily journalism had been a familiar outlet for Fisher since the turn of the century, when he published articles on health. His charts and columns appeared in the *Hartford Courant*, the *Philadelphia Inquirer*, and many of the major newspapers.[103]

Karsten pushed the sales force to travel to regional newspaper editors throughout the country to try to "sell" them on the merits of including Fisher's Business Page in their papers every Monday. The Index Number Institute salesmen hoped to make Fisher's academic prominence a key selling point. Karsten directed his sales force to accentuate the "[s]cientific nature of our laboratory, its scientific origin and the scientific nature of its work."[104] This eventually was a successful approach, as Fisher's page appeared in dozens of newspapers. But it required a lot of work: one salesman canvassed seventy-nine newspapers in spring 1928, traveling throughout New York, New Jersey, Pennsylvania, Maryland, New England, and parts of Canada.[105] Many of the editors insisted that Fisher's syndicate not only supply the news stories and indexes but also help bring in business advertisements that would run on the page. This brought Fisher's syndicate into greater connection with large manufacturers and other companies, as they scrambled to find advertisers.[106]

With Karl Karsten and a sales team behind him, Fisher had gone from being a "mere" academic economist who issued the occasional forecast to a major pundit who expressed his thoughts clearly and boldly. Such prominent periodicals as the *New York Times* and the *Wall Street Journal* sought out his predictions.

In 1929, Fisher hoped to expand the audience of his forecasting service to the general public by publishing a brief guide on how to use the Fisher indexes in forecasting. It explained, in very simple language, Fisher's idea that a rising price level (or a decline in purchasing power) showed "that the volume of money and credit available is increasing faster than its utilization in the production and exchange of goods and services." If the price level was rising, the brochure instructed businesspeople, "Know in advance what will need to be ordered. See that inventories do not get low. Be particularly alert as to 'sensitive commodities'—those goods or supplies which experience indicates may soonest encounter shortage on sharply advancing quotations."[107] Conversely, a declining price level hurt borrowers and helped creditors, signaling the need for opposite action.

Fisher's forecasting business entered a new phase in the late 1920s. At that time, while Roger Babson was sending his salesmen out to address Rotary Clubs to gain subscribers, Fisher was trying to increase the number of newspapers that carried his Business Page and thereby reach more people. In December 1928, he met with the board of the Index Number Institute. Karsten, the company's president, estimated that the institute was suffering losses in these efforts to expand.[108] Fisher, however, was undeterred by the red ink. In early 1929 he gave instructions to the staff to "go ahead full steam."[109] Over the summer he expanded his home offices, spending more than $30,000 to build new workrooms and buy new office equipment.[110]

While Fisher was desperately trying to reach a popular audience, his work in mathematical economics was attracting a group of young economists. In April 1929, Ragnar Frisch (age thirty-four) and Charles F. Roos (age twenty-eight) approached Fisher. They wanted to start a new academic society based on the application of mathematical and statistical methods to economics. Frisch was a Norwegian who had studied economics and received his Ph.D. in mathematical statistics from the University of Oslo. He had come to the United States in 1927 on a fellowship from the Rockefeller Foundation and met Fisher. Roos, who had received his Ph.D. from the Rice Institute, was a professor at Cornell at the time. Frisch and Roos, both of whom became major figures in the field of econometrics, convinced Fisher that there was now enough interest in mathematical economics to start a society—thanks in no small part to Fisher's own pioneering contributions. Fisher agreed to be a founding member of the Econometric Society.[111]

DEBT AND DEFLATION

In the fall of 1929, Irving Fisher, aged sixty-two, was at his busiest. He was giving speeches on the benefits of stable money, serving on the board of Rand-Kardex, managing his investments, purchasing stocks on margin, teaching at Yale, and sending missives to President Herbert Hoover and congressmen on the subject of monetary reform. He was shifting his attention from New Haven and New York to Washington, D.C., while his house at 460 Prospect Street buzzed with the work of economists, secretaries, and assistants.

Forecasting was a central part of Fisher's life. He was a well-known figure and, like Herbert Hoover, a promoter of the New Era Optimism. In September 1929, Fisher engaged in a war of words with Roger Babson, provoked by Babson's comments that a severe stock market crash was on the way. This became an ominous moment in Fisher's career. He did not believe that the share prices on the stock market were overvalued. On September 6, 1929, he argued: "[T]here may be a recession of stock prices but not anything in the nature of a crash."[112] On October 15, at a meeting of the Purchasing Agents Association in New York City, Fisher gave a talk defending the work of the investment trusts. In it, he said (infamously) that stock prices had reached "what looks like a permanently high plateau."[113]

Fisher had great faith that recent gains in industrial productive capacities had permanently altered the economy for the better. He was particularly impressed by the new managerial efficiencies he observed in America's firms. He believed that real gains had been made by businesses plowing their earnings back into research and development rather than paying out dividends. He noted the widespread use of electricity in production and the high number of new patents. He felt the rise in stock prices during the 1920s had been justified and would soon rebound from the fall 1929 crash. "For the immediate future, at least, the outlook is bright," he concluded.[114] If anything, he thought shares were undervalued. Two days before "Black Thursday" (October 24), the *New York Times* reported: "Fisher says prices of stocks are low."[115]

When Babson's prediction seemed confirmed in the days of the stock market crash of late October, Fisher was stunned—but he remained optimistic. In November 1929, Fisher claimed that the crash had been the "shaking out of the lunatic fringe." He wrote, "It was the psychology of panic. It was mob psychology, and it was not, primarily, that the price level of the market was unsoundly high."[116] He drew attention to the high volume of stocks bought on brokers' loans—something he, too, had done in excess. A sober analysis of the situation, Fisher said, was that stocks were not overvalued and that the crash resulted largely from the "piling up of margin accounts during 1929" and then panicked selling.[117]

But such reasoning did little to repair the damage to Fisher's reputation. In December 1929 the *Outlook and Independent* noted, "The Wall Street upheaval which sank Irving Fisher's stock to a new low sent Roger Babson's skyward."[118] Fisher was ridiculed as a misguided "expert" who had misled the public.

Babson relished the moment. He called Fisher "one of the greatest economists in the world today and a most useful and unselfish citizen." But he argued that Fisher fundamentally misunderstood human nature and its role in the economy. Fisher faltered because "he thinks the world is ruled by figures instead of feelings, or by theories instead of by styles." Babson went on to point out that human beings often simply follow trends rather than pursue the most rational course of action. "An economist might figure out that high shoes and long skirts are better for women in the Winter time than low shoes and high skirts, but all the economists in the world could not make women change until the style changed.... In the same way styles rule Wall Street."[119] Babson thought Fisher had no capacity to understand swings in temperament or mood among the public. This remark had some merit. In fact, Fisher had some capacity to judge the irrational elements of the economy—hence his remark about the lunatic fringe. But he viewed them as merely temporary disturbances to the real economy that would vanish rather than (as Babson did) integral and enduring parts.

Fisher persistently released upbeat forecasts in subsequent months. In January 1930, Fisher claimed that it "would not be surprising if by next month the worst of the recession will have been felt and improvement looked for."[120] In February 1930, a mere four months after the crash, Fisher published *The Stock Market Crash—And After*. He argued that the factors leading to the crash derived, perhaps counterintuitively, from America's "unexampled prosperity" that would rapidly reassert itself. The cataclysm of the previous fall, he suggested, was a largely superficial affair. "The effects of the crash were largely psychological" and would soon pass.

Even the continued bad times did not dampen his optimism for the economy. In December 1930, Fisher acknowledged the severity of the economic troubles but still thought the worst was over and expected a rise in commodity prices to come perhaps by the following spring.[121] In early 1931, well before the 1932 nadir, Fisher wrote, "The industrial giant has become conscious again. He is beginning to move around slowly in an effort to regain his feet, as the cobwebs from a knockout blow gradually clear from his brain."[122]

Throughout the early 1930s, Fisher insisted that the lingering depression could be solved through monetary policy. Through his correspondence and newspaper editorials, he tried to pressure the Federal Reserve to expand the money supply. In 1931 he wrote, for instance, "No single factor would be as helpful to business as a cessation in the commodity price decline that has been continued for the past two years."[123] Before his death in 1928, the governor of the Federal Reserve Bank of New York, Benjamin Strong, had taken the correct countercyclical policies to maintain monetary stability, Fisher asserted. "He did it by putting money in circulation when other people were taking it out and by taking it out when they were putting it in."[124]

In 1933 Fisher came up with a new theory to help explain the lingering hard times. His "debt-deflation" theory focused, like much of Fisher's work, on monetary and banking policy but put great emphasis on the role of debt. The problem with the economic situation, Fisher argued, was that the overinvestment and overspeculation had been conducted with borrowed money. American households had taken on great debt (through the purchase of cars and houses and through investing) and European governments had also borrowed great sums. When stock prices collapsed, businesses, banks, and households sought to improve their financial condition. This led to distress selling, pushing stock prices down further, and to reduced bank deposits. The velocity of money slowed and prices continued to fall. Fisher believed that only reinflation would help the economy; he advocated a return to the 1926 price level through open market operations of the Federal Reserve and other actions—and he wrote persistently to President Roosevelt to pursue this course, but to no avail.[125]

Fisher kept the Index Number Institute and his news syndicate going for a few years, advertising in the *New York Times* and hiring a new sales staff on commission, preferably those with "acquaintance with better class business and financial firms."[126] His employee Royal Meeker wrote many of the articles for the Index Number Institute in the early 1930s, but he left the company in 1936, prompting Fisher to sell it to the Institute of Applied Econometrics.[127]

Eventually Fisher's activities at 460 Prospect Street wound down. Karl Karsten continued as the head of the Index Number Institute until 1933, when he left for the first of several positions with federal agencies, though he increasingly directed his energies elsewhere. He produced his own book, *Scientific Forecasting: Its Methods and Application to Practical Business and to Stock Market Operations* (1931). He also toiled on an unpublished novel, *Horse in a Limousine*, about a future world so rich that even horses could afford chauffeurs.

Fisher himself still had his handsome salary as a professor, and he received fees for being a director of Remington Rand and Sonotone. But these could not support the lifestyle he had built at 460 Prospect Street and he was deeply in debt from his previous stock purchases. Fisher did not diversify his investment portfolio and his Remington Rand stock dropped from $58 a share in 1929 to $1 in 1933. He was also required by the Internal Revenue Service to pay $61,000 in back taxes on money earned in 1927 and 1928.[128] Within this context of embarrassment and debt, Fisher remained a whirlwind of activity promoting his myriad causes. He lectured and wrote three books on the importance of Prohibition.[129]

His personal situation grew increasingly dire. Fisher borrowed heavily from his sister-in-law, who had inherited money from the Hazard fortune. In 1936, he persuaded Yale to purchase his grand house on Prospect Street and grant his family a life-tenancy under a modest rent. Even under those terms he was forced to leave in 1939 because he could no longer pay the rent. At that time, Fisher was in debt to Caroline Hazard $750,000 and owed interest payments of $3,800 per month to his brokers and rent to Yale for his home.[130] In January 1940, before the Fishers' planned move from the Prospect Street home, his wife died of a heart attack while they were visiting California. Her death was a grievous loss for him; the two had been married forty-seven years. Fisher, whose two remaining children were grown, moved into a modest apartment. In 1947, Fisher died of cancer a few months after being honored at the Yale Club of New York on the occasion of his eightieth birthday.[131]

FISHER AS FORECASTER

The irony of Irving Fisher's life was the gulf between the misery in which his career and personal life wound down and the reverence he attracted among a small group of young economists who would come to dominate the profession. While Fisher's reputation as a popular prophet and pundit sank in the

1930s, he was making significant contributions to the field of forecasting. In 1930, the professional association of mathematical economists that Frisch and Roos had proposed in 1929 came to fruition. Its first organizational meeting took place in December 1930 at the American Economic Association's meeting in Cleveland, where the group voted to call themselves the Econometric Society, borrowing a term coined by Ragnar Frisch.[132]

In 1932 Fisher expressed his hope for the burgeoning movement in a letter to his wife: "I hope they [the new generation of economists] may make Economics a truer science and more like the older sciences." He remembered how the scientific approach of his teacher Josiah Willard Gibbs had transformed thermodynamics; Fisher had the hope of similarly transforming the foundations of economics by applying Gibbs's methods: "For years I was greatly disappointed because there seemed so little market for my wares and so much resistance to their novelty. But now of a sudden I'm realizing that the seed planted really took root."[133]

Though he was wrong about the movements of the stock market and the business landscape in 1929 and the early 1930s, he was in a broader sense more right than anyone else in his insights into the causal mechanisms of a capitalist economy. Fisher believed that the Great Depression was made much worse by the contraction of the money supply, something the Federal Reserve should have prevented. In this he has had many followers, including Milton Friedman and Anna Schwartz in *A Monetary History of the United States, 1867–1960*.[134] The latter point was emphasized in Friedman and Schwartz's book on the subject and became a consensus view shared by John Kenneth Galbraith and others.

Moreover, Fisher's contributions to forecasting, and to economics more broadly, have long outshone those of his competitors. These contributions were threefold: his brilliant formulation of the Equation of Exchange and his subsequent writings on monetary phenomena; his sense that changes in business practice and in technology could have lasting effects on industrial productivity; and his advocacy for the use of mathematics and statistics in economics that changed the shape of the field.

Admiration for Fisher has grown markedly in the years since his death, to the extent that there have even been efforts to defend Fisher's defiant optimism in the years after 1929—to claim that he had been right all along about the stock market and its valuation at the time of the colossal crash.[135] While Fisher's influence on businessmen in the 1920s is not clear, his influence on businesspeople from the 1970s onward is undoubted: today's mathematical approach and dominant belief in the efficiency of markets would be unthinkable without Fisher.[136]

As one of Fisher's biographers wrote of the great economist, "With Fisher, everything was cut and dried, practical and pragmatic, the variables all well specified.... He ignored or dismissed, or assumed away all the great imponderables."[137] Fisher's life had indeed been filled with turbulent excesses and tragic "imponderables": with the early loss of his father and sister and the tragic death of his daughter Margaret; with the gain and loss of a great deal of money; with the rise of both successful business and academic careers, and the fall of the former; and with his own health problems. This was the context in which Fisher undertook a monumental struggle to impose reason and predictability upon the world by embracing the scientific method.

CHAPTER 3

John Moody: The Bright Light of Transparency
||||||||||||||||||||||||||||||||||||||||||||||||||||||||||||||||||||||||||||||||

John Moody (1868–1958) established himself as a leading forecaster in the 1910s and 1920s while building one of the largest business-information companies of the twentieth century. Forecasting was just one of Moody's interests. His name is best known today in the ratings industry. Moody's Investors Service became the most influential of the Big Three credit ratings agencies and today is a company of tremendous power and size.[1] His interest in amassing data about the health of individual firms and the securities they offered informed his approach to forecasting, which, in today's terminology, was more oriented to micro- rather than macroeconomics. But this was not a distinction recognized at the time.

Throughout his career, Moody was an advocate for transparency in financial markets. He perceived that Wall Street was changing rapidly in the early twentieth century. Railroads were the biggest companies in the country, but industrial firms were gaining in size and importance and some, like Standard Oil and U.S. Steel, were massive. New brokerage houses seemed to open daily in Manhattan and stock ownership was growing more widespread. The men and women who owned the stocks and bonds of railroad companies had a right to know the financial conditions of these concerns, argued Moody. The "railroads are not owned by a small group of capitalists of great wealth, as is erroneously supposed in some quarters, but by a large number (between one and two millions) of individuals in this and other countries, whose average holdings range from $700 to $1,500 each," wrote Moody in 1909.[2] These investors did not control the railroads, Moody acknowledged, but the group of investors did *own* them. Securities ownership, though still confined to 12 percent of the population by 1929, was no longer simply the province of plutocrats.

But ordinary investors had little access to information in a period when companies seldom printed annual reports. Moody believed that the publication and analyses of corporate statistics would make the financial markets fairer and more "scientific" in orientation. He developed his business-information publishing company out of both his desire to shine a light into the dark corners of Wall Street and his own relentless effort to secure a personal fortune. Moody built his empire several times over, including losing everything in the Panic of 1907 and starting again from scratch.

Roger Babson used the language of meteorology to describe business activity, creating "business barometers." Irving Fisher borrowed the terms of physics when he described the economy as an intricate machine whose mechanisms could be best understood through application of mathematical analysis. Moody's worldview, informed perhaps by his love for English literature, was Dickensian in nature. His writings describe an economy energized by the aspirations of entrepreneurs and by powerful industries. In his view, business leaders and their firms were the main actors in the economy. They commercialized inventions, hired people, and made investment decisions. They created the buildings and bridges that dominated the physical landscape, the clothes that people wore, the transportation that moved goods and people about, and so many of the wondrous inventions of the period—bottled sodas, safety razors, cash registers, adding machines, bicycles, telephones, and so on. But the economy was also filled with speculators and swindlers. Bucket shops, where people wagered on securities but did not actually purchase them, were magnets for—in the Wall Street parlance of the day—"lambs," or naïve investors, who were "sheared" by unscrupulous operators.[3]

Moody spent a big part of his life forecasting. He did not espouse a single model for making predictions. He was suspicious of theory and thought his clients would be uninterested in reading academic treatises. Moody was fond of the writings of the acerbic H. L. Mencken and distrusted the conformity and confidence of the 1920s. "It was the era of Babbittry, and like many who classified themselves with the intelligentsia, I became 'Menckenized,'" Moody wrote of that period in his autobiography *The Long Road Home* (1933). "That is to say, I fell in line with the intellectual racketeers, seeing our modern world as the acme of hypocrisy, and almost losing faith in the good intentions of mankind."[4] He was skeptical of professors, market theorists, and bureaucratic reformers.

In part because of this skepticism, Moody based his forecasts on the acquisition of vast amounts of news and other information about the large firms of the day and their operations and about the personalities of their leaders. By 1900, when the young Moody published his first *Manual of Industrial and Miscellaneous Securities*, men like Andrew Mellon, John D. Rockefeller, and J. P. Morgan exerted an unprecedented level of influence on the nation's economy. Moody profiled these leaders in books like *Railroad Builders* (1919) and *Masters of Capital* (1921).[5]

While Babson looked at industrial output to help determine the health of the economy and Fisher examined money, prices, and interest rates, Moody looked at the financial data of corporations, news that poured in on tickers, the price-earnings ratios of securities, and other information that he collected in his firm's massive library. He also focused on another important part of the economy: expectations. Expectations, like output and money, play an important role in a nation's economy. They can drive an economy to crisis during, for instance, bank runs; they can also produce booms in stock prices during periods of optimism. Expectations, then, can have very real consequences. Indeed, governments and private businesses today go to great extremes to try to manage the expectations of businesspeople, consumers, and investors.[6] Since its inception in 1966, the U.S. Consumer Confidence Index, calculated annually by the nonprofit business membership and research group organization the Conference Board, has been an important indicator of the nation's economic health.

In forecasting, Moody was particularly interested in the expectations of business leaders for profits—and even tried, in the mid-1920s, to create a method for analyzing them systematically. Mostly, though, Moody approached forecasting using his knowledge of business leaders and their plans, his ratings of securities, and his survey of general news. His predictions were not based on historical trends or changes to the price level but on deep analysis of current financial information. If Babson was an oracle who noted the recurrence of historic trends and Fisher was a prodigy who illuminated the cause of economic change, Moody was a Wall Street analyst who persistently recorded the day-to-day activities of businesspeople and their firms, seeing them in aggregate as representing the economy.

Though working in the Wall Street area, Moody focused most of his attention on making sense of general business conditions rather than predicting changes in the stock market—and his story provides a chance to draw a distinction between these two endeavors. For many business analysts of the time, and today, the stock market provides a barometer of future general economic activity. This was, for instance, the view of Charles Dow: trends in the stock market foreshadowed ups and downs in manufacturing and employment. Moody believed the opposite, that activity in the stock market actually followed changes in general business. He argued that investors tended to purchase securities when business was good, and they had surplus funds, and sold them when they encountered financial difficulties—and that this behavior, en masse, made stock purchases lag changes in the "real" economy. One article from an economist at Moody's firm spelled out the company position: "Close study reveals the fact that the stock market is a creature of trade, and a trailer after it, and not a leader or a maker of trade conditions."[7]

Moreover, Moody did not believe, like Babson and Fisher, that capitalist economies have natural equilibrium points. Babson argued that there was an internal logic to markets that, in tune with the laws of gravity, made everything even out—not just in business but in all aspects of life. Fisher perceived that there was a mathematical logic to economic relationships of prices, the velocity of money, and total output. Moody did not seem to have any such sense. Instead he saw capitalist economies as more chaotic—terrifying in their capacity to bring ruin and exhilarating in their ability to create fortunes. The best way to forecast was to gather, organize, and analyze all the news and information one could and to use judgment and even intuition to try to be one step ahead of the rest.

FROM JERSEY CITY TO WALL STREET

John Moody was a New Jersey native, born just three years after the Civil War ended. He recalled the Jersey City of his early childhood as hastily built. In his 1933 memoir, Moody wrote, "horse cars jangled along the cobble-stoned or unpaved streets" and "the buildings, even in the business section, were mostly wooden and only three stories or less."[8] When Moody was five years old, the family moved to a more rural area around nearby Bayonne.[9]

Moody's father spent much of his working life as a clerk at one of the nation's leading shipping concerns, the Adams Express Company. According to his son, however, he was "impractical" and "romantic," frequently investing in the stock market and in get-rich-quick schemes. He lost a fortune in the Panic of 1873, including the money intended for his children's college education. Moody left school after the eighth grade to support his family. Despite these losses, Moody's father failed to learn from experience. He continued investing in the stock market whenever he heard a good tip; after the panic of 1879, Moody described his father's holdings, in the slang of the day, as again "beautifully 'trimmed.'"[10] These experiences had lasting effect on Moody, who never ceased to see Wall Street as something of a casino; he eventually came to believe, however, that if he could supply better information to investors, he would improve their odds. This belief in the importance of transparency shaped much of his career.

In 1883, at fifteen years of age, Moody began working at a woodenware wholesale house on Washington Street in lower Manhattan. He earned three dollars per week—the equivalent of about $65 today—running errands, delivering mops and pails, shining shoes, and sweeping, all the while quietly plotting his escape from his menial duties.

To compensate for the early conclusion of his formal education, Moody took correspondence courses and read a great deal, including topics in political economy and history. Moody completed the four-year correspondence course of the Chautauqua Literary and Scientific Circle, a movement begun in 1878 that provided the means of acquiring a college-level education to thousands of Americans.[11] Moody's literary bent also became apparent early. He sold stories to *Boy's World* magazine for $3. In later years, he supplemented his income by writing "pot boilers" for boys' magazines. He also briefly published a small literary magazine, *Hyperion*, though it lost money.[12] Moody's high energy level and his ambition in writing foreshadowed his later success as an entrepreneur and publisher.

In May 1890, Moody secured a Wall Street job with the help of his mother's cousin George Foster Peabody (1852–1938), who was a partner at the financial house of Spencer Trask & Company. The position was a huge break in the life of a boy with no clear path. The company's founder, Spencer Trask (1844–1909), was best known for financing Thomas Edison's lightbulb and serving as president of the New York Edison Company. The investment firm also underwrote railway construction in the Southwest and in Mexico. Though Moody's work at Spencer Trask was not glamorous—he was hired as an errand boy and a "stamp licker" at $20 a month—Wall Street was a dramatic contrast to the world he had seen thus far. His new surroundings had soft carpets and roll-top desks and employees who spoke calmly and did not swear.[13]

Moody rose quickly at Spencer Trask. He demonstrated a capability with numbers and soon became a statistician and a specialist in the analysis of securities, drawing a high salary of $3,000 per year (about $75,000 today). He gained knowledge about all aspects of Wall Street. According to his memoir, he "acquired the reputation of being the walking statistical table of the business."[14]

Despite his promotion at Spencer Trask, Moody ran into trouble. He followed in his father's footsteps, losing money as fast as he made it at local bucket shops. These gambling dens were common around Wall Street. Moody believed that they functioned primarily as places where the clerks of banks and brokerage houses went to copy the investments that their bosses and managers were carrying out on the New York Stock Exchange. Moody joined a pool with other clerks from Spencer Trask and borrowed money to invest in railroad stocks, but when these investments dropped in value in 1893, three years after he joined the firm, Moody again was left in debt.[15] (Moody railed against bucket shops later in life. "Pure betting is done in bucket-shops," he wrote in 1906. It "is of no use to the community, is destructive to the morals and pockets of young men, and cannot be too severely censured.")[16]

In 1899 Moody married Brooklyn resident Anna M. Addison (1877–1965), who, like Moody, had a strong interest in the arts.[17] As a newlywed, Moody began to chafe at the life of a salary-man. By then he was Spencer Trask's head of research, but he felt he had little chance for advancement, at least anytime soon. Rather than wait for the promotion that might never come, he began a new career as a publisher of business information—a move that eventually led him to forecasting.

Around the time of Moody's marriage, an article by the financial journalist Thomas F. Woodlock in the *Wall Street Journal* on the need for more business statistics about individual firms gave Moody the idea for which he had been waiting. At Spencer Trask, where his responsibilities included studying and analyzing specific railroads, mines, and other potential firms for investment, Moody became aware of the growing demand among businesspeople and investors for statistical information. "During the year 1898," Moody wrote in his memoirs, "an insistent demand arose in Wall Street for some reliable publication which would supply complete information and statistics on industrial corporations, and more particularly on their numerous stock and bond issues,—which were flowing into the financial markets in ever increasing volume."[18] Moody went to visit Woodlock and discussed the sort of publication that could meet this need.[19] Like Babson, Moody decided to print a directory of industrial corporations and the securities they offered. This was Moody's first significant move toward rendering the mysteries of Wall Street visible to outsiders.

MOODY'S FORERUNNERS

Moody's idea was to compile a publication, or manual, of statistics of industrial corporations, including manufacturers and mining companies. Standard Oil and Carnegie Steel were the biggest and best known, but the number of industrial firms was rapidly increasing and more of them were issuing shares to the public. There was little information about these new firms, aside from Charles H. Nicoll's *Manual of Statistics—Stock Exchange Handbook*, first published in 1879, which covered about four hundred firms but provided little financial information.[20] Moody decided to print a directory of industrial corporations and the securities they offered. He chose to include companies listed on the Boston, Philadelphia, and Chicago exchanges, as well as the New York Stock Exchange.[21]

All forecasters were influenced by past traditions. Whereas Babson drew on the work of meteorologists and the prophet Samuel Benner, and Fisher on the mathematical economics of Rudolf Auspitz and Richard Lieben, Moody benefited from the work of Henry Varnum Poor. Poor was a pioneer in providing financial and statistical information about the railroad industry.[22]

In the late nineteenth century, Poor's Railroad Manual Company was the most influential publisher in the field of business information. Henry Varnum Poor was an early business analyst, the first important figure in the field. He was born in Maine and practiced as a lawyer in the city of Bangor. He learned the railroad business from his brother, who helped develop Maine's railroads. In 1849 Poor published the *American Railroad Journal*. Poor took his editorial role seriously and began to expand coverage of individual companies, including financial performance data. In 1860 he published *A History of the Railroads and the Canals of the United States*. With his son, Henry William (1844–1915), Poor founded the H. V. and H. W. Poor Company, which eventually became Poor's Railroad Manual Company. Demand for information on railroads soared after the Civil War: railroads were among the first industries to require immense outlays of capital and hence sold large quantities of securities to meet their upfront costs. In 1868 the company printed the *Manual of the Railroads of the United States*, which became highly popular, selling 2,500 copies in a few months. Poor's books guided investors to the financial health of different railroad lines. The *Manual* was updated annually and became the leading source of information for railroad investors, both in the United States and abroad.[23]

Poor and his staff were so well trained that they set the standards for the next generation of business statisticians in the country.[24] In 1900 railroads were still synonymous with big business and were the leading firms issuing securities for public purchase, but industrial enterprises were growing. Poor had even published the *Handbook of Investment Securities* from 1890 to 1893 that treated industrial companies, but he had stopped publishing it during the depression, leaving that field open.[25]

Lacking the $20,000 to $30,000 that Moody thought necessary to launch the business, he moved boldly. He got some financial help from Eliphalet Nott Potter, a colleague at Spencer Trask, and began canvassing Wall Street firms for preorders in order to raise money to fund the writing of the book.

Moody remembered encountering resistance from old Wall Street hands who preferred to guard their "insider" information. "If you begin to flaunt too many facts, there won't be much inside knowledge left to work on," he later remembered one banker telling him. "You will be spoiling our game."[26] The quotes may very well be apocryphal—we have only Moody's word for it, and he was very fond of representing himself as a public-minded crusader for corporate transparency—but the trend was real: more financial statistics about firms were becoming public in the early decades of the century, changing the culture of Wall Street.[27]

Moody created a detailed prospectus, a "humdinger" with enough promises to make Wall Street "turn somersaults," he said. He sent out five thousand copies of the prospectus along with blank order forms. He mailed it to the entire New York Stock Exchange directory and to selected bankers, brokers, and insurance company executives throughout the country. He had printed the flyers on credit and spent around two hundred dollars of his own money on postage. But his instincts proved correct. He received several hundred orders—for a book that did not yet exist.[28]

Moody then set about working tirelessly on the *Manual*, with the help of his wife, Anna. He completed it about seven or eight months later and it was published in 1900. Running to over 1,100 pages, the *Manual* had statistics on

1,800 industrial companies and was bound in red to distinguish it from Poor's green-covered publications on railroads. Moody's manual had twelve sections, including ones on steel and iron, automobiles, mining, telephone and telegraph, and textiles. It listed company names, balance sheets, dates of incorporation, and outstanding securities (date of issue and value).[29] The firms it covered had issued a total capital of $9.3 billion—a colossal amount of securities that, together with the railroads, were fueling the growth of the nation. Though not nearly as well edited as Poor's manuals, it would improve over the years.

The first edition of the manual met with success of storybook proportions. Moody shrewdly had waited until after the distraction of the 1900 presidential election was over. When pro-business Republican William McKinley earned a second term and fought off the populist challenge of William Jennings Bryan, the stock market rallied—as did the market for investment advice. Moody published 5,000 copies of the 1900 manual and sold them all at $5. His profits on the manual exceeded $5,000. Moody recalled in an autobiographical essay that he was so satisfied at the time that it seemed like "rainbows were shining all around me."[30]

Moody expanded his sales effort. In 1901 he opened offices at 35 Nassau Street and hired Louis Holschuh, who later became president of the company, to deliver the *Manual* all over Manhattan and hired away one of Poor's salesmen, Orland Lewis (a "monumental windbag" but effective salesman, according to Moody), to work the Philadelphia area. Moody also set up sales agencies in Chicago, Pittsburgh, London, and Amsterdam. In 1902 he went on a sales tour with stops in Cleveland, Chicago, Omaha, Denver, and several cities in California, with pamphlets "boosting the Manual to the skies."[31] Onboard the train, he dropped circulars on every seat. In retrospect, Moody estimated that the publication gained a national reputation by about 1903. At that time Moody had fifteen to twenty employees in his office.

Moody faced competition in these years, especially from Luther Blake's Standard Statistics Bureau, a firm that, like Moody's, offered financial details on individual companies. After arriving in New York City from Fayetteville, Tennessee, Blake (1874–1953) took a job at Laidlaw and Company, a brokerage, operating their wire department. In 1904 he began keeping a scrapbook and had the idea of printing, on cards, facts about a hundred leading companies.[32] Moody's *Manual* was already well established, but Blake's business promised to provide more frequent updates about individual firms.

Maiden Lane and Nassau Street, 1921. Moody's office was along Nassau Street. New York emerged as the nation's business center in the years after the Civil War. It became a place where tycoons like Andrew Carnegie, James Buchanan Duke, and John D. Rockefeller migrated. J. P. Morgan, who was born in Connecticut, started his own private bank in New York in 1861 and spent the rest of his life centered there, becoming to many the very symbol of capitalism itself. Source: Photo 721877F American Studio, Photographic views of New York City, 1870s–1970s, Millstein Division of United States History, Local History & Genealogy, New York Public Library, Astor, Lenox and Tilden Foundations.

In 1906 Blake started Standard Statistics, using bellboys from the Calumet Hotel to deliver his news cards. Within the first two years he had secured three hundred subscribers (including J. P. Morgan & Co., Kuhn, Loeb & Co., and National City Bank), all of whom paid $5 per month. The big move for Blake was the purchase, in 1913, of the Babson Stock & Bond Card System, giving him complete control over this type of news-card service.[33] The following year, Blake incorporated the firm. For years, Moody's and Standard Statistics were the two largest suppliers of business information in lower Manhattan; they did not have identical products but rather coexisted as two behemoths serving a booming audience.

Moody's more direct competition in the field of corporate information was the Poor publishing company. In 1904, Poor's brought out a volume on industrial companies and public utilities. Poor's books were more expensive: Poor's two volumes on railroads and industrials sold for $14, while Moody's single volume covered both for $10.[34] Moody could have expected this competition, since he had started out his industrial manual by copying Poor's volume on railroads; but while the Moody and Standard companies seemed to coexist peacefully, the relationship with Poor's eventually became bitter.

FORECASTING A FIRM-CENTERED ECONOMY

Continuing his rise, Moody founded the Moody Publishing Company in 1903 with capital of $125,000. The company had two new lines of business. One was a Bureau of Corporation Statistics, a financial library of two thousand volumes with news clippings and other data on individual firms. The library became a busy center for researchers from private firms.

The second business Moody started was a book-publishing company specializing in works on finance and economics. Moody wrote some of the books himself, including a five-hundred-page tome called *The Truth about the Trusts* (1904), which offered his opinions on one of the most controversial features of the turn-of-the-century business landscape: trust companies, which had become notorious as a result of their size and influence. *The Truth about the Trusts* showed Moody's belief that the economy comprised a landscape of firms and that large companies determined the country's economic future. Beginning in the late nineteenth century American firms had increasingly exploited this legal device to get around competition law and develop informal cartels. In the course of doing research for other publications, Moody had collected mountains of financial information about individual firms and large trusts: in copper, sugar, and in the telephone industry.

Moody was a supporter of trusts. Unlike Louis Brandeis, whose *The Curse of Bigness* remains one of the most famous critiques of large, horizontally and vertically integrated corporations, Moody saw them as a natural evolution of business: "Instead of the growth of the Trust movement being an achievement to be laid at the door of Mr. Morgan or Mr. Rockefeller, or any other leader of men, it should be laid at the door of nature." The trust, Moody continued, "*is the natural outcome or evolution of societary conditions and ethical standards which are recognized and established among men today as being necessary elements in the development of civilization.*"[35] Moody saw the devel-

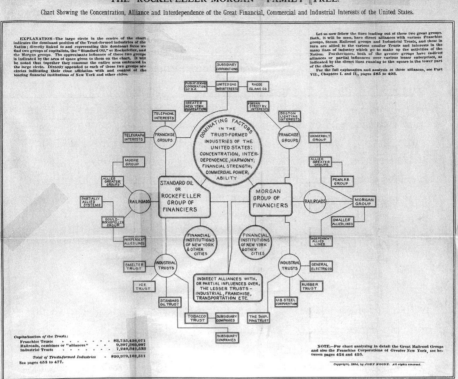

Moody's view of the economy. In this 1904 chart, Moody encapsulates a firm-centered view of the economy, in this case showing the dominance of the Morgan banking interests and Rockefeller's Standard Oil. Moody wrote at the top of the chart, "The large circle in the center of the chart indicates the dominant position of the Trust-formed industries of the Nation; directly linked to and representing this dominant force we find two groups of capitalists, the Standard Oil, or Rockefeller, and the Morgan groups. The approximate influence of these two groups is indicated by the area of space given to them on the chart. It should be noted that together they consumed the entire area embraced in the large circle. Directly appended to each of these two groups are circles indicating their close affiliation with and control of the leading financial institutions in New York and other cities." Moody's diagram was unique among the forecasters; it resembled something of a family tree of capitalism. Source: John Moody, *The Truth about the Trusts: A Description and Analysis of the American Trust Movement* (New York: Moody Publishing Company, 1904), between pages viii and ix.

opment of large banks and financial companies as parallel to the large manufacturing trusts. Large-scale business was necessary in several industries to
produce efficiently, Moody reasoned.

As his good fortune continued, Moody outdid himself with new enterprises and new investments. In 1904 Moody formed the Moody Corporation with $1,000,000 in capital (about $21 million today) to coordinate his
many ventures. A year later he started *Moody's Magazine*, a glossy publication
filled with pieces by notable journalists, businesspeople, and economists, including Irving Fisher, who wrote about the Equation of Exchange. Moody
also made other investments, many of them financed with borrowed money,
in endless schemes to get rich. He acquired an expensive printing plant in
New Jersey to produce his publications, a brick-making factory in New York,
and even a gold mine in Nevada.

THE PANIC OF 1907

With all of these businesses, Moody found himself overextended with the
onset of financial panic in 1907. The event arrived unexpectedly, Moody recalled, "destroying values by the billions, replacing confidence with fear and
foreboding, annihilating credit and driving interest rates up to the moon."
His "house of cards collapsed with the rest, and all my business interests fell
in ruin at my feet."[36] When the panic hit, Moody was thirty-nine years old and
the father of two young boys, John and Ernest, aged seven and three. Faced
with his failure and monumental debts, Moody contemplated suicide while
staring out at the water off the Atlantic shore. Moody said of the period that he
"learned that uncontrolled optimism is no asset at all, but a great liability."[37]

Moody's newspaper lost subscribers, the gold mine turned up nothing but
mud, and the brick-making factory found little demand for its product during hard times. The printing plant, in particular, proved to be a burden, for
it forced Moody to pay huge fixed costs, in terms of plant operation, debt on
the equipment, and payroll. Moody sold *Moody's Magazine* to publisher Augustin Ferrin, who continued to run it out of Moody's offices at 35 Nassau
Street. Moody called him an "ambitious literary lamb" who "sunk capital into
[the magazine] for ... eight years" until it failed.[38]

Moody survived by keeping creditors at bay. He celebrated his own "extraordinary finesse in the art of stalling."[39] Though he was over $100,000 in

debt, Moody avoided personal bankruptcy through the work of a lawyer who helped him rearrange repayment schedules and get extensions on his loans. In autumn 1907, Moody wrote: "I had been a great donator, a great lender, a great borrower, a great endorser. I had thought all along that I was a great builder; but now, for the first time, I discovered that I was only a great optimist!"[40] He could not keep his business concerns out of receivership, however, and in February 1908 was forced to sell his manual company to a group of creditors including his company's treasurer and former Wall Street colleague, Eliphalet Potter. Potter, who had known Roger Babson for years, arranged for Babson to purchase the company.

Losing control of his business publishing empire was bad enough; worse was to watch it go to Roger Babson. Babson later made moralistic comments about the former owner of his new enterprises. "Unfortunately, John had a New York training instead of a New England training," Babson explained in his 1935 autobiography, suggesting (somewhat accurately) that Moody was too eager to simply get rich rather than to grow a business slowly.[41] Babson took over ownership of the *Manual*, the copyright to the "Moody" name for use in the publication, and the printing press. Babson and his colleague Roy Porter, an editor, began publishing *Moody's Manual* in 1908 and did so for the next sixteen years. Babson added advertisements to the manual to increase revenue, a new feature that generated over $20,000 in the first year it was offered. The new company, recalled Porter, hired "practically all" of their information compilers from Poor's.[42] Moody's 1907 losses would affect him for years to come, pushing him to become more of an analyst and forecaster, with his own identity, than a mere provider of information.

FROM STATISTICS TO ANALYSIS

After the 1907 panic subsided, Moody returned to work and started to rebuild his publishing business in the summer of 1908—in a far different economic climate than the booming years in which he had begun. He chose to reenter the field of providing economic information but now with increased competition from Roger Babson, publisher and owner of *Moody's Manual*, and from Poor's and Standard Statistics.

Moody could not simply re-create the publications that had made him rich before the panic; he was banned from doing so by his agreement with

Babson. His key insight as he rebuilt his business empire—and one that would lead him to forecasting—was that there was a need for business publications that provided opinions, rather than mere facts, to aid decision making. In 1909 Moody founded Analyses Publishing, which operated out of his old Nassau Street offices.[43]

Moody entered the forecasting field directly—although he had offered his predictions informally in the business press for years—with the start of *Moody's Weekly Review of Financial Conditions*, also called *Moody's Weekly Letter*, and with his *Monthly Analyses of Business Conditions*. Moody claimed that the idea for forecasting came from customers who regularly sought his views about the market.

Moody distinguished his newsletter from "the usual market tipping services." There was, he wrote, "nothing like a weekly service designed primarily for investors rather than for mere speculators. Roger Babson was issuing a shallow superficial service and James K. Brookmire of St. Louis had put out a so-called 'scientific' one, but this was too high-brow to get a wide circulation." Luther Blake of Standard Statistics Bureau seemed to have spread himself too thin with side enterprises that lost money rather than earned it. "I promptly sponged him off as a serious competitor," Moody concluded.[44]

Just as he had done for his original manual, Moody canvassed bankers and brokers and investors in Manhattan to gain their subscriptions prior to publishing his first issue of the forecasting letter. He returned to the same customers who had read *Moody's Magazine*, for he had kept a copy of the subscription list after selling the periodical—something Roy Porter, of Babson's, criticized as "piracy."[45]

Moody regained his position in the business information field as quickly as he had lost it. He had more than 100 subscribers within a week, who were paying him $50 to $60 for an annual subscription to the newsletter. By 1911 the *Weekly Review* made profits of $18,210; and, in the following year, $21,665.[46]

Moody also started another business at the same time, one that proved crucial to his forecasting endeavors. He started his ratings agency, Moody's Analyses Publishing. In forming the business, Moody had several historical predecessors. By far the closest parallel was in the nineteenth-century credit-reporting agencies, which were established in the mercantile field to help dry goods merchants and other suppliers determine the creditworthiness of shopkeepers and salespeople.[47] The largest and best known of the nineteenth-

century credit ratings agencies was Lewis and Arthur Tappan's Mercantile
Credit Agency, founded in 1841. Tappan and his brother were wealthy silk
traders who were also active in the antislavery movement. In their silk business they learned to assess the creditworthiness of customers. Using their
extensive abolitionist connections, they set up a network of correspondents
throughout the Northeast to collect reports about the reliability of individual merchants. Their business grew quickly and they were able to engage some
180 correspondents by 1843. Customers of the mercantile credit agency,
most of whom were Manhattan wholesalers, came to Tappan's New York offices, where they could hear these reports read to them, at a whisper, to retain
confidentiality. Tappan's successors at the firm were Benjamin Douglass and
Robert Graham Dun, who re-founded the firm as R. G. Dun & Company
in 1859.

By the time Dun took control of the firm, the field of credit reports was
competitive. In 1849, John M. Bradstreet of Cincinnati began to collect, sell,
and market credit reports. He used a different model than the one the Tappan brothers had originated. In Bradstreet's system, written reports on individual merchants were not kept in-house but were mailed to his clients
and placed in loose-leaf binders. In 1857 Bradstreet moved to New York and
began publishing credit reports in the form of reference books. He introduced a rating system of A through E to indicate levels of creditworthiness.
In 1909, when Moody started his bond-rating business, he also used a letter
code similar to Bradstreet's to indicate his confidence in a security.[48]

The first edition of Moody's *Analyses of Railroad Investments* contained
ratings of 1,200 bond issues and hundreds of stocks and details of the issuing firms. For each firm, he included a description of the railroad line, as well
as its location, mileage, equipment, income, expenses, and balance sheet.
Moody was careful to distinguish this publication from his original manual.
"This is not a mere 'manual' or statistical record of American railroads,"
he wrote in the introduction. "It is much more than this. While it contains
all the statistical records and other information required by the Banker,
Broker, Financial Institution and Individual Investor ... it also contains expert analysis of the railroad systems, showing the Physical Condition, Earning Power, Financial Characteristics and General Credit and standing of
each of the Companies."[49] The *Analyses* advanced Moody's agenda of transparency while also giving him valuable data to assess the general health of the
economy.

To make his ratings Moody had to judge the railroad's earning capacities. In doing so, he looked at territory, freight tonnage, passenger and freight density, and its balance sheet and existing bond and stock issues. Moody, like Babson and Fisher, assembled a massive data-gathering center, subscribing to trade journals, newspapers, government reports, and news wire services. Moody also had canvassers collecting information from the exchanges and individual firms.

Moody rated each issue from "Aaa" (highest class) to "E" (very weak or defaulted). The "A" class was regarded as investment grade; the "B" had a "speculative tinge." These categories are still in use more than a century later, though Moody dropped the lowest rating categories.[50] Such ratings have much in common with forecasts: a statement of confidence in an investment product is akin to predicting a high investment return; a statement of low confidence is a predictor that losses are likely.

For Moody, his *Analyses* had the noble intent of leveling the playing field and making it harder for industry insiders to mislead the investing public. Moody claimed that his ratings faced opposition from the business interests who believed they would be damaged by the transparency he promoted.[51] Corporations objected if their bonds received a lower rating than they thought appropriate—but, unlike the situation today, where companies pay enormous fees to be rated, they did not directly fund the ratings agency and hence had no leverage to wield over the raters.

Despite the objections of some parties, Moody quickly made money with his ratings. Recognizing a good idea when they saw it, other companies followed Moody into the securities rating business. In 1922 Poor's Publishing began rating corporate bonds and municipal securities. Standard Statistics did the same the following year. John Knowles Fitch (1880–1943), who had founded the Fitch Publishing Company in lower Manhattan in 1913, began publishing ratings books in 1924. These companies dominated the field for decades: Moody's, Poor's, Standard, and Fitch.[52]

Forming the ratings agency was a major achievement. Irving Fisher had written that the value of a security was the present value of its future payments. Moody in his ratings business did not formulate this idea in a mathematical way, but he was far ahead of most bankers in recognizing it. Investors, Moody argued, needed to value securities on what they expected to earn from them rather than studies of past price trends. Estimated future earnings derived from knowledge of the issuer's resources for growth, patents, managerial expertise, and market position vis-à-vis its competitors. Also by 1929, Moody was calculating price-earnings ratios as a better indicator of stock value than simply looking at share price.[53]

MOODY'S INVESTORS SERVICE

In 1914 Moody founded Moody's Investors Service, which served as an umbrella corporation to run both the ratings manual and the *Weekly Letter*. The company was, as Moody put it in a slogan, "founded to endure and investors make secure." World events would challenge Moody's optimistic ambitions, but by the end of World War I, he had secured a triumphant reputation as a forecaster.

In the summer of 1914, undeterred by escalating international tensions, Moody went to Europe to meet with business leaders and intellectuals and to tour the historical sites. The outbreak of World War I forced his return.[54] The war had an immediate impact on Moody's new business. The five-year-old *Weekly Review* had a net profit of $17,875 in 1914, but cancellations came in as soon as exchanges in Europe and the United States were closed (the New York Stock Exchange closed in August and did not fully reopen until December). Moody later recalled: "Everybody was bearish, including all the forecasters.... Roger Babson said he was thinking of closing up shop for good; he wrote me in November that unless the Exchange opened soon, I would lose my shirt if I kept going. Of course I put this down as a Babson trick."[55] In fact Babson was selling off several businesses at this point. He sold the Stock & Bond Card System to Luther Blake and his interest in Moody Manual Company to Roy W. Porter, though he remained a shareholder.[56]

Moody cut his workforce drastically by firing half of his employees and reducing weekly payroll expense from $200 to $45. But he continued sending the *Weekly Review* to his former subscribers, free of charge. He seemed on the cusp of another business bankruptcy; the company had just $5,000 left in the bank. Despite these challenges, Moody saw the outbreak of war as an opportunity to improve his reputation as a Wall Street pundit. Leading forecasters were predicting desolation and penury in Europe's future and difficult times ahead for the United States and its exporters.[57]

Moody had also held this view through mid-October 1914 but then began to feel differently. He put together a glossy, very bullish forecast for

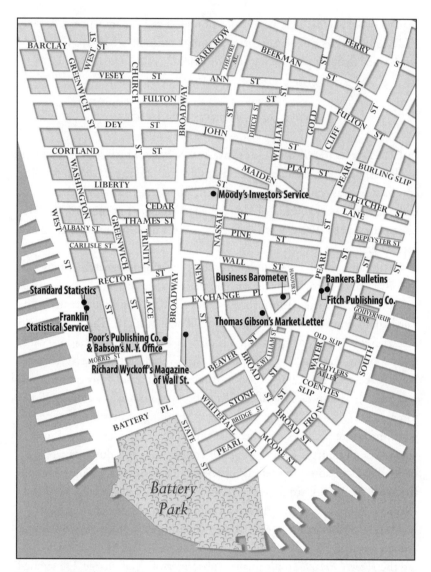

Prominent Wall Street–area forecasting agencies, c. 1927. Moody operated his extensive businesses, including forecasting, securities ratings, publishing, and other services, in lower Manhattan—the center of the country's forecasting activities and business information industry. Being in New York brought immediate access to many of the nation's leading businesspeople. Nearly all of the forecasters lived in New York at some point in their career: Roger Babson learned about the securities business there; and Warren Persons and Homer Vanderblue, both of the Harvard Economic Service, sought fortunes there in the late 1920s in the booming investment trust business. Thomas Gibson's *Weekly Market Letter* was published at 15 William Street, just south of Wall Street. The Franklin Statistical Service the bond market for 1915, which included a historical report on the effect of the U.S. Civil War and the Franco-Prussian War on bond prices, arguing that bond markets outside of the war-torn areas had prospered. Moody's forecast also noted that England and France had recently begun placing orders for munitions and other material with U.S. manufacturers and that foreign exchange was increasingly being done in the dollar, bringing gold to the United States.[58]

In December 1914 Moody mailed out his optimistic forecast, predicting a rally as soon as markets reopened in January. He sent this with a graph of bond prices free of charge to brokers and investors across the nation, from Wall Street to the regional exchanges; to every member of Congress; and to the nation's leading newspapers. "It created a sensation and got an immense amount of publicity," recalled Moody. "Luckily for us, the stock market failed to slump at the opening, but after a little backing and filling, began its long climb which did not begin to slacken until the autumn of 1915."[59] The Dow Jones Industrial Average rose from 60 at the start of 1915 to 100 by the year's end.[60] The stocks Moody recommended, such as Bethlehem Steel (a major supplier of armor plate and ordnance), turned out to be good bets. The accuracy of his forecast of an upswing in business conditions cemented Moody's reputation on Wall Street.

Moody's Optimistic Economy

Moody's business grew substantially after World War I and he devoted time to writing forecasts in his *Weekly Letter*. By 1920 he had over ten thousand clients. More than five hundred banks and brokerages in New York City were regular subscribers, as were several thousand banks and other financial

---

published the *Weekly Analysis of Business, Industry and Finance*. The Fitch Publishing Company, founded by John Knowles Fitch (1880–1943), published the ratings service, the *Fitch Bond Book* and the weekly newsletters, with frequent forecasts, the *Fitch Bond Record*, and the *Fitch Stock Record*. Also nearby were the only two companies that could compete with Moody's in terms of scale: Poor's Publishing Company, which kept a massive library with files on 250,000 corporations, and Standard Statistics Company. Source: Much of the information in this section is from Illinois Chamber of Commerce, *Commercial Services* (not published, 1927).

MAY 28 1920

Number 602

May 27, 1920

Moody's
Investment
Letters

MOODY'S INVESTORS SERVICE

JOHN MOODY, President

35 Nassau Street, New York

Telephone, 2947-8-9 Rector

Founders of Moody's System of Investment Ratings

Moody's
Analyses of
Investments

WEEKLY REVIEW OF FINANCIAL CONDITIONS

A BULLISH BREAK: If the market can ever be said to break in a bullish manner, it did so during the past ten days. To the margin trader who is long of stocks, all breaks are alike in that they all represent losses; but to the investor in long term securities a decline which paves the way for future prosperity is not much different from a clearance sale. In a genuine sale of this sort the merchant takes a paper loss on a portion of his stock of goods in that the gross margin is insufficient to cover expenses and charges; but incidentally he gets rid of goods which are getting stale, and threaten to depreciate by 30 to 50 per cent. in market value. So, too, a break in the security markets if it is incidental to the restoration of sound credit conditions is not an unmixed evil.

This, moreover, is just the sort of a decline which we have been experiencing. It means, as we said last week, "readjustment without panic." Cuts in goods prices are diminishing the demand for bank loans, and the sale of stocks and bonds by merchants and manufacturers is providing working capital which would otherwise have to be obtained at the banks. Inventories are being reduced all along the line, and this means that the nation's stock of goods and materials is passing from the hands of producers and merchants into the hands of consumers. Incidentally, the producers and merchants are thereby enabled to pay off bank loans.

If this price cutting were due to overproduction, there might be cause for alarm; but it is not due to any such thing. There is practically no overproduction in any of our industries, and the cutting of retail, wholesale and manufacturers' prices is due almost solely to overvaluation. Prices are going down not because we are producing too much, but because we are producing too little. It is artificial restriction of output that has put prices so high that the banks can no longer finance the volume of the nation's business. If outputs had been larger, prices would have been lower, and thrift would presumably have been greater—in which case the typical business man would have maintained with his bank a larger excess of deposits over borrowings—and there would have been no money famine.

Otherwise expressed, when this shortage of loanable funds or working capital is eliminated, prices will stop going down and business will expand. Notwithstanding the fool's paradise that the majority have been living in, we have not escaped the consequences of the war destruction of capital. Just as after the Civil War and the Napoleonic struggle, the reconstruction of the world's industries now creates plenty of business, provided only there is capital enough to finance it. The most important question about the business situation for the next ten years is likely to be the question of capital supply just as was the case from 1815 to 1825, and from 1865 to 1875. Hence, in cutting prices, reducing bank loans to normal, and replenishing capital supplies, we are laying the foundation for prosperity next year or perhaps a little later.

Price-Cutting: Merchants and manufacturers have always looked with horror upon price cutting; but now it is the only way out. There is no other possible way to check the rise in operating expenses. For wages, costs of materials and interest charges there is no sky top until prices are broken. The sellers of both labor and materials must be humbled into a reasonable frame of mind, and this cannot be done by any other means. If our banks had $60,-

Moody's *Weekly Letter* (officially titled the *Weekly Review of Financial Conditions*), May 27, 1920.

institutions outside the city. At this time, Moody had four volumes of his credit-rating manual to sell: railroads, industrials, public utilities, and a new volume on foreign and American government securities.

Moody charged $100 per year for his complete service, which included the *Weekly Letter*, ratings books, and monthly updates. Of this period, Moody later wrote, "Both the volume of business and profits kept on climbing in 1920 ... and at the same time [we] called the turn perfectly in our *Weekly Review* on the business recession and bear market of that year, [and] we nearly doubled our Gross and Net over 1919."[61]

Moody's forecasts and his thoughts about business appeared not only in his newsletter but also in popular magazines. In 1921 Moody published a lengthy, five-page, optimistic forecast for the future of war-ravaged Europe in the *Saturday Evening Post*. "No sun sets without [human beings] adding something to the reproduction and recreation of wealth," wrote Moody. "Slowly but surely men and women by the sweat of their brows, the ingenuity of their minds and the industry of their hands are once again making use of the creative forces of Nature in the fields and setting the wheels of industry to work." America would play a significant role in its rebuilding, Moody argued, predicting years of prosperity for the United States.[62]

In 1922, in an article in the *American Magazine*, Moody, who was described as "almost an oracle in the financial world," forecast twenty or thirty years of general trends in prosperity—meaning through to the 1940s and 1950s. The "constructive period" had come, he wrote. "It began when a considerable number of business men realized that the only sound way to 'make money' is to produce something as economically and efficiently as possible, and to market it in the same manner."[63]

In 1924 Moody began a series of popular articles in *Forbes* magazine on investing; these were later published as *Profitable Investing: Fundamentals of the Science of Investing* (Forbes, 1925). The volume contained strong warnings against speculation and get-rich-quick schemes and advocated diversification and the importance of being an "intelligent investor" who used ratings and other available information. Moody also traveled frequently to give talks, usually bullish ones on bonds and stocks. He advertised heavily in the *New York Times* and *Wall Street Journal*. All of these efforts bolstered his image as a commonsense prophet who knew the ways of Wall Street and all its players.

Moody sold a remarkable 24,000 copies of the manuals in 1924 and the-firm's revenues passed $1,000,000. The company's revenues increased from $1.4 million in 1926 to $1.8 million in 1928. Net profits were $214,000 in 1926 and $271,000 in 1928. In addition to reaping financial rewards, Moody's publications became standard tools for assessing risk among investors.[64]

Moody's rise coincided with the growing importance of Wall Street. By the end of World War I, New York was an international financial capital to rival London, Paris, and Vienna. Prior to then, European financial markets were in many ways more sophisticated than those in the United States. But American capital markets developed rapidly in the late nineteenth and early twentieth centuries. By the end of the war, U.S. financial markets were in better shape than those in European centers, with the exception perhaps of London. By that point, the United States had built a central bank and Europe was recovering from war.[65] The United States moved from being a debtor nation to being a creditor. "We used to be a borrowing nation, paying tribute in millions of dollars annually to other countries," Moody exclaimed. "Now they pay millions to us."[66] By that time, as well, investors and bankers in New York had begun to finance industrial and public utility companies as well as railroads. The number of industrial stocks listed on the New York Stock Exchange rose from 20 in 1898 to 173 in 1915.[67]

By 1924, Moody paid $100,000 to repurchase the rights to the name *Moody's Manual* from Roger Babson and his associate Roy Porter. He thought this was a very good deal. He wrote in a memoir that he was ready to pay $250,000 had they asked.[68]

The mid-1920s were also times of expansion for the firm, both in terms of its distribution and in terms of its data-gathering operation and consultancy. The company opened regional offices in Chicago and Los Angeles to provide services to local clients and to gather information. In 1925 Moody established a European subsidiary, Moody's Investors Service Ltd., London.[69]

Moody attributed his success to four things: resisting outside control, providing good morale in the workplace, leading by example (hard work by the owners), and little regulatory intervention. He was also helped, he added, by the generally high demand for business information in the 1920s: "In those flush Wall Street days, most prosperous dealers and traders were easy marks on every handout."[70]

John Moody from the
American Magazine,
September 1922.

But this undersells Moody's real achievement. From his days working at Spencer Trask forward, Moody had acquired a tremendous bird's-eye view of business. He, like many of the clients he served, was entirely future-oriented in his business ambitions—always adding to his services, reorganizing his company, adding new branches, and securing new audiences. His forecasts reflected this sense of mastery over the details of individual firms and also a sense of which industries offered opportunities.

FORECASTING METHODS

Moody never published an article describing his method of forecasting. He rejected simple or mechanical ways of judging the trend of business activity, distrusting the notion that business trends moved in a uniform or reliable sequence.[71]

Moody did not theorize on the nature of the business cycle. When pushed, he gave an explanation of the business cycle in psychological terms, not unlike Babson: "Business must alternate from good to bad and back again, because it can do nothing else. A cycle is merely this inevitable alternation. Most business changes are due to universal human traits and instincts, or, in other words, to psychology as expressed in mercantile affairs. Successes tend to make even the greatest of men over-confident, while failures make us all humble." But he did not believe, like Babson, that there was an exact equivalence between ups and downs. He did not think that business cycles were alike; he believed there were many variations in their underlying causes and consequences. The "business situation is the sum total of a vast number of ever-changing factors."[72]

Indeed, the type of data that Babson and Moody gathered could hardly be more different. Babson focused on collecting and publishing economic data, as part of what today we would describe as "technical analysis." Moody assembled masses of details of individual firms and securities, and completed what today would be known as "fundamental analysis." Babson's advice tended to focus more on the *timing* of investments, as he claimed his data showed the ups and downs of the cycle. Moody's advice more often focused on *where* to place investments—which company or security.[73]

However, Babson did at times offer advice about individual firms and Moody about broader economic trends. Moody, for instance, developed a trade barometer index that also resembled Babson's composite index, in that it comprised an agglomeration of statistical series, including lumber prices, coal production, commodity prices, interest rates, and other items. But Moody believed that the forecaster needed to include all available business news, financial figures, and other economic information—and use the barometer as only one tool among many. The official position of the company was that chart reading was a "post-mortem and not a diagnosis."[74] Charts said what had happened and not what was coming.

Moody advocated focusing investments on specific firms after carefully examining their balance sheets and management. He made a clear distinction between investment and speculation. Investing required analysis and some measure of safe return over time. Investment was an analytical endeavor unlike speculation based only on heard-on-the-street gossip.

Moody included forecasts about individual firms, entire industries, and the national economy. In all of these areas, he maintained a focus on businesspeople and their innovations, plans, and expectations. He worked out his ideas about the importance of entrepreneurs and businessmen in determining the future of the country in several books published just after World War I. In *The Railroad Builders: A Chronicle of the Welding of the States* (1919), Moody described the triumph of business invention in conquering the country: "The United States as we know it today is largely the result of mechanical inventions, and in particular of agricultural machinery and the railroad."[75] In *The Masters of Capital: A Chronicle of Wall Street* (1921), he described the careers of J. P. Morgan, Andrew Carnegie, E. H. Harriman, James J. Hill, and John D. Rockefeller. This group, in Moody's story, had brought a revolution in the nature of business and capitalization.

Under the old meanings of "capital," Moody wrote, predominating in the early nineteenth century, companies tended to value their property based on its replacement cost or original cost. But after the rise of new machinery and efficient methods of management, companies came to perceive their true value was in their future capacity to earn profits: "It was found that the limit of capitalization was by no means reached when *present* earning power alone was capitalized, for in a growing country like the United States, with population practically doubling every generation, future earning power was seen to be vastly greater."[76] For Moody, this future orientation toward innovation, building, and capitalization had brought great wealth to the United States. *Railroad Builders* and *Masters of Capital* were both hefty productions that showcased Moody's ability to tell a sweeping historical narrative from the biographical perspective of business and industry leaders.

This was the type of rich analysis Moody brought to his forecasting. Among the many kinds of information that intrigued him, expectations held a special place. Moody was keenly interested in learning about the expectations for future profits by leading businesspeople. He wrote, "If the margins are fat there will be a great rush to capture them and a big boom. But thin margins mean small inducements, and tend to restrict activity."[77] This information was naturally extremely difficult to attain: in trying to determine the expectations for profits, Moody surveyed Wall Street and contacted his employees in branch offices and his salesmen. He also employed analysts to do industrial studies in which they investigated the trends in costs in specific industries: if the costs of raw materials were rising for a particular manufacturing sector, profits might be expected to narrow.

Moody also sought more methodical industry-level forecasts by introducing in 1922 an "index of operating costs," which included the costs of factory labor, fuel and light, rent, and raw materials. This index was compared with an index of commodity prices to determine the prospects of the industry. If the production costs seemed to be encroaching on price, Moody expected business leaders in that industry to adjust their plans downward. Similarly, if prices were escalating and costs declining, managers would adjust their plans in the opposite direction.[78] But such devices never altered Moody's focus on individual firms and their health and on the expectations of business leaders. He remained an avid collector of news and a believer in the need for judgment to make sense of it.

Moody found that a growing number of businesspeople were approaching investing analytically in the 1920s and were looking for the rich range of statistics and information that he provided. Some of this interest was encouraged by commercial schools and by colleges. The number of chief executives who attended college then was still small but growing. Among the chief executives at the top two hundred firms, one quarter had gone to college (a far higher proportion than in the general population); MIT and Columbia were the most attended.[79]

Some clients used Moody's statistics and advice as the basis of their own forecasts. After the turn of the century American Telephone and Telegraph became a leader in the field in using business statistics and in developing methods of business forecasting, thanks to the efforts of president Theodore Vail and statisticians Malcolm Rorty and Walter Gifford.[80] Macy's, the famous New York department store, began generating forecasts of general business conditions as early as 1919. The demand for forecasts came from the owners, Percy and Jesse Straus, who sought information about the markets and about the store's competitors. It was also prompted by the store's expanding operations and by the Strauses' belief in the scientific management practices they had heard about at Harvard.[81] After the 1920–21 recession, Harvard graduate Henry S. Dennison, of the paper goods company Dennison Manufacturing, became acutely interested in using statistics to produce forecasts of demand for paper.[82] All made use of Moody's data.

An Optimist in Uncertain Times

Moody began 1928 on a wave of optimism. His firm had no funded debt, growing wholly on its own profits. In July, Moody moved from 35 Nassau Street to modern headquarters at 65 Broadway on the upper floors of the

Adams Express Building. In doing this, Moody may have been following a rival, Standard Statistics, which had moved into new three-floor headquarters on Varick Street in 1927.[83] But whatever his motivation, Moody was not alone in seeking new real estate. The built environment of Wall Street was being transformed by optimistic corporate leaders in the late 1920s.[84]

Like Irving Fisher, Moody was full of confidence then, and his reputation among investors remained high. He later recalled, "Wherever I went during 1928 or in the spring of 1929, whether to business or social gatherings, to dinners, lectures, concerts, theaters or churches, I was invariably buttonholed for my opinion of this or that stock-market movement or tip."[85] His ratings books were selling well. Clients could subscribe at rates of $150 to $350 a year, selecting from a range of publications and individual advisory services.

With his flourishing business, Moody took the company public in 1928. He later viewed this as a disastrous mistake, saying that he had been "affected by the virus" of optimism following the election of Herbert Hoover and had succumbed to the pleas of bankers looking for underwritings. Moody bought out the shares of several other investors. All of this loaded Moody with 32,000 of 60,000 shares of common stock just prior to the 1929 crash.[86]

Throughout the late 1920s, Moody devoted more time to leisure. He spent weeks in his summer home in Merriewold Park, in upstate New York. He recalled of this period a growing distaste for a life spent solely in business: "I nowadays viewed with horror certain rich old men I sometimes saw in Wall Street; men whose whole lives had been money-making, and who had amassed great wealth, but in the feebleness of old age continued to toddle about adding just a little more to their already swollen fortunes."[87]

Moody's stature in Merriewold had some similarities to Babson's in Wellesley. He owned several of the town's properties, repaired town gates and other public structures, and funded community activities. He and his wife owned an Adirondack-style home called The Ledge. Anna Moody bought art and held many parties, inviting New York and European celebrities and artists. In addition to The Ledge, Moody built his own personal retreat on Merriewold Lake, which he called Camp Solitude.[88] This was a place for him to meditate and write.

Moody's view of Wall Street often emphasized its chaotic nature; he failed to develop, like Babson and Fisher, a theory intended to rationalize the workings of capitalism. Instead Moody embarked on a lifelong search for spirituality, which he viewed as in opposition to his business work. This, again, was unlike Babson and Fisher, who tended to view all of their outside activities, whether they pertained to religion, Prohibition, or health, as inseparable from their business activities.

Moody became an obsessive reader of works on religion and spirituality. He studied Madame Blavatsky and Theosophy, and Buddhism, and he "dipped into the fog of Christian Science."[89] In the late 1920s, especially following the tragic death of his son John Edmund from typhoid fever on a trip to Europe, he turned increasingly to the structured theological world of Catholicism.

Moody also became a frequent traveler, spending time in England and in Rome in particular. In the summer of 1929 he embarked on a three-month vacation in Europe. He returned to New York in September 1929, thinking that a speculative boom might be under way but one that would not end until spring 1930 at the earliest. He expressed these feelings in his October 7, 1929, newsletter shortly before the crash. He believed that the fundamentals of the economy were fine, but there was a growing nervousness among investors due to the high amount of margin buying that had occurred.[90]

The October crash took Moody by surprise, as it did so many others. On the morning of the single worst day of the sell-off, October 28, Moody's *Weekly Letter* commented on the previous week's liquidation: "We are convinced that it represents nothing more or less than a speculators' frenzy of fear for the time being—in other words, a technical condition of the market rather than a reflection of radically changing underlying conditions, which, in point of fact, remain relatively stable."[91] That day the Dow Jones average went down 13 percent.

With those words, Moody joined the other forecasters who failed to anticipate the greatest economic cataclysm yet to affect the United States. After missing the stock market crash, Moody was embarrassed that his nemesis, Roger Babson, had gained popular recognition for predicting it. Moody found it difficult to comprehend what had happened.[92] In November 1929, the *Monthly Analyses of Business Conditions* noted that "the recession will probably be accentuated and prolonged by the feeling of pessimism which spread from the stock market into business." But the newsletter also expressed some puzzlement: "The extent of net paper losses and their effect can hardly be measured for the country as a whole."[93]

Moody's forecasts became more optimistic as spring approached. In April 1930, the *Weekly Letter* noted, "the inescapable conclusion is that we are not facing a business depression."[94] But when things did not improve over the summer, Moody's returned to write about the inability of businessmen and investors to form clear expectations. In July the newsletter reported, "the recent conservatism in buying [is] caused by lower purchasing power and accentuated by psychological uncertainties."[95]

Moody missed the continuing depression in part because managers at firms became uncertain about future profit. It was as if he had been watching executives fly kites on the wind of their hopes, but then there was no movement at all to watch. For a forecaster like Moody, who based his predictions on the expectations of business leaders, the prolonged period of uncertainty during the Depression rendered unworkable his method of surveying business executives and examining statistics for undervalued securities.

Moody's revenues in 1929 had risen to $3.6 million. They still exceeded $3 million in 1930, but in 1931 revenues plummeted to $500,000. The firm's takings would not reach 1929 levels for twenty-five years, though they were above $2 million in 1932.[96] *Manual* circulation in 1929 had exceeded 37,000 volumes; by 1932 it was down to fewer than 26,000. Moody's introduced radical cost cutting in these years. The firm slashed its payroll, cutting salaries 20 percent or more and reducing staff.

In the 1930s, Moody began to gradually move away from producing forecasts, focusing more on securities ratings and providing consulting services to individual clients. As many bonds defaulted in the early 1930s, the fear of loss increased and investors again began to purchase Moody's ratings books.[97]

Moody exerted a significant influence in the world of investment and securities analysis. When he announced in the 1930s that he could no longer interpret the signals of Wall Street, he canceled the *Weekly Letter* and decided to move Moody's Investors Service more solidly toward securities ratings. Unlike the *Weekly Letter*, which had also offered forecasts of the state of the business cycle, his company's securities ratings confined their assessment to the reliability of individual firms or other corporate bodies, such as municipalities, which issued securities. As it turned out, it was a decision that would eventually vault the company to prominence. In the 1930s, government officials and investors demanded more transparency in the securities markets. The Securities and Exchange Act of 1934 created the Securities and Exchange Commission in order to oversee federal securities laws and regulate the securities industry. An ensuing 1936 law prohibited banks from investing in speculative securities; banks were only permitted to hold investment-grade bonds. This proved to be a boon to Moody's Investors Service (as well as other ratings services like Standard & Poor's and Fitch) because it required all securities to receive ratings. Moody's became the preeminent ratings company of the twentieth century.

THE LONG ROAD HOME

In the early 1930s, religion occupied an increasing portion of Moody's time and thoughts. He wrote two autobiographical books, *The Long Road Home* (1933) and *Fast by the Road* (1942), before retiring as president of the company in 1944. Neither book contained much about business or a celebration of his business life. In that way, they make a stark contrast to Roger Babson's *Actions and Reactions* (1935), an autobiography that celebrated Babson's life and set the stage for his presidential run. In *The Long Road Home*, Moody quickly covered his business adventures, his triumphs, and disillusionments in Wall Street; the real subject was spiritual awakening and his embrace of Catholicism, which he called "coming home." *Fast by the Road* was the continuing story of his "pilgrimage." He wrote: "I now found myself using the phrase, 'Good-bye to all that,' in connection with many things that I had left behind."[98] In 1946 Moody published a 360-page biography of John Henry Newman, a nineteenth-century Anglican clergyman who converted to Roman Catholicism. Moody devoted much of his time to the Catholic Church and was made a Knight Commander of the Order of the Holy Sepulchre of Jerusalem.[99] In 1957 Moody moved to La Jolla, California, where he died one year later.

With his interests in Catholicism and religious history, Moody retreated from the ephemeral and future-oriented world of Wall Street—a world in which trading activity could be feverish in the morning and eerily silent by the afternoon. In some ways, he continued to exhibit his exhaustive search for information and even truth. Among forecasters, Moody was the foremost advocate of transparency in financial markets. He believed that knowledge of the financial health of individual firms and objective judgment of their security offerings would elevate the decision making of investors and managers. He had mastered a huge amount of knowledge of the intricacies of Wall Street throughout his professional life, enough so that he attracted a following among those who sought his advice and predictions. But the business

world remained chaotic and unfathomable, one that eluded theoretical con-
ceptualizations. In Catholicism he had found something else. "This great
Mother Church of the Christian Faith has brought me the inestimable bless-
ing of perfect peace," he wrote. "Where all was doubt before, she gives me
certainty."[100]

Gallery of Business and Forecasting Charts

Forecasters made use of an array of graphs, charts, and diagrams. The intuitive appeal of the Babsonchart, for instance, with its normal line and its equal periods of "action" and "reaction," was critical to Roger Babson's success. In devising a way to represent the economy visually, he was part of a broader effort that was gaining popularity in the early twentieth century. Alternately informative and hackneyed, business charts of all types, showing not only forecasts but a whole range of economic information, proliferated in newsletters, newspapers, and magazines.

Some charts served mostly to emphasize trends over time in agricultural output, stock prices, or industrial production, for instance. Time-series graphs, though newly popular, were hardly new. They dated to the tenth or eleventh century, when they were used to record planetary orbits. In the eighteenth century time-series charts were used in scientific writings—such as for seasonal variations in temperature. William Playfair (1759–1823), a Scottish political economist, published the *Commercial and Political Atlas* (1786), which contained forty-four charts, many of time-series data, on trade balances, government debt, and other topics. This was a landmark book, and Playfair's graphs are today highly sought after for their artistry.[1] But charts served other purposes than describing change over time. Some were used to organize work, for instance. The Gantt Chart used colorful bars to illustrate the completion of tasks during a complex project. The chart, devised by the mechanical engineer and consultant Henry Gantt (1861–1919), was employed to keep track of mobilization efforts during World War I and to monitor the progress of the construction of the Hoover Dam in the 1930s.[2]

In 1923 Carl Snyder (1869–1946), a statistician at the New York Federal Reserve, observed, "In and since the War the use and development of charts has been almost phenomenal—so large, indeed, that at least one able economist who is interested in such things thinks that we as a country have gone chart-mad."[3] But where Snyder saw madness in the contemporary zeal for charts, others saw evidence of a new rational age. Karl G. Karsten, the founder of Karsten Forekastograf and a close associate of Irving Fisher's, produced a

724-page tome, *Charts and Graphs (1923)*, which featured about five hundred graphs made by various authors. He perceived that the "language" of American business was becoming more visual. This new orientation was nothing more than the "natural evolution" of civilization that began with the rise of "clear-cut thinking" in the Renaissance and blossomed with the coming of professional statisticians in the nineteenth century and the rise of modern chart makers (of which he, of course, was one) in the early twentieth. "A world turning to saner and richer civilization will be a world turning to charts," Karsten wrote.[4]

Graphs, Karsten recognized, benefited from the new range of available data distributed by federal and local governments and trade associations. By the end of World War I, businesspeople could find statistics on imports, immigration, commodity prices, business failures, pig-iron production, crop output, and myriad other items.[5] Charts made trends in this mass of data suddenly become visible. The more data available, the more trends were discernible.

Forecasters claimed to be able to point out which trends were important for predicting future economic change, which were misleading, and which were inconsequential. But their graphs and diagrams also often stood for metaphors to make sense of the economy. The two most common metaphors were to portray the economy as a vast atmosphere or as a great machine. Each signified different ideas about how economies operated and how they could be influenced. What follows are a few examples of such charts, selected largely from forecasters other than those profiled in this book, to give a wider sense of the field.

THE ECONOMY AS ATMOSPHERE

Many analysts and chart makers compared the economy to an atomosphere or other natural phenomena. In explaining the source of economic power in the United States, John Moody drew a family tree of the Rockefeller and Morgan interests. His use of the term "tree," family or not, enlisted an image of nature. Trees were ancient symbols, powerful and resilient. Important events transpired under their leaves; the New York Stock Exchange was formed under the Buttonwood Tree, or so legend has it.[6] In Moody's diagrams, firms, like trees, covered the American landscape.

More commonly, forecasters and other business-writers of the early twentieth century compared the economy to the atmosphere and to weather systems. Roger Babson's charts, especially, had similarities to the meteorological charts developed at the time; he also included the word "barometer" in his forecasting chart titles as did the Harvard Economic Service. James H. Brookmire (1869–1946) created some of the most imaginative weather-related economic forecasting charts of the early twentieth century. In 1910, Brookmire, the son of a prominent St. Louis merchant, founded the Brookmire Economic Chart Company in his home city; the company opened a New York office in 1913.[7]

Brookmire published large economic charts describing different aspects of the American economy. *A Graphic Record of Fundamental Political and Industrial Conditions as a Barometer to the Financial and Business Situation for the Period Beginning 1885* (1910) was a beautiful volume, published on thick paper in vibrant colors of red, green, and yellow. In it, Brookmire included graphs of industrial production, bank deposits, crop output, and cotton and wool production (with projections of the sheep population in America for many years in the future). He also produced his own "barometer" to indicate where business was headed. Whereas Babson tried to create a single aggregate series to indicate business activity (drawn mostly from production figures), Brookmire began to experiment with the idea of using leading indicators, an important contribution later pursued with more statistical rigor by the Harvard Economic Service.[8] Brookmire's barometer (see next page), depicted three indexes of economic sectors—business activity, the stock market (an index of thirty-two stocks), and banking resources. The chart emphasized the cyclicality of the capitalist system as the three barometric indexes were thought to go up and down in sequence. In it, business activity led stock market activity, which, in turn, led banking activity. As one went up, the others followed. The barometer was a visually appealing device, as the reader could quickly see the current state of each of the three economic areas.[9]

THE MECHANICAL ECONOMY

While some business analysts and forecasters compared the economy to natural phenomena, others saw something more mechanical. Irving Fisher frequently likened the economy to a machine. His weighing-scale chart, shown

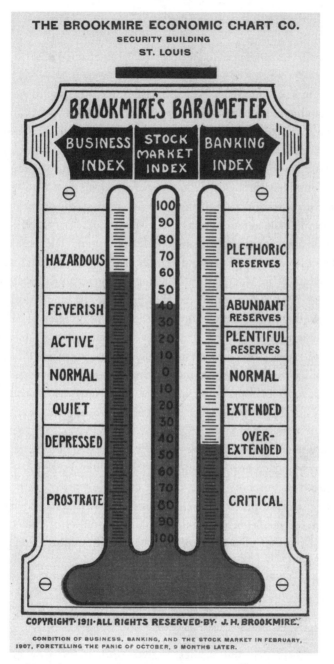

James H. Brookmire's barometer. The small print reads, "Condition of business, banking, and the stock market in February, 1907, foretelling the panic of October, 9 months later." James H. Brookmire, *The Brookmire Economic Charts: A Graphic Record of Fundamental, Political and Industrial Conditions as a Barometer to the Financial and Business Situation …* (St. Louis: Brookmire Economic Chart Co., 1913).

in chapter 2, was functional in purpose, indicating that if one of the elements on the scale were moved (like the amount of money), then the other elements (prices and output) would also have to move for the economy to return to equilibrium. In his graph, it is clear that monetary policy could alter, for instance, the total volume of output in the economy. Fisher also pursued a different mechanical analogy when created a hydraulic machine, also shown in chapter 2, in which water flowed through cisterns to demonstrate the circulation of money through the economy of a great city.

But Fisher was not the only one who, in creating a diagram to illustrate the economy, likened money to a liquid. Malcolm C. Rorty (1859–1936), a statistician and forecaster for American Telephone and Telegraph and a co-founder of the National Bureau of Economic Research, did so as well in his 1922 diagram "The Round Flow of Money Income and Expenditure" (see next page).[10] "At the top of the diagram the total of all individual incomes flows in through pipes representing the three primary factors in all productive operations," wrote Rorty. The inflow of money came from salary and wages (constituting 68 percent), return on capital (24 percent), and natural resources. The outflow of this money then went to rent, to government agencies, and to retail and wholesale distribution, and other sources. Eventually money circled around to fill the tank of individual incomes again.[11]

This mechanical vision expressed entirely different political sensibilities than the comparison with nature—for the atmosphere is ancient, vast, and pitiless, while machines are man-made and, though powerful, can be re-engineered. The machine-oriented image created a sense of the interdependence of economic institutions. The system of pipes, in Rorty's diagram, was massive, yet seemed controllable through the fine-tuning of water flows—or in the case of money, by taxing, or borrowing, or by adjusting interest rates, for instance.

The Geography of Business

Still other forecasters and business analysts made use of geographic maps. These also presented economic activity in familiar terms. The United States, for example, had frontiers of entrepreneurial activity, regions of established business, areas of agricultural output, and centers of industry and trade. Both Brookmire and Babson produced U.S. maps that indicated areas of high and

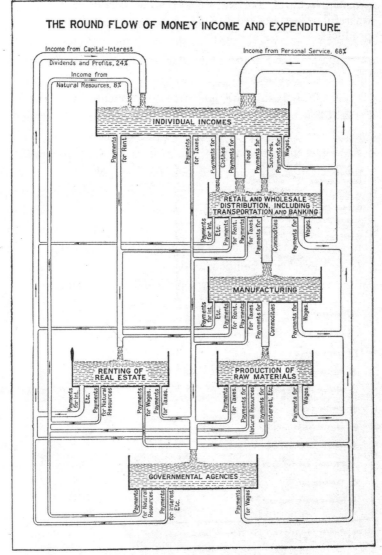

THE ROUND FLOW OF MONEY INCOME AND EXPENDITURE

Permission of Mr. Malcolm C. Rorty.

"The Round Flow of Money Income and Expenditure," in Malcolm C. Rorty, *Some Problems in Current Economics* (Chicago: A. W. Shaw Co., 1922), 63.

low "business activity"—giving that term, often only defined in the footnotes if at all, a seemingly tangible and measurable presence.

In a crudely drawn map of the United States from 1925 (see below), Karl Karsten showed American states in relative proportion to their population and shaded according to the extent of their business activity, with the darkest states (New Hampshire and Vermont) representing poor levels. The chart revealed the relative geographic distribution of business enterprise and population—still very weighted toward New England, Pennsylvania (with the rise of the steel industry in Pittsburgh), and Illinois (with the growth of Chicago and its meatpacking plants and grain industry). New York, especially, looked like a balloon about to burst in the area around Manhattan. The graph also displayed a "good" amount of business activity in the less populated areas of California, Texas, and Louisiana. The greatest business opportunities, Karsten argued, were to be found in the lightly shaded states (Massachusetts, New York, Illinois, Texas, Louisiana, and others in the dotted pattern) at the present time, since they were "thickly populated states in a 'trading mood.' "[12]

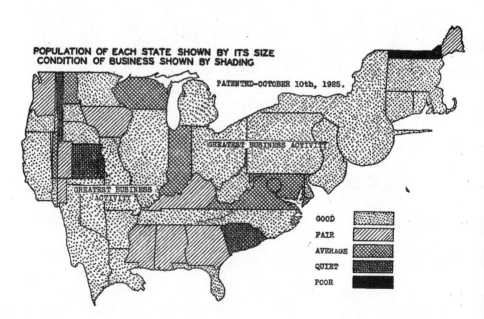

Karsten "Map of Business Conditions," 1925. Source: Karl Karsten Papers, Library of Congress, Washington, D.C.

CHARTING THE BUSINESS CYCLE

Finally, other charts sought to illustrate the very rhythm and heartbeat of economic activity by rendering the business cycle itself. The idea of a business cycle was seldom expressed before the publication of Wesley Mitchell's *Business Cycles* (1913), but it became the leading subject of interest among economists (and many popular business writers) in the decades afterward. Each of the dozens of authors who wrote on the subject defined the cycle differently. Joseph Schumpeter's 1,095-page, two-volume book, *Business Cycles: A Theoretical, Historical, and Statistical Analysis of the Capitalist Process* (1939), summed up in his subtitle the all-inclusive nature of the topic. In his analysis, he tried to create a synthesis of a jumble of cycles: Juglars (eight- to ten-year cycles named for Clément Juglar), Kitchins (forty-month cycles named for Joseph Kitchin), and Kondratievs (fifty- to sixty-year cycles named for Nikolai Kondratiev).[13]

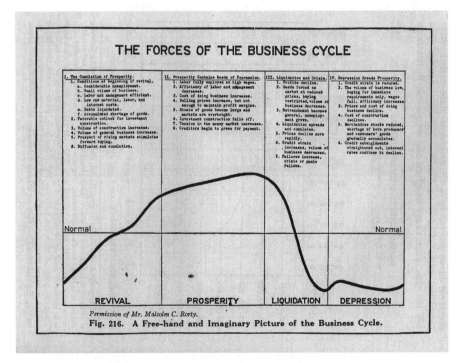

Fig. 216.   A Free-hand and Imaginary Picture of the Business Cycle.

"The Forces of the Business Cycle," in Malcolm C. Rorty, *Some Problems in Current Economics* (Chicago: A. W. Shaw Co., 1922), 78.

Malcolm Rorty depicted the business cycle with a simple, freehand line, in his book, *Some Problems in Current Economics* (1922). In this graph on the preceding page, capitalist economies had four discernible phases: revival, prosperity, liquidation, and depression. Above each of these four, Rorty included a list of economic conditions common to each to help readers determine the end of one phase and the start of the next. Note that the chart showed an especially sharp drop of business activity during times of liquidation or crisis. Rorty included the following signs of such a "panic-filled" period: profits decline, goods are forced on the market at reduced prices, unemployment grows, prices decline rapidly, and business failures proliferate.

Others tried to chart the workings of the cycle. In Brookmire's "Cycle Chart of Business and Banking" (1912), he showed how the ups and downs of business activity tended to deplete and then free up banking resources (see below). As business activity ran from "normal" to "prostrate," banking resources climbed from "normal" to "abundant" and even "plethoric." When business activity subsequently climbed to "feverish" and "hazardous," at the peak of the cycle, banking resources fell to "overextended" and even "critical."

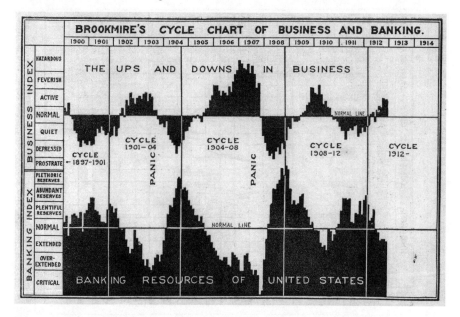

James H. Brookmire's "Cycle Chart of Business and Banking." Source: James H. Brookmire, *The Brookmire Economic Charts: A Graphic Record of Fundamental, Political and Industrial Conditions as a Barometer to the Financial and Business Situation ...* (St. Louis: Brookmire Economic Chart Co., 1913).

* * *

Together the many charts and graphs encouraged the idea that capitalism was both logical and understandable, in the way that one could make sense of the weather by looking at a meteorological chart, or a system of aqueducts by consulting a blueprint, or geographic distance by studying a map. They encouraged a sense of comfort, familiarity, and confidence in the marketplace—and, importantly, its predictability.[14] Forecasting charts depicted the economy as a separate phenomenon, divorced from labor strife, cultural difference, and even events like war and natural disaster. In this way, the graphs were as important for what they left out, as for what they included. Still, all forecasters profiled in this book made use of such illustrations, and they became part of the daily dialogue about the economic future.

CHAPTER 4

C. J. Bullock and Warren Persons: The Harvard ABC Chart

IIIIIIIIIIIIIIIIIIIIIIIIIIIIIIIIIIIIIIIIIIIIIIIIIIIIIIIIIIIIIIIIIIIIIIIIIIIIIIIIIIIIIIIIIIIIIIIIIIIIIII

In many ways, Charles Jesse Bullock (1869–1941) and Warren M. Persons (1878–1937) of the Harvard Economic Service created the most influential forecasting agency of the early twentieth century.[1] Prior to its rise, forecasting was largely an entrepreneurial adventure. Roger Babson and John Moody both had a staff working for them, but their agencies were extensions of their personalities. Irving Fisher was a professor at Yale for his entire professional career, but he formed the Index Number Institute, which produced his forecasts, with his own money and operated it out of his basement at 460 Prospect Street.

The Harvard Economic Service was an entirely different type of organization. It was rooted within the university's Economics Department and funded by the school's Committee for Economic Research and the Rockefeller Foundation. The forecasting group had its offices on the Harvard campus and reported to the university's president, Abbott Lawrence Lowell. Bullock thought that only a university setting, with high standards for objective research and far removed from the temptations of Wall Street, would provide the right frame of mind to produce forecasts. Bullock was also more ambitious than many of his rivals in the forecasting industry. He hoped to build a truly global organization that compared the boom-and-bust cycles of capitalist economies in many different nations. He contacted leading economists in countries throughout the world and urged them to set up "economic observatories" similar to Harvard's. His most significant international collaboration came with Cambridge University's John Maynard Keynes, who was the premier economist of his generation but also a keen investor who managed his university's endowment. For all of these reasons, the Harvard Economic Service's forecasting method was celebrated, criticized, and copied around the world.

Bullock ran every facet of the organization, recruiting personnel and overseeing its advertising and promotion. Through his connections to Harvard alumni, he was in touch with leading business figures in New York's financial houses and in the country's manufacturing industries. Though its subscription list remained relatively small—at about two thousand, it was between one-sixth and one-fifth of the size of a more popular service like Babson's or Moody's—it constituted a veritable who's who of business, government, and intellectual leaders.

Bullock was an established figure in Harvard's Department of Economics, but he was not a renowned scholar. When he formed the Economic Service, Bullock had been at Harvard for thirteen years and had made only one major contribution, an article on the law of diminishing returns.[2] The launching of the Harvard Economic Service, which Bullock oversaw at age forty-six, was an ambitious effort to place Harvard at the forefront of economic research and to secure his own legacy.

Though Bullock ran the Harvard Economic Service, he did not create the group's forecasting model—that was done by statistician Warren Persons. The Harvard Economic Service did not highlight changes in output, as did Babson, or in the price level, as did Fisher, or examine financial news, as did Moody. Instead Persons built a leading-indicator model that charted the interrelation of three aspects of the economy—speculation, business, and money—on a single three-curve graph, with curve "A" standing for speculation; "B" for business; and "C" for money. The Harvard Economic Service's ABC chart, as it was called, is a parent to the leading and lagging indicators developed by the National Bureau of Economic Research and used widely today by business and government. The group also studied historical rhythms in the movements of speculation, business, and money in order to compare the present with the past. They did not search historical data for recurrent patterns as Babson had but instead looked for analogies when making their forecasts: What past period, going by the ABC chart, most resembled the current?

Like Irving Fisher, Persons was an expert on the construction of index numbers and his work contributed to the growth of that field.[3] But Persons's approach to forecasting was far different from Fisher's. Whereas Fisher pioneered a mathematical model that sought to illuminate the causes of periods of expansion and recession, Persons was a pure statistician who focused on gathering and dissecting empirical data. Persons understood the economy through series of statistics that he then placed on economic charts. If detailed enough, these pictures could be put together like a movie, to be watched and interpreted. This, he thought, was the best way to understand economic movements—through observation. Fisher, of course, had an entirely different viewpoint. He wanted, instead, to understand causality in the economy. To him, the goal was not to create a series of pictures of the past but to create a mathematical formula (or even a machine) that simulated the way the economy worked.[4]

In a larger sense, Persons and Fisher had different ideas about what "science" should be—a dichotomy that went all the way back to the empiricist Francis Bacon and the theorist René Descartes. Was the best path to making sense of the economy through mathematical theory that might reveal the economy's timeless inner workings, as Fisher pioneered? Or was it through impartial empirical historical observation, as Persons suggested? Without observation, how could one know how theory and reality aligned? In 1928 Bullock wrote to Harvard's president, Abbott Lawrence Lowell, "The [Harvard Economic Service] has already done a good deal to call economic theory down from the sky and make it travel along the solid highway of verifiable and measurable fact."[5]

Critics later called the type of approach used by Persons, and by economist Wesley Mitchell, as "measurement without theory."[6] As opposed to forecasting methods based on mathematical models of the economy—like those of the econometricians and Keynesians who predominated after the 1930s—the Harvard group refined an approach to forecasting that did not attempt to take the structure and internal relations of the economy into account.[7] Members of the Harvard Economic Service were skeptical that any single theory could explain the complexity of economic activity that they observed. As their effort to build a network of international collaborators showed, they pursued empirical inductive reasoning (rather than theoretical deductive reasoning) with great ambition. In the 1920s, at least, observation was a more popular and compelling way of understanding economics than Fisher's approach, which had yet to take off.

More than any of the other forecasters profiled in this book, the Harvard team celebrated the idea of using the world's most elite institutions and most creative minds to solve the problem of forecasting. By doing so, they hoped to wrest the field away from entrepreneurs like Roger Babson and John Moody. In 1929, the renowned Harvard economist Frank W. Taussig (1859–1940) said of the Harvard Economic Service: "Nothing of this sort—the application of the highest scholarship under academic auspices to the perplexing oscillations and irregularities of modern trade and industry—had ever been tried before."[8]

HARVARD'S ECONOMICS DEPARTMENT

In the late nineteenth century Harvard was but one of several American universities trying to distinguish itself in the field of economics. Johns Hopkins and Columbia had the best reputations, and other prestigious centers included those at Wisconsin, Yale, Princeton, Pennsylvania, and the new University of Chicago, which opened in 1892.[9]

In 1897 Harvard made economics a separate department within the division of History, Government, and Economics, a grouping that says much about the interrelated nature of all three disciplines at the turn of the twentieth century. The field was not like it is today, with mathematics at its center. It was instead a study of what is now called political economy, with a mixture of history, philosophy, and politics, including the study of tariffs and regulation.[10]

Irving Fisher had been ahead of his time in introducing mathematics into the study of economics; only a handful of scholars did so in the early twentieth century, and most were in Europe. The Harvard Economics Department did not offer courses in mathematical economics in the first three decades of the twentieth century, with the exception of a course taught by Allyn Young around 1911. The economist Joseph Schumpeter introduced a course in mathematics for economists in 1933, which was subsequently taken on by others.[11]

Around the turn of the century, Frank W. Taussig was the dominating presence in the Harvard Economics Department. From 1886, when he received a law degree, until 1935, he taught economics at Harvard with only a few interruptions. He was regarded as one of the best teachers of his generation and wrote the foremost economics textbook, *The Principles of Economics*

(1911). He was deeply interested in business and published a statistical study of America's business elite; he also devoted a great amount of time to public service, including a three-year stint as chairman of the U.S. Tariff Commission under Woodrow Wilson.

Other influential members of the department included Thomas Nixon Carver, who became an authority on rural and agricultural economics; and William Z. Ripley, who became the country's leading authority on railway regulation and railway financing and who studied trusts and corporations. Ripley edited a well-known book, *Trusts, Pools, and Corporations* (1905), and published *Railroads: Rates and Regulation* (1912) and *Railroads: Finance and Organization* (1915).[12] Another member of the department was Edwin F. Gay, an economic historian who played an important role in the forecasting industry both by being part of the Harvard Economic Service and, as mentioned in the next chapter of this book, by founding, with Wesley Mitchell, the National Bureau of Economic Research (NBER).[13] In 1908 Gay was selected as the first dean of Harvard's new Graduate School of Business Administration, which initially shared a campus and some faculty with the Economics Department before it moved, in 1927, across the Charles River to its current Boston home. Both Gay and his successor as dean of Harvard's business school, Wallace Donham, were board members of the Harvard Economic Service.[14]

Charles J. Bullock joined the Economics Department in 1903. He had received a Ph.D. from Boston University, writing his dissertation on the finances of the United States in the years just after the American Revolution. He was a specialist in financial history, especially on tariffs and taxes. Bullock made his reputation by promoting economic research and advising Massachusetts's and other state governments on taxation, rather than through teaching or scholarship. Later Paul Samuelson recalled Bullock as a man of impressive classical learning. "Bullock's fiefdom was public finance, and he brought to it a knowledge of Greek and Latin and perhaps some smattering of Hebrew and Aramaic," he wrote. "In case you are too dull to guess how that confers deep insight into taxation and fiscal policy, Bullock's writings would have driven home to you that throughout all history unbalanced budgets contrived the downfall of Greece and the decline of Rome."[15]

Another of Bullock's former students, the Harvard economist Edward Mason, remembered him as an indifferent teacher who seldom updated his courses: "Even in 1919–1920 [about a dozen years before Bullock retired] when I took his course in Public Finance, his lecture notes had a distinct tinge of yellow."[16]

Bullock also became a strong advocate of empirical research. In 1915 he published an article in Harvard's alumni magazine titled "The Need for an Endowment in Economic Research." Bullock noted the new possibilities for empirical research given the rising availability of data from the U.S. government and from private sources, including Standard Statistics, Babson's, and Moody's. But he argued that the real benefit of these new resources was not being recognized because of the expense of conducting rigorous research and lack of scholarship. He believed that academic groups rather than government bureaus or private entrepreneurs should be responsible for collecting and analyzing economic statistics. "It also seems clear," he wrote, "that a university devoted to scientific studies and dedicated to the pursuit of truth is a most fit institution to receive such endowments."[17] Bullock argued that objectivity in forecasting could be achieved *only* in a university setting, where the profit motive was secondary—and financial support could come from the school and from foundations to supplement whatever was made through subscriptions.

In 1917 Bullock helped organize the Harvard University Committee on Economic Research and, through it, hoped to enable Harvard to achieve recognition in the field of economic research.[18] The directorship of the committee was a mixture of businesspeople, government bureaucrats, and academics. Among them were Nicholas Biddle, a scion of the famous Philadelphia banking family; Edwin Gay; Wallace Donham; and New York state senator and later treasury secretary Ogden L. Mills.[19]

By the 1920s the committee had become the highest-funded research activity of the Harvard Economics Department, absorbing the time of several faculty members.[20] Over the course of the decade, funding came from the Rockefeller Foundation, several private companies, wealthy individuals, and subscriptions to the group's publications.[21] The central activity of the Harvard Committee on Economic Research was sponsoring the Harvard Economic Service, the forecasting group that began publishing its predictions in the quarterly *Review of Economic Statistics*, founded 1917, and its *Weekly Letter*, started in 1922. Bullock believed the Harvard Economic Service could be a truly revolutionary organization and would constitute his main contribution to the field of economics and to the university. His first task after the war was to build a staff on a budget of $5,000 contributed by alumni.[22]

Warren Persons

In the fall of 1918, Bullock brought Warren Persons from Colorado College to help build the Harvard Economic Service. Persons was a wunderkind in the field of statistics who had just published an article on building a forecasting model. Bullock viewed him as someone who could provide a framework for the Harvard Economic Service's forecasting goals and be a workhorse to churn through the mass of data Bullock hoped to collect.

Persons's own career had not been smooth. Like Roger Babson and Irving Fisher, Persons was shadowed for much of his life by tuberculosis. In 1910, at the age of thirty-two, Persons was teaching at Dartmouth College when he was diagnosed with the disease. He promptly moved with his wife, Irmagarde, to Colorado, where in a few years his condition began to improve.[23] He became a professor of economics at Colorado College, in Colorado Springs, the "TB Mecca of the West" that was also briefly home to Babson and Fisher. While there, he finished a Ph.D. dissertation for the University of Wisconsin about the distribution of wealth and income, and was appointed dean of Colorado College's Department of Business Administration and Banking.[24]

Persons's scholarly interest was in the statistical analysis of time-series data—and little else.[25] According to one of Persons's students, "In [his statistics] course, as elsewhere, [Persons] held staunchly to the view that statistics is much more than a collection of numerical facts; that it is, on the contrary, a method and a logic; that it is an applied science in which, therefore, it is just as necessary to scrutinize the premises as the logic and mathematics."[26] Statistics, then, was Persons's way of making sense of the world. In a mid-1920s speech on some "fundamental concepts" of the field, Persons included the fact that "statistics may be effectively utilized not merely to describe the past, but as a basis for estimating present and future tendencies." Statistical analysis provided a way to interpret the "complex world of affairs in which we are immersed" that required not only the collection of facts but the creation of "special methods ... for summarizing these data."

The statistician was an "explorer" who could grasp the important and essential detail in a sea of numbers and draw a general inference. While the natural scientist could set up an experiment and run it again and again until a conclusion was found, the statistician (like other social scientists) had to study the "relentlessly hurrying stream" of events and make use of data often accumulated by accident rather than design. Persons rejected the role of probability theory in making predictions about the future because, he said, probability implied randomness to unfolding events—like, for instance, the probability of turning over a red card rather than a black one in a deck. But economic phenomena were not random and the best way to predict was to gather and analyze statistical data.[27]

One Harvard professor recalled, "Persons was considered to be something of a statistical wizard by his colleagues in the Economic Service."[28] Persons had caught Bullock's attention with a 1916 *American Economic Review* article on "business barometers." More than his contemporaries, Persons saw the potential for forecasting to enter many different facets of life in the early twentieth century. He described the growing market for forecasting tools among economists and sociologists who "need such a barometer when dealing with the phenomena of a dynamic society." Government officials, likewise, would find forecasting useful in formulating unemployment policy or undertaking large projects. Manufacturers, investors, and retailers would welcome information on coming economic trends "when considering the desirability of making extensions to their plants or of contracting or expanding their purchases, sales, or commitments."[29]

In his business barometers article, Persons argued for an approach to forecasting based on statistical methods and the deep collection of empirical data about the business cycle. This would allow him to observe the workings of the cycle and see which elements in an economy anticipated cyclical trends, which were concurrent with the cycle, and which ones lagged them. His approach would eventually become the Harvard Economic Service's famous ABC curves.

Like the other forecasters, Persons felt it necessary to disparage the work of his competitors in order to promote his own approach—which he saw as the strictest statistical reasoning in both data selection and interpretation.[30] He described Babson, Moody, and James Brookmire as small fish, not far from bucket-shop owners or even astrologers. Babson's theory was nonsense, he argued. Moody had no training in statistics. Brookmire, whose leading-indicator charts looked similar to Persons's, used only the crudest statistical methods.[31] Fisher had a reasonable theory, but his data were unreliable.

Persons's role at the Harvard Economic Service was to edit the quarterly journal, *Review of Economic Statistics*, to teach statistics, and to develop his forecasting model. With Bullock, he also formulated the predictions of the Service, as they appeared in the *Weekly Letter*, starting in 1922. By fall of that

Charles J. Bullock (left) and Warren Persons (right) from the 1920 Harvard Class Album, pages 18 and 24. Source: Harvard University Archives, HUD 320.04.

year Bullock had recruited Homer Vanderblue, from Northwestern, to edit the *Weekly Letter* and write on general business conditions.[32] Vanderblue, a salesman as well as an economist with a Ph.D. from Harvard, would aim to make the *Letter* more friendly and easier to read. He is remembered today for his great collection of first-edition works of economic history, which form part of the core of Harvard Business School's collection in that field.[33]

METHODOLOGY

Persons's first undertaking at Harvard was to publish a lengthy series of articles on forecasting methodology in the *Review of Economic Statistics*.[34] He devoted the first three regular issues (January, April, and May) and four of the monthly supplements to a discussion of his forecasting methods, writing several articles himself. He produced a total of two hundred pages of methodological articles in 1919 alone. These articles were later published in a folio-sized volume, *Indices of Business Conditions* (1919).

Persons devoted much space to explaining how to combine statistical series of very different types of information: crop yields, pig-iron prices, bank deposits, interest rates, and so on. How could these different types of data be compared to observe their role in the business cycle? This entailed comparing items that not only were in different units (prices on the one hand and output on the other, for instance) but varied seasonally (some time series, like crops, were highly seasonal and others were not). How, too, could fluctuations in time series be compared when some industries were growing and others not? Finally, what type of information should be looked at to make sense of the business cycle?

Persons conducted an intense plotting of a wide variety of data series from trade publications and government sources.[35] He wanted to see how different economic data series related to one another. For example, did they rise and fall at the same time? In what patterns and sequences?

Persons believed that each data series was composed of a secular trend (a regular increase or decrease over the whole period under consideration), seasonal variation (the movement of items within the year), and the underlying cyclical fluctuations (the value secured by the removal of secular trends and seasonal variation). Using his own pioneering statistical methods, he adjusted these data series to eliminate seasonal variances and secular growth. At the core of Persons's idea was the thought that by getting rid of "disturbances," he would reveal the true nature of the business cycle. It was a bit like looking for a whale in a deep and dark sea. Could the actual, moving business cycle be brought into sight by looking closer and closer?

Persons's efforts in this area differed from Fisher's approach; the latter believed the business cycle was in many ways a "myth" or an "illusion" brought about by monetary factors. For Fisher, who argued that the booms and depressions were in part due to periods of inflation and deflation, the effort to remove secular and seasonal changes was tantamount to tossing out the baby with the bathwater. He wrote: "Some of the agencies have tried to 'eliminate the secular trend' from the price level, a procedure almost useless not only because the price level cannot properly be said to have any secular trend, or long time tendency in one direction, but also because, to eliminate any such supposed trend is to throw away a part of the rise or fall, which, as we shall see, is so vital a factor."[36] To some extent, of course, this charge about neglecting an essential factor could be leveled at all the forecasters: by necessity they had to focus on some things and ignore others. Babson's critique of Fisher's refusal to pay attention to consumers and their stylish whims was not dissimilar to Fisher's complaints about Persons. In both cases, the forecasters were criticized for presumably looking at the wrong thing.

Persons devised his method while studying the relation of different economic series. The idea was that although all factors in an economy were affected by the highs and lows of a business cycle, they did not move up and down simultaneously. "Some factors appear to lag behind, rising and falling many months after the rest," a Harvard Economic Service report noted. "Other factors appear to lead the movement; they begin the rise and they begin the fall; they can be used to suggest when the turn of the cycle from rise to fall or vice versa is approaching."[37]

In order to measure the predictive qualities of individual data series, Persons compared the movements of each to a standard series representing general business conditions—in this case, wholesale commodity prices. Persons included those series that had the highest correlation with wholesale prices in his index of business activity. He also made note of all the data series that seemed to lead and lag the movements of these commodity prices.[38]

Today such statistical work could easily be done on a computer, but then it was a difficult affair. Each of the nearly two dozen corrected data series was graphed on a sheet of translucent paper and compared with the others plotted on their own sheets. The comparisons were made over an illuminated box that Persons's group had designed. Three observers examined the charts and recorded the degree of correlation as "high," "moderate," or "low" and judged the duration of lag in months. Persons noted that over 190 such observations of graphs on the illuminated box were made in the formation of the ABC models.[39]

Persons concluded that when the data series were sorted chronologically, the series that fluctuated first, either upward or downward, had to do with investment and speculation; those that lagged behind the "speculative group" had to do with business and industrial activity; and finally, the third group, which lagged behind the "business group," had to do with banking conditions and interest rates.[40]

Persons created three economic indexes: on speculation (Group A), business activity (Group B), and banking (Group C).[41] He superimposed the three composite indexes on a single chart that would present all three cyclical movements together, thus revealing the features of the general economy. Persons believed that he had found a way to dissect the sequences of cyclical

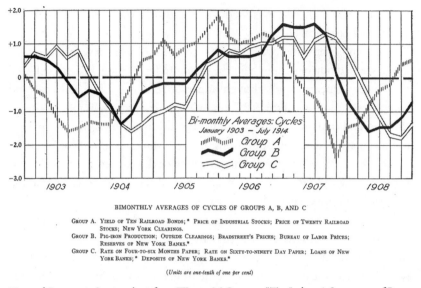

BIMONTHLY AVERAGES OF CYCLES OF GROUPS A, B, AND C

Group A. Yield of Ten Railroad Bonds;* Price of Industrial Stocks; Price of Twenty Railroad
Stocks; New York Clearings.
Group B. Pig-iron Production; Outside Clearings; Bradstreet's Prices; Bureau of Labor Prices;
Reserves of New York Banks.*
Group C. Rate on Four-to-six Months Paper; Rate on Sixty-to-ninety Day Paper; Loans of New
York Banks;* Deposits of New York Banks.*

(Units are one-tenth of one per cent)

Harvard Economic Service chart from Warren M. Persons, "The Index: A Statement of Results," *Review of Economic Statistics* 1:2 (April 1919): 112. Persons wrote, "Group A forecasted
Group B, while Group C lagged behind Group B, and afforded some indication of the future
movement of Group A. Together they afforded a reasonably accurate summary of the course
of business in a period including all phases of the business cycle. In other words, these three
averages constituted an intelligible index of business conditions which, when properly interpreted, threw light upon future tendencies as well as upon current movements." Quote from
Persons in Edwin S. Mason, "The Harvard Department of Economics from the Beginning to
World War II," *Quarterly Journal of Economics* 97:3 (August 1982): 415–16.

agitation. He discerned a pattern in which speculation, business activity, and
banking credit flowed somewhat predictably. As Persons explained it: the
major fluctuations of *speculation* (A) preceded those of *general business* (B) by
four to ten months, and the major fluctuations of *general business* preceded
those of *banking* (C) by two to eight months.[42] The Harvard group viewed
this as an "an important economic discovery," which showed "that there
[was] an established sequence in movements in the speculative, business, and
money markets which [could] be measured statistically and shown graphically on an index chart."[43]

At the heart of the Harvard group's method was the idea that analogous
patterns of economic change found in past periods of depression and expansion
would reemerge in the future. Historical comparisons had to be undertaken

with care, however. Persons's methods called for experts to make detailed analyses of historical analogies.

The trends, showing data from 1903 to 1914, of one curve following the other, seemed obvious enough on the graph. In forecasting, Persons believed that history repeated itself, though imperfectly. Only skilled analysts could compare the motions of the ABC curves at present with their movements in the past and find analogous situations. He also monitored the activities of the speculative curve for rapid drops. In explaining the coming of the 1907 panic, for instance, he noted a sharp decline of the A-curve.[47] After the disruption of World War I, Persons believed that his research revealed that the pattern of the ABC curves had returned.

Persons understood history as a data set rather than as ideas and events: "The past is not exactly like the present and future; it is only more or less similar."[44] But the more complete and rigorous the statistical portrait of the past, the better the understanding of the future. Persons emphasized that the appropriate way to use the Harvard Economic Service's chart was to supplement its statistical analysis with economic analysis that would bring to bear external data not embodied in the chart; that is to say, the chart needed to be interpreted by professional economists, like those in the Harvard Economics Department, rather than by laymen—just as a trained medical doctor would examine an x-ray.[45]

Persons emphasized that his approach to forecasting was based on *empirical* rather than *theoretical* criteria. He did not advance a theory to explain why this relationship held; he was not interested in understanding causation.[46] This new empirical approach to forecasting was different than Fisher's, which focused on theory and causation. In some ways his approach was more similar to that of the trend analysts, like Roger Babson and James Brookmire. But Persons's methods were of an entirely new level of statistical sophistication. His work, with Bullock, brought a higher level of prestige to the field of business barometers.

SELLING PREDICTIONS

The Harvard Economic Service began on a positive note. One fateful prediction in 1920 propelled it from the cloisters of the academy into the ranks of the commercial forecasters. Early that year the Harvard group issued a warning that the dislocation caused by the end of war in November 1918 was far from over. The transition from several years of a wartime economy to peacetime conditions would cause significant economic shocks. Demobilization would swell the ranks of the unemployed and the drop in demand for U.S. agricultural products as Europe returned to producing its own food would deepen the distress.

As it happened, they were right. Beginning in January 1920, the United States experienced eighteen months of recession. The predicted surge in unemployment was indeed severe, but the crisis was also accompanied by a period of extreme deflation—the largest one-year percentage price decline in the previous century and a half of data: the index of wholesale prices of all commodities fell by 37 percent from 1920 to 1921.[48]

Buoyed by their success in correctly predicting the 1920 downturn, Charles Bullock and the rest of the Harvard Economic Service moved to market their forecasts aggressively to decision makers in business and government, focusing their efforts in particular on Harvard alumni by hosting dinners at the school. At the first dinner, to which all subscribers were invited, Persons explained his index of business conditions to about forty executives, including company presidents and treasurers.[49] This was the core audience Bullock and Persons wanted to reach, not casual investors but leading businesspeople who would promote the reputation of the Harvard Economic Service and verify their claims that the ABC curves were useful in practical affairs.

In 1922 the Harvard Economic Service began printing its *Weekly Letter* on economic conditions as a commercial publication to supplement their scholarly quarterly, the *Review of Economic Statistics*, in which the group discussed its methodologies. It was a large and handsome quarterly, printed on high-quality paper, perhaps owing to the prosperous early years of the Harvard Economic Service.[50]

The *Weekly Letter* became the group's main forecasting channel and was intended to appeal to executives; their approach was different from that of Babson, who marketed to the hoi polloi.[51] Bullock then hired a business manager, who was "on the road almost continuously from fall 1919 to spring 1920," touring cities and meeting with businesspeople and increasing the number of subscribers.[52] Harvard's newsletter was met with a great deal of enthusiasm in these years.

By summer 1923, the Harvard Economic Service had grown to a staff of thirty-eight, which included fourteen economists and statisticians, some of whom were also members of the Harvard faculty. The total expanded to forty-three in 1924.[53] Throughout the 1920s, a subscription to the Service cost $100 per year (or about $1,100 today). Subscribers received the *Weekly Letter* on the general economic situation as well as the quarterly *Review of Economic Statistics*, which presented longer, more detailed academic articles on business conditions and was edited by Persons. Thus the group aimed to hit two audiences: business executives, who would read the *Weekly Letter*, and academics, who would spend time with the quarterly journal.

From the fall of 1921 to the spring of 1922, around the time it introduced the *Weekly Letter*, the Service conducted an extensive campaign of newspaper advertising and direct mailings. It spent $35,000 in advertising and received, reportedly, about $62,000 in new business (the equivalent of about $806,000 today).

The Harvard Economic Service was innovative in its methods: it used direct mail to target businesspeople. In 1922, the service had sent 440,000 pieces of direct mail to approximately 110,000 individuals, firms, and corporations; their response showed that large companies were the best prospects and that the Service did not appeal to firms with capital of less than $500,000. Circulars sent to presidents and treasurers yielded the best results. The Harvard group also hired salesmen to sell the service, on commission, in New York, Philadelphia, Cleveland, Chicago, and Toronto.[54]

Some subscribers purchased the service for its indexes of specific industries; some for the forecasts; and some because it stimulated their own thinking about the course of business. An executive from Consolidated Steel wrote that the *Weekly Letter* was "looked forward to as a basis on which to mold our own opinions on the fundamental conditions which it analyzes." The chief statistician at American Telephone and Telegraph (AT&T) noted, "We make regular use of the publications of [the] Bureau and I think, on the whole, find them to be of more value in our economic and statistical work."[55] AT&T used forecasts to help determine when and where to open new plants and when to purchase raw materials.

Harvard Economic Service leaders were bullish about their forecasts. In December 1922, C. J. Bullock wrote to John Maynard Keynes: "Our work has grown considerably during the year, and we now have a surprisingly large number of business concerns that are basing their plans for the year 1923 exclusively upon our forecasts."[56] The subscriber list grew from 740 in 1921 to 2,395 in 1924.[57] Even at its height, though, the Harvard Economic Service

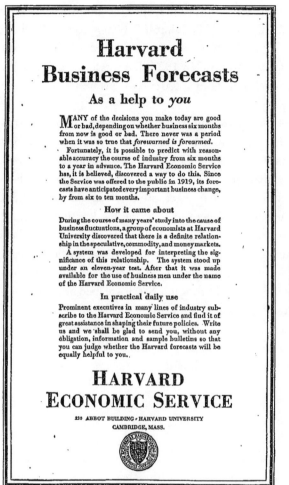

An advertisement for the Harvard Economic Service from the *New York Times*, October 5, 1923, p. 27.

had only one-fifth or one-sixth the subscribers that Moody or Babson could boast. Bullock made a decision in the early 1920s not to pursue a mass audience. He therefore reduced spending on the sales force and newspaper advertising and instead concentrated on direct mail and on retaining current subscribers. In fiscal year 1925–26, the Harvard group stopped spending money on a commission-based sales force. They hired a new business manager and engaged a salaried sales representative in New York to concentrate on securing renewals.[58]

These cutbacks reduced expenditures and helped the group realize a huge profit in fiscal year 1926–27 of $47,700 (almost $600,000 today). Without much marketing, however, the Harvard Economic Service lost subscriptions, which fell from 2,395 in 1924 to 1,567 by 1927. The Service then decided to aim for a core subscription list of about 1,200 and to operate at a small profit of $5,000 or $10,000 per year.[59]

But the influence of the forecasting service went beyond its formal subscribers at big companies. The ABC curves excited interest among members of Harvard's Economics Department and likely its student population as well. Paul Samuelson recalled that for some, the Service promised "a philosopher's stone that would tell customers when to get into the wild and woolly stock market of the 1920s and when to get out." During the Roaring Twenties, Samuelson recalled, the investment firm of Jackson and Curtis had offices located just outside the walls of Harvard Yard and was popular with students and the occasional assistant professor who wished to try their hand in the markets.[60] The activities of the Harvard Economic Service helped bring the speculative excitement of the booming economy to the Cambridge campus.[61]

The other big audience for the Harvard Economic Service was abroad. Bullock reached out to economists throughout the world to take an interest in the exciting activities going on at Harvard.

INTERNATIONAL ACTIVITIES

The Harvard Economic Service was the first forecasting enterprise to construct a truly international organization. Other agencies had made some overseas connections: Babson had opened European offices in 1912;[62] Fisher had corresponded with economists throughout the world; and Moody had opened an office in London in 1925.[63] For the most part, however, all three ultimately focused on the United States. The domestic economy was home to their subscriber base and the subject of most of their predictions. The notion of a global system was largely beyond their purview.

The Harvard Economic Service, by contrast, perceived the increasingly global nature of economic affairs. It set up a network of collaborating economists to monitor business conditions throughout the world and share insight into local economic conditions. As early as 1920, Bullock had expressed his ambition to better understand international business.[64] Over the next decade, he developed contacts with leading economists in Britain, France, Italy, Germany, Austria, and Canada, and the influence of the Harvard method spread. Jan Tinbergen of the Centraal Bureau Voor de Statistiek (Central Bureau of Statistics of the Netherlands) became infatuated with Harvard's work—before criticizing it.[65] Economists in other countries developed forecasting charts based on—and sometimes in opposition to—the Harvard group's model.[66] The international bureaus often followed the outlines of the Harvard service but substituted their own data series to conform to differences in their home economies.[67]

The most fruitful international collaborations were with economists at the London & Cambridge Economic Service. In December 1921, John Maynard Keynes of the University of Cambridge wrote to the Harvard Committee on Economic Research proposing cooperation between the Harvard economists and a group he had organized in Britain.[68] Keynes's biographer, Robert Skidelsky, noted that the economist took an interest in "business barometers" in the early 1920s and was "for a while captivated by them."[69]

Keynes had been collaborating with William H. Beveridge, the director of the London School of Economics (LSE), and Arthur L. Bowley, a statistically and mathematically inclined member of the LSE's faculty, on the formation of a British forecasting service. In February 1922, Bullock went to London to meet with them and reached an agreement of cooperation between the newly formed London & Cambridge Economic Service and Harvard's Committee on Economic Research.[70] Bullock promised that Harvard would underwrite some of the British group's activities. Keynes helped publicize the Harvard Economic Service's barometer throughout Europe by describing it in his Reconstruction Supplements for the *Manchester Commercial Guardian*, the first of which appeared in April 1922.[71]

The London & Cambridge Economic Service published its *Monthly Bulletin* on economic conditions from 1923 to 1951. Like Harvard's *Weekly Letter*, the reports from the London & Cambridge service contained a general economic outlook and forecast. Keynes concentrated on "special memoranda," or in-depth looks at specific economic issues of the day.[72] Overall, the London & Cambridge Economic Service had five hundred subscribers to their regular service, mostly in Britain.[73]

In June 1922, the Harvard Economic Service's *Weekly Letter* began to include the British index, courtesy of the publishing exchange agreement. In the first issue of Britain's own *Monthly Bulletin*, William H. Beveridge praised the Harvard service, noting that "the trade cycle, though irregular in length and range, is certainly not without laws. A long step forward to the discovery of these laws has been made in the past few years through the work of the Harvard University Committee on Economic Research."[74] Bullock wrote to Keynes that he thought the British *Bulletin* was well on its way toward becoming "indispensable to merchants throughout the world."[75]

But some differences of opinion began to emerge. Keynes's correspondence with Bullock in the 1920s reveals the growing divergence between his view of economic fluctuations and that of the American forecasters. It highlights his interest in moving beyond the Harvard group's purely observational approach to business barometers. In their correspondence, Keynes began to push Bullock to clarify the aims and ideas of the Harvard Economic Service, some of which contradicted Keynes's own economic ideas. The two differed, for example, about the role of government policy in economic cycles. The Harvard Economic Service was committed to a view of their forecasts as scientific and impartial, remote from politics and policy. Keynes, by contrast, saw the government and economic realms as intertwined, and felt that the Harvard service mistakenly perceived business cycles as being inevitable and, in some sense, even natural.

In a letter to Bullock in early 1925, Keynes expressed reservations about Persons's ideas of forecasting and the importance of historical analogy. The "Trade Cycle," as he called it, could not be understood merely by "the investigation of past events" and was not "something unalterable in its broad outlines and independent of policy." On the contrary, he continued, "I think that it could be largely eliminated and that it certainly depends on such things as the policy of the Federal Reserve Board more than anything else." Warren Persons, he observed perceptively, "is more inclined to liken it to a natural phenomenon such as the tides." In the same letter, Keynes wondered if the Harvard Economic Service had put itself in the precarious position of opposing the flattening of business cycles, as it thrived on predicting the next wave. "I feel it would be a great pity if the Service were to get into the state of mind of having, so to speak a vested interest in the due recurrence of the boom and slump according to program," Keynes wrote.[76] This was a major indictment against the entrepreneurial incentives of the forecasting industry.

Rather than respond to this challenge, Bullock retreated into the Service's oft-repeated refusal to engage in policy advocacy: "Until our Service is more firmly established, we cannot afford to be advocates of anything, because such a course would confuse our subscribers."[77] He restated the Harvard position that historical investigation was of prime importance and that government policy was not the focus of the Service.

Unlike Keynes, Bullock believed that the central banks were about as powerless to prevent economic cycles as were governments to regulate the weather. As he wrote to his English colleague about the Federal Reserve, "They sometimes seem to think that they have it in their power to prevent real booms and real depressions from occurring; but, if so, they overestimate their wisdom and power."[78]

Keynes continued to be a frequent critic of the Harvard *Weekly Letter* through the late 1920s, passing constructive comments along to Bullock in private correspondence. But, for the most part, the British economist increasingly distanced himself from the forecasting project. His public references to the Harvard Economic Service or its London & Cambridge counterpart dried up, and when Bullock tried to convince Keynes to come to Harvard for a term in the fall of 1928, he declined.[79] Instead, Keyes devoted himself to the line of thought that culminated in his 1936 *General Theory of Employment, Interest, and Money*: that merely predicting economic fluctuations was far too modest a goal. Governments could—and should—devote themselves to minimizing the business cycle, thus minimizing the unemployment, labor unrest, and other human distress that it engendered.

* * *

Across the Channel, Bullock forged a successful connection with the French economist and statistician Lucien March. March had been a director of the department Statistique Generale de la France since 1910.[80] He published an international index of prices starting in 1917 in the *Revue politique et parlementaire*. In January 1923, March started a quarterly journal, which was published without any university sponsorship. In June 1923 Bullock wrote to March, trying to persuade him to take his journal to the University of Paris so that it could be affiliated with a major research university.[81] The following year March did just that, aided by a contribution of $2,500 from the Harvard Committee on Economic Research toward expenses. In 1924–25, the Harvard Economic Service began to print a French index.[82]

Bullock then made connections with economists in Italy, Germany, and Austria. His initial Italian contact was Professor Constantino Ottolenghi of the University of Turin, an expert on price levels in Italy, but Ottolenghi lacked funds and, despite Bullock's wish to help, the Harvard service could not extend another offer of financial support.[83] In 1924, Professor Corrado Gini of the University of Padua wrote to Harvard about potential collaboration. Unlike Ottolenghi, Gini had the endorsement of the Federation of Italian Industries. In November 1925, Gini visited Cambridge, Massachusetts, and met with members of the Harvard Economic Service. Shortly afterward, he began publishing a quarterly bulletin, *Vita economica italiana*, under the joint auspices of the Universities of Rome and Padua.[84]

The situation in Germany proved to be more complicated. The Weimar Republic (1919–33) would seem to be a fruitful site for collaboration, given that it had the most developed program of quantitative economic research on the continent. Thanks to the Imperial Statistical Office and the Berlin Institute for Business-Cycle Research, founded in 1925, the Weimar Republic "sponsored efforts in empirical, policy-oriented economic research that were unprecedented in German history and without parallel in contemporary western Europe," noted one historian.[85] But personal and political issues hampered effective collaboration. For one thing, Bullock was not willing to cooperate with the Imperial Statistical Office, preferring that the service be run entirely out of a university.[86] A further difficulty had to do with language. The work of the major scholar in the field, Ernst Wagemann, head of the Imperial Statistical Office and professor at the University of Berlin, was, not surprisingly, in German, and both Keynes and Bullock had difficulty getting someone they trusted to evaluate its quality.[87] Another reason for the initial hesitancy, aside from Wagemann's connection with the imperial office, was Wagemann's personality, which Bullock found high-handed and arrogant.[88] Bullock instead began collaborating with another economist at the University of Frankfurt, though eventually he changed his mind because Wagemann had greater resources at his disposal. "I have gained the impression that he is not more pretentious than any German economist would be who managed to start an institute for research in Berlin with ample resources," Bullock wrote reassuringly to Keynes.[89] Bullock and Wagemann became frequent correspondents.[90]

Indeed, Wagemann's own early work was heavily influenced by the publications of both the Harvard Economic Service and the London & Cambridge Economic Service.[91] One of Wagemann's German contemporaries considered his work "nothing more than an inadequate imitation of the Harvard Committee."[92] But Wagemann had one asset his American counterparts did not: the vast store of statistical data collected by the German state during the Weimar Republic. Unlike the Americans, who had no national agency collecting official statistics, Wagemann was able to work with a clear measure of national income.[93] (After 1933, however, the German statistical state moved in a radically different direction, as the nation's statisticians put themselves at the service of the Third Reich and full-blown totalitarian planning.)[94]

While Bullock was eventually able to find a workable solution for gaining data from Germany, he was unable to do the same in Austria. Bullock had less success finding data and colleagues there, despite that country's collection of renowned economists. In 1926 the Österreichisches Institut für Konjunkturforschung (Austrian Institute for Business Cycle Research) was founded at the initiative of Ludwig von Mises. Friedrich von Hayek, Mises's pupil, served as director from 1927 to 1931. Von Hayek had become fascinated by the idea of researching of business cycles while on a visit to New York in 1923.[95] He attended courses at Columbia and at the New School for Social Research, where he was in touch with Wesley Mitchell and heard about the barometers being constructed at Harvard.[96]

In April 1927, von Hayek wrote to Bullock, "It shall be our great pleasure ... to collaborate with the Harvard Economic Service." But, he confessed, "our work is ... in a far less definite stage than yours," and, moreover, he felt that a direct affiliation with the University of Vienna was impossible at the time owing to the lack of appropriate faculty in statistics. Von Hayek hoped that by summer 1927 he could forward "in the first Bulletin a preliminary sketch of a kind of Harvard Barometer for the year 1896 [to] June 1914 and some elements for such a barometer for the time since 1923."[97] The Austrian Institute and the Harvard Economic Service agreed on a publication exchange, but in the opinion of Harvard economists, the "time [had] not yet come for considering the establishment of permanent relations."[98] In June 1927, the Austrian Institute began publication of a monthly bulletin, *Monatsberichte des Österreichischen Instituts für Konjunkturforschung* (Monthly Reports of the Austrian Institute for Economic Research).[99]

The Harvard Economic Service also collaborated with Nikolai Kondratiev, the famous Russian economist who pioneered the theory of long-wave economic cycles of fifty or sixty years in Western capitalist countries. After publishing his first book, in Russian, *The World Economy and Its Conjunctures During and After the War* (1922), Kondratiev visited several European countries from 1924 to 1925 and toured the United States. His goal was to study agricultural economies and regulation in capitalist societies.[100] In the United Kingdom, Kondratiev met with Keynes. In the United States, he met with Wesley Mitchell of Columbia and Irving Fisher of Yale, and visited Harvard in December 1924. Kondratiev's official report of the trip did not mention his visit to Cambridge, Massachusetts, probably due to fears that bourgeois connections would have jeopardized his standing at home. The Harvard Economic Service's annual report similarly omitted mention of the visit. As a result of his visit to Harvard, however, Kondratiev initiated a tentative exchange and supplied the Harvard Economics Department with information on economic fluctuations in Soviet Russia.[101]

Kondratiev was most fascinated by long-term economic waves, as opposed to the shorter fluctuations that interested Persons and Bullock. But a year after his visit to Cambridge, he reviewed favorably the research of the Harvard Economic Service in a 1926 article on forecasting, "The Problem of Foresight." He called Harvard's publications "exceptionally major work" toward "a practical solution to the problem of forecasting the phases of the cycle." In the same article, he also reviewed Babson's barometer, calling it "the least perfect infantile form," and the work of the earlier American forecaster Samuel Benner, which he dismissed as "equally imperfect."[102] The window of time in which Soviet economists could publish freely and have foreign contacts was brief, however. Kondratiev's interest in the fluctuations of economic output—to say nothing of his public support for creating economic incentives for agricultural workers—was in sharp relief to the coercive policies of the Five-Year Plans that followed the end of the less restrictive New Economic Policy in 1928. By 1930 he was in prison, a victim of Stalin's purges. He continued to write books from prison but was executed in 1938.[103]

These many international connections, and others still in Canada, New Zealand, Hungary, Poland, and Romania, gave the Harvard Economic Service a broad international scope. By the mid-1920s, Harvard's *Weekly Letter* contained an international barometer that included information from numerous countries. The scholarly connections persisted, too. In June 1928, the London & Cambridge Economic Service held the first international conference for economic forecasting at the London School of Economics. All the foreign correspondents of the Harvard Economic Service attended, with the exception of the representatives from Warsaw and Bucharest and Professors Gini and Ottolenghi of Italy.[104] The conference's major outcome was an agreement on mutual exchange of information among all parties and the formation of two committees, one on information exchange and the other on the standardization of methods.[105] The participants appointed a committee to "consider scientific problems common to" all.[106] The conference was mostly significant, however, for bringing this distinguished group together. Friedrich von Hayek remembered it as the first time he met John Maynard Keynes. Their competing visions of government intervention and free markets would set the terms of debate in policy-oriented economics for decades to come.[107]

In addition to fostering essential connections within the rapidly emerging field of statistical economics, the Harvard group's international efforts highlighted the extent to which forecasting systems were creatures of the political systems in which they were created. In Europe, particularly the parts of continental Europe where the state took an active role in fostering industrialization, forecasting was typically undertaken by state agencies, like the Weimar Republic's Imperial Statistical Office. In the United States, by contrast, where the state took a more hands-off role in the economy, forecasting was more typically an entrepreneurial endeavor.

CRITICISM AND CRISIS

Despite its international connections, the Harvard Economic Service faced challenges on several fronts—more than its competitors had encountered. On the one hand, a barrage of criticism came from rival forecasters. Bullock's and Persons's dedication to transparency in forecasting methods opened them up to attack in a way that forecasters with more opaque methods avoided. In 1922, Ray Vance, the head of the Brookmire Economic Service, complained that the Harvard service focused solely on short-term trends of the next quarter or season and that the model itself gave no sense of the *magnitude* of impending periods of boom or slump.[108] In 1924, Roger Babson echoed this complaint about severity in an article in the *Annals of the American Academy of Political and Social Science*.[109]

But by far the most damning criticism came from academic economists. Here the fight surrounding the Harvard Economic Service was about methodology—and all the more severe because the Harvard group's rivals were economists competing not for customers but for academic prestige. The attacks damaged the Harvard group's morale, as well as their reputation as accurate forecasters. But the controversy did exactly what scholarly exchanges are supposed to do: expand the frontiers of knowledge and enlarge the world of ideas. From the attacks on the Harvard Economic Service came insights that enriched the work of several eminent economists and contributed to the founding of an entirely new subfield in the social sciences.

The opening salvo in this battle came from New Haven–based economist Karl Karsten, Irving Fisher's colleague and sometime employee. In 1926 Karsten, who almost certainly showed his essay to Fisher, published "A New Interpretation" in the *Journal of the American Statistical Association*, in which he accused the Harvard group of misunderstanding the data they had collected.[110] The famous A, B, and C curves were not, as Harvard claimed, true "mutually self-predicting" lags in the specified sequence of speculation, business, and money. The Harvard Economic Service's graphs were simply points in time that did not illustrate how economies worked. "By what occult powers the speculating world in mass could accomplish a thing which no speculator seems able to do individually, and that is correctly to divine and discount the future of business, for between six months and a year in advance," Karsten wondered.[111] Making matters even worse, Karsten wrote a letter to Harvard's president, Abbott Lawrence Lowell, accusing Persons and other Service staff members of trying to suppress another article by him that was going to appear in the *New York Times Annalist* by writing to that paper's editor. Karsten complained, "I am amazed at this attempt upon academic freedom of discussion."[112]

In his defense, Bullock wrote a letter to all the members of Harvard's Committee on Economic Research, saying that Karsten's article was not well thought out and was, in fact, "unbelievably bad."

> His principal contention is that our Curve B really forecasts Curve A. In order to prove that, he first turns it upside down. Then he discovers that its trend isn't right, and changes its trend. To change his trend, he looks at Curve A in order to determine the significant points on Curve B, and thus fits Curve B to a large extent to Curve A. Having thus fitted Curve B to Curve A in advance, he then studies the correlation between his doctored B Curve and the A Curve, and naturally finds a high correlation. Of course the result he obtains was of his own manufacture, and not at all in the original data. The article will probably be a good thing in the end, and will "clear the air." It will also disclose who some of our enemies are, a thing which it has been hard for some of our friends to believe.[113]

But the episode rattled him. In his letter Bullock asked that everyone be on the lookout for any articles that cited Karsten favorably, as that would make visible the Harvard group's enemies. Bullock, Persons, and their recently hired colleague W. L. Crum responded to the article by Karsten, point by point, in the April 1927 issue of the *Review of Economic Statistics*, saying that his article made "absurd conclusions."[114] But the charge that the Harvard group paid no attention to understanding the *causes* of economic cycles resurfaced later in the 1920s and 1930s in more potent critiques, especially with the work of economist Jan Tinbergen, a pioneer of macroeconomic modeling and co-winner of the first Nobel Prize in economics. Tinbergen focused his macroeconomic analysis on policy and the belief that economists could forecast the effect of policy "instruments" on desired economic "targets."[115]

The next attack also included substantive criticism: the charge that prophecies were self-fulfilling. This was the accusation of the German Austrian economist Oskar Morgenstern (1902–77). Morgenstern spent 1926–27 as Honorary Research Fellow at Harvard, where he became familiar with the forecasting efforts of the Economics Department, but also attended the private seminars of Harvard's philosopher-mathematician Alfred North Whitehead and "struggled," as he later put it, with the writings of Bertrand Russell, Ludwig Wittgenstein, and Hermann Weyl on logic. "One of the problems that naturally sprang to my attention" in this setting, he later recounted, "was that of the influence of predictions on the predicted events."[116] The problem with any trusted forecast was that it would influence the course of the economy it was forecasting because it would lead the economic players involved to take actions that would change the economy's course—thus rendering the whole process vastly more complicated.

Morgenstern used his time at Harvard to write a book-length appraisal of economic forecasting that he published in Austria in 1928 as *Wirtschaftsprognose: Eine Untersuchung ihrer Voraussetzungen und Möglichkeiten* (Economic Forecasting: An Investigation of Their Prerequisites and Possibilities). In it, he dismissed the Harvard Economic Service's ABC curves on the grounds that an economy was too complex for regular patterns to be discerned, as forecasters were attempting to do. But he also offered what he later called an "epistemological" critique, writing that he found the entire enterprise of business forecasting, as currently practiced, inherently impossible. "[A]ny widely accepted forecast," Morgenstern contended, "itself sets up reactions which doom it to failure." To illustrate his point, Morgenstern made an analogy to the pursuit by Sherlock Holmes of the criminal master-mind Professor Moriarty in the popular series of detective novels by Arthur Conan Doyle.[117] The narrative premise of the struggle is that both men, intellectually closely matched, attempt to guess what their rival was likely to do. "One may be easily convinced," Morgenstern wrote, "that here lies an insoluble paradox." The analogy, he suggested, was direct: economic forecasting was in essence little more than a futile effort on the part of one party to out-think another. "And the situation is not improved," he continued, "but, rather, greatly aggravated if we assume [the presence of] more than two individuals," as there necessarily would be in a real-world example. "Always, there is exhibited an endless chain of reciprocally conjectural reactions and counter-reactions."[118]

Morgenstern continued to pursue the line of thought raised by his criticisms of forecasting through what would become a hugely influential career. He became professor at the University of Vienna and director of the Austrian Institute for Business Cycle Research from 1931 to 1938. He returned to the Holmes-Moriarty example in a 1935 article on foresight and economic equilibrium. When the Nazis declared him "politically unbearable" and dismissed him from his posts in 1938, he accepted an offer from the Princeton Institute for Advanced Studies, where he struck up a close working relationship with the mathematician J. von Neumann, who had been pursuing related ideas in his own research since the late 1920s. Their subsequent collaboration resulted in the publication of their major work, *The Theory of Games and Economic Behavior* (1944). Morgenstern regarded this book—which also made use of the Holmes-Moriarty example—as a natural outgrowth of his 1928 *Wirtschaftsprognose*. In it, he and von Neumann offered a radical reconceptualization of the basic problems of competition and collaboration as a game of strategy among several agents, as well as an important and novel approach to utility theory. Though it took decades to be accepted—it remained controversial even at the time of Morgenstern's death in 1977—"game theory" has permeated the social sciences, from economics to political science and international relations.[119]

These criticisms, voiced by Keynes, Karsten, Morgenstern, and other scholars, revealed one of the difficulties of being transparent in one's methodology. Entrepreneurial forecasters (like Roger Babson and John Moody) seldom published discussions of their methods in any great detail, as Persons had done. This allowed other economists to test, and even try to replicate, the Harvard Economic Service's models. But the critiques also showcase the outlooks and limitations of respective disciplinary approaches: statistical approaches that were more focused on description than on causation, for instance; or mathematical ones that tended to narrowly focus on a few key variables.

The complexity of economies eclipsed academic boundaries and called for a multidisciplinary approach. But the restrictions of academic boundaries were not the Harvard Economic Service's only problem. In the late 1920s, it ran into increasing problems owing to its place within a university—the very setting that Bullock had thought would be ideal.

POWERFUL ALUMNI

The next crisis to hit the Harvard Economic Service in the mid-1920s was not intellectual but institutional. Harvard president Abbott Lawrence Lowell had grown increasingly uneasy with a for-profit, business-oriented institution at the university. Lowell, who was in office from 1909 to 1933, came from a prominent Boston family and had an aristocratic bearing. But he undertook several steps aimed at democratizing the university. For instance, he founded Harvard's Extension School, which offered classes to the public (it is still a thriving institution). Another of his most lasting legacies was his decision to require all freshmen to live in college dorms. The purpose of this was to bring social classes together, as Harvard's most wealthy students had taken to living in a section of Cambridge nicknamed the "Gold Coast" because it was so exclusive. Lowell also oversaw the building of the great residential houses for Harvard undergraduates that now line the Charles River.[120]

The Harvard Economic Service did not seem to fit with Lowell's agenda. Even as early as 1923, Lowell expressed the idea that the Harvard Economic Service was "felt to be in the nature of a business which the University ought not to undertake."[121] By the middle of the decade, plans were being made to separate the Harvard Economic Service from the university. In 1928 the group was given a new name: the Harvard Economic *Society* (rather than *Service*). It was reorganized as a Massachusetts corporation, whose purpose was "scientific and educational and not commercial." Annual dues remained at $100.

The exact nature of the society's relationship with the school was for a time ambiguous. The group, after all, had moved just a few blocks down

Massachusetts Avenue in Harvard Square. The announcement stated that "[t]he original Directing Members are the same individuals who up to this time have constituted the Harvard University Committee on Economic Research and, by gentlemen's agreement, provision has been made under which all future Directing Members shall be persons in sympathy with the aims and ideals which have guided all our work," and further stated that the "ultimate control of the Society" rested with Harvard University.[122] The new society tried to imitate its old Harvard-sponsored publication. It kept the crimson binding and the gold letters for their annual volumes. It also tried to mirror the layout, down to imitating the Harvard seal on their front matter with a similar corporate seal.

Full secession came toward the end of the 1920s, however. In the summer of 1928, Lowell wrote to Bullock, saying that he had consulted with the Harvard Corporation, and its directors had demanded that the Harvard Economic Society and the university be wholly separate and that the "so-called gentlemen's agreement had better be cancelled."[123]

The biggest loss to the society at the time of its incorporation as a private concern came with the departure of staff to more lucrative positions at private companies. Two senior figures left in the late 1920s, a time when speculation on Wall Street, and increasingly on Main Street, took on aspects of a mania.

In 1928 Persons resigned his position as editor of the *Review of Economic Statistics* to become a vice president of the National Investors Corporation, which had been organized by a former business manager of the Harvard Economic Service.[124] He also established his own company, Warren M. Persons and Associates, Consulting Economists and Engineers, in New York, with clients including AT&T, American Tobacco Company, and Philco Radio.[125] Persons had given the Harvard Economic Service its model and had overseen its predictions for a decade. He created a set of core statistical techniques for preparing and comparing time-series data that were widely influential. But he came to believe, as would Bullock in the 1930s, that in the form of his ABC curves he had something more valuable in the booming market than could be realized in his position at Harvard. In 1929 Homer Vanderblue also entered private business, becoming vice president of the Tri-Continental Corporation, an investment management firm.[126]

The first meeting of the new and legally independent Harvard Economic Society was held in mid-November 1928 and featured speeches by economic statisticians from General Motors and AT&T and by W. Randolph Burgess of the Federal Reserve Bank of New York.[127] Without Persons, Bullock and the mathematical economist W. L. Crum oversaw the production of the *Review of Economic Statistics* and the *Weekly Letter* as the stock market kept climbing in 1928 and early 1929.

The new organization had fewer subscribers than its predecessor, but, at least temporarily, it remained profitable because of low marketing expenses. The 1928 annual report noted that the yearly income from all sources was $109,150 and total expenses $86,284.[128] In May 1928, Bullock succeeded in getting funds from the Laura Spelman Rockefeller Memorial to supplement their revenue.[129]

So stood the Harvard Economic Society in 1929—stripped of its institutional home and some of its key longtime personnel. If this weren't bad enough, the stock market crash took the organization completely and humiliatingly by surprise.

The Harvard Group and the Depression

The Harvard Economic Society, which had maintained optimism following Roger Babson's gloomy predictions, expressed uncertainty immediately after the October 1929 crash. On November 16 the *Weekly Letter* noted, "The unprecedented declines in stock prices ... make it difficult to estimate at present the amount of injury which will be done to business."[130] But by the end of the month, the group seemed heartened that interest rates had not risen sharply. It declared that the current crisis would not be as bad as the previous one, nine years before. The *Weekly Letter* reported, "While the extent of the damage to business can not yet be appraised, it is clear that serious and prolonged business depression, like that of 1920–21, is out of the question."[131]

In December, the agency remained optimistic and predicted a recovery by spring. In its message of December 21, 1929, the society foresaw two or three more months of "slack business" due to a "spirit of caution" and an effort by merchants to restrict inventories in the wake of the market crash. Looking at "historical precedents," they concluded that a depression was "improbable." They predicted a "recovery of business next spring, with further improvement in the fall, so that 1930, as a whole, should prove at least a fairly good year."[132] The society continued to issue optimistic forecasts through the spring. When economic conditions did not improve by the summer, the society attributed the situation to the pessimistic attitude of investors and predicted improvement in the last half of 1930.

By the fall of 1930, the society admitted that the downturn in industrial production was more serious than anticipated. "Our view that the decline in business would not go beyond a recession has not been borne out by this year's developments, since first the duration and now the magnitude of the decline indicate a depression," the agency wrote. However, the society still maintained that the crisis of 1920–21 was a worst-case scenario: "But our statement that, with money easy, commodity speculation absent, and commercial credits in good condition, this country did not face a depression of such extreme severity as that of 1921 seems to be in process of justification."[133]

By late fall 1930, however, after the Dow Jones Industrial Average dropped from 294 in the spring to barely 170, the Harvard Economic Society had turned pessimistic about prospects for business: "Business is now much reduced, but neither the statistical evidence nor the present economic situation gives assurance that it has yet reached bottom." Further decline "seems to be indicated," they reported.[134]

Despite the gloomy message, the society interpreted every minor uptick in their speculation curve (A) as a sign that business recovery was at hand. While the overall trend over the months following 1929 was downward, there were periods when securities prices moved up—and this was interpreted as an impending return of prosperity. They were in good company. Even among the more pessimistic market observers in this period, none thought the Depression would last as long as it did (twelve years).

The Harvard Economic Society also suffered because the international network Bullock had worked to create shattered in the 1930s. It fell apart under the pressures of worldwide depression, the rise of dictators in Italy, Germany, and the USSR, and, ultimately, world war.

But incorrect predictions and dissolved international partnerships were not the society's only problems. In the January 8, 1931, edition of Harvard's *Alumni Bulletin*, William P. Everts, a Boston lawyer and highly engaged alumnus of the class of 1900, charged that the frequency of incorrect forecasts by the Harvard group beginning in the mid-1920s had actually contributed to the stock market crash and its aftermath. The combination of the society's prestige and its "optimistic tones," he wrote, "helped to push the market up higher and higher and made the inevitable crash so much the greater, and then helped to delay the real recovery by its ill-tempered optimism." Everts accused the Harvard group of other erroneous predictions, and cited examples from the decade.[135]

Everts also compared the Harvard Economic Society unfavorably to Roger Babson's service. He implied that the Harvard-based economists did not possess the courage to make pessimistic predictions because the society feared angering its clientele, whereas Babson had no such reservation: "To show what I mean, shortly after Roger W. Babson, the writer of a rival bulletin, came out with his famous speech, a few weeks before the crash, on October, 1929, in which he predicted an eighty-point break in the stock market, the highest official of the National City Bank called him on the telephone and insisted on talking to him although he was sick in bed, for the purpose of inducing him to change his attitude and join the other optimistic financial writers." In the wake of such pressure, Everts claimed (most likely falling for a bit of Babson self-promotion), Babson had maintained his forecast of a depression. But the Harvard society had chosen to join the optimistic consensus.[136]

Two days later, President Lowell's office issued a press release saying that the university was not responsible for "the effect of prophecies by the Harvard Economic Society, Incorporated, as the institutions were entirely separate."[137] The affair was reported in the *New York Times* under the headline "Harvard Denies Onus for Trade Predictions."[138]

A few days after the article in the *New York Times*, Bullock wrote to Lowell suggesting that Everts's letter was "misleading, inaccurate, and on the whole very unfair." He admitted that the society had underestimated the severity and duration of the economic problems facing the United States in the months since the market crash. But the incorrect predictions did not stem from outside pressure. Rather, he asserted, their predictions—though wrong—were made for the right reasons. As it always had, the society had made its optimistic predictions based on statistical analysis and *"strict adherence to historic precedents."* On every other occasion, he stressed, conditions had continued serene.[139] Here Bullock signaled the main problem with making sense of the 1929 stock market crash and the ensuing economic contraction: it was an unprecedented economic event.

The society continued to issue forecasts after Everts's letter appeared in the *Alumni Bulletin.* But the days of the group were numbered. In the late summer and fall of 1931, the Harvard society focused even more on the global financial problem. The analogy that the group most promoted, the 1920–21 depression, no longer made sense in 1931, for at that point, according to the historical analogy, the depression should have been over. Its *Weekly Letter* of August 22, 1931, reported, "We regard the European situation still as the dominant factor; and, since its course cannot be foreseen, we find it possible at present to make only a conditional forecast of the course of business in the United States during the remainder of the year."[140] The report concluded that a depression was likely to continue until the "disturbances" in Europe were over.

In November 1931, Bullock announced that the Harvard Economic Society would soon end its *Weekly Letter* but would continue publishing the quarterly *Review of Economic Statistics*. The new service would focus less on forecasting. The subscription fee under the new terms would fall from $100 per year, for the weekly service and quarterly journal, to $10 per year, for the quarterly alone.[141] In his explanatory letter to subscribers Bullock gave many reasons for this change, including inadequate funds to pay senior staff, excessive strain and overwork, and heavily reduced revenues. But he explained the real reason to President Lowell in a personal letter that same month. The society, he explained, had been "influenced to a considerable extent by a desire to avoid a repetition of such trouble as we had over the Everts letter in the *Alumni Bulletin* early this year."[142]

The experience of the members of the Harvard Economic Society demonstrated, among other things, the problem of having a fixed mind-set (or, as economists would say, being "path dependent"). The group had promoted the ABC models for over a decade. But in the early 1930s when the Harvard Economic Society consistently missed its prediction, it could hardly say that the model had all along been worthless. In this way, the society faced a problem that less academically inclined forecasting organizations like Moody's, which had never explicitly stated a model, did not.

The *Weekly Letter* ceased to be published at the end of 1931, marking the end of the Harvard Economic Society's forecasting endeavors, though the *Review of Economic Statistics* continued in print.[143] Soon after, Bullock and Crum tried to restore their reputations. In 1932 they published an article titled "The Harvard Index of Economic Conditions: Interpretation and Performance, 1919–1931," in the *Review of Economic Statistics*. Bullock and Crum argued, a bit defensively, that, in fact, the chart had been right in the fall of 1929 but that they had doubted what they were seeing. The chart had

CHART I. — THE MONTHLY INDEX CHART

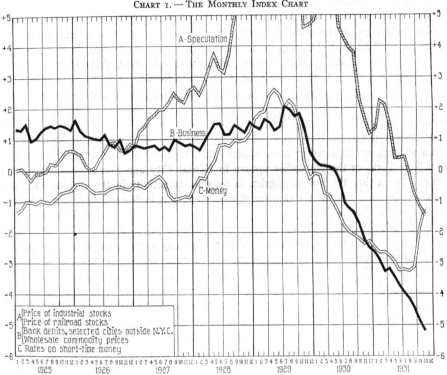

Harvard Economic Society, *Weekly Letter*, December 19, 1931. At this point the curves were clearly out of rhythm.

correctly captured the "basic difference" between the "high prosperity in general business" and the "violent inflation in speculation." Bullock and Crum wrote that they would have seen this if they had relied on a more "mechanical" interpretation of the curves.

> Again in the spring of 1929, the chart gave a new and much more emphatic warning [than it had the previous summer] of a cyclical decline to depression. Curve A dropped sharply for a few months; and further sharp advances occurred in Curve C, already at a very high level. These developments in the chart pointed emphatically toward a reversal of the cyclical movement in business, and their mechanical reading would have spelled the coming of depression. Had the chart been taken at face value in June 1929, the forecast of a cyclical depression would have been unavoidable.[144]

The course forward, Bullock and Crum reasoned, lay in more empirical work and less second-guessing by chart readers. Forecasters needed to have the strong will not to be afraid to tell customers of impending crises.

But perhaps a bigger problem for the Harvard Economic Society was its directors' continued belief in the inevitability of cycles during a time when politicians and businesspeople were looking for *cures* to the depression. In the 1930s, Bullock maintained his faith that government could do little to change economic conditions. He compared current prospects for effective action to those faced by "King Canute" and his "efforts to control the tide"— referring to the story of a Danish Viking king of the late tenth and early eleventh centuries who commanded the tide to halt and not wet his feet; but when this failed, he realized the weakness of kingly power and the majesty of god.[145]

Such confidence in the Harvard Economic Service's methods led Bullock to attempt a second career on Wall Street in the 1930s making use of the ABC curves. When Bullock ended the *Weekly Review* in 1931, he had intended to spend several years in Harvard's Widener Library, working on a manuscript on the early history of economic thought. But Bullock, like Persons and Vanderblue, became drawn into the stock market and to the tempting possibility of making a fortune.

In New York, Persons struggled, however. He found it harder to abandon the stance of the academic than it had been to abandon the academy. One of his colleagues noted that consulting did not come easy to Persons: "So determined was he … to retain his integrity as a scientist in pursuit of the truth, that he usually frightened prospective clients away."[146] He had the talents of a statistician rather than an entrepreneur.

Charles Bullock was not wealthy. In 1927 he wrote that he had no personal investments in any trusts, "except a very small trust in the Bullock family of which I am the trustee."[147] Gradually Bullock came to do work for a relative at Kidder, Peabody, becoming a paid consultant and still relying on the Harvard ABC curves. Outside of his relatives on Wall Street, though, Bullock had little success in selling his forecasts. In the fall of 1934, he confessed to a colleague, "With economic conditions as they are, business men are not much interested in statistical and economic analysis, and are inclined to think of little except what the Administration at Washington is going to do to them next."[148] They were less interested, at least, in the type of analysis Bullock provided.

Still, Bullock made one last try to revive the society, as he explained in a letter to the chairman of Wells Fargo: "When it appeared clear last fall that we could not go on without help, I sent a letter, of which you received a copy, to some three hundred twenty of our oldest and most interested members and subscribers; but the result was only thirty-six or thirty-seven $100 contributions."[149] In 1935 the Harvard Economic Society closed, and its quarterly journal was moved to the Department of Economics, where it was renamed the *Review of Economics and Statistics*, edited by distinguished economist Seymour Edwin Harris.[150] Today it is an elite journal published by MIT Press.[151]

After concluding that the market for forecasts was moribund, Bullock wrote to a friend in 1935 that he felt a sense of freedom: "I feel a very great sense of relief from a heavy burden and responsibility which has taken a good deal out of me, and if continued would have pretty well chained me to my desk for the few remaining years of my scientific activity."[152]

CLOSING DOWN

The closing of the Harvard Economic Society and Bullock's retirement from the Economics Department coincided with other changes at Harvard. Frank Taussig, the luminary of the department for all of Bullock's time there, retired in 1935. The department gained status with the arrival of the Austrian-born economist Joseph Schumpeter in 1936, who had previously been a visitor there. Schumpeter was perhaps the most knowledgeable economist in the world and, among other things, a leading expert on business cycles. He was skeptical of efforts to extract cycles from "normal" economic behavior: "Cycles are not, like tonsils, separable things that might be treated by themselves but are, like the beat of the heart, of the essence of the organism that displays them." Moreover, he doubted the ability to predict them, suggesting that while doctors might be able to advise patients about their general health, they could not determine whether a healthy patient would be struck by a brick upon leaving the hospital.[153]

Schumpeter quickly sized up the Harvard Economic Society. He applauded the group for its efforts and felt that it had succeeded by achieving a "rough common sense" through its statistical methods. But he felt that, at its center, was a misconception. Persons and Bullock had believed that their forecasting methods were based purely on observation. In fact, they were following a clear theoretical path.

> The constructors of the Harvard Barometer emphasized for the benefit of their readers and also believed themselves that they were not using any of that discredited and discrediting monster, economic theory. Professor Persons was quite prone to reply to theoretical objections by pointing to the hundreds of correlation coefficients that had been figured out under his direction. As a matter of fact, however, they did use a theory that was all the more dangerous because it was subconscious: they used what may be termed the Marshallian theory of evolution. That is to say … they assumed that the structure of the economy evolves in a steady or smooth fashion that may be represented (except for occasional changes in gradient, "breaks") by linear trends and that cycles are upward or downward deviations from such trends and constitute a separate and separable phenomenon.[154]

Though Persons argued that his approach was nontheoretical, Schumpeter pointed out that it had a clear conceptual framework. Persons, for instance, began with the belief that economic fluctuations had secular, seasonal, and cyclical components. He also believed that there were "accidental" fluctuations caused by exogenous shocks, as well as inherent cyclical patterns.[155]

This was an essential point about the Harvard Economic Service—and forecasting generally. All predictive efforts, even those claiming to simply reveal past patterns or to be based solely on observation, contain deeply embedded assumptions. Persons, a dyed-in-the-wool statistician, never examined the theoretical basis behind his methods. Bullock, whose lengthy exchanges with Keynes and other economists might have alerted him to this issue, never broke away from the theoretical assumptions of the ABC model even when its underlying ideas about equilibrium were challenged by economic realities. His inability to escape the mind-set embodied in the forecasting model, even when it was clearly not working, added to his deep frustration during the Depression.

Ironically, the greatest legacy of the organization was in the promotion of leading, coincident, and lagging indicators used in econometrics, rather than statistical observation. The ABC barometers were forerunners of indicators developed at places like the National Bureau of Economic Research by Arthur F. Burns (1904–87), Geoffrey Moore, and others. The work also influenced post–World War II government economists, such as Julius Shiskin (1913–78), who headed the Economic Research and Analysis Division at the U.S. Census Bureau and developed computerized methods for business-cycle tracking.[156]

But the history of the Harvard Economic Society also serves as a cautionary tale of the commercial ventures undertaken by universities. The issue was not simply about forecasting but about the conflicts of "gown" and "town." The commercial pressures of the marketplace played a big role in the story of the society.[157] The excitement it generated in the early and mid-1920s reached Harvard students, faculty, and alumni alike. "A number of economist stars, young and old, dropped a bundle in the 1929 crash," wrote Paul Samuelson in his recollection of the Harvard forecasting group.[158] These same enthusiastic followers became bitter in the early 1930s with the Harvard Economic Society's cheery predictions. Samuelson, who had no formal role in the forecasting organization, recalled even hearing regular complaints from his dentist, who had followed the advice of the Harvard Economic Service. It was not the first or the last of such ventures, of course. The problem of universities "in the marketplace," as Derek Bok, Harvard president from 1971 to 1991, called it, became vastly greater in the late twentieth century.[159]

CHAPTER 5

Wesley Mitchell and Herbert Hoover: Forecasting as Policy

||||||||||||||||||||||||||||||||||||||||||||||||||||||||||||||||||||||||||||||||||||||||||||||||||||||

This chapter differs from the others in this book in that it does not focus on a private forecasting agency but on the role of the Department of Commerce, and other government agencies, in supporting and promoting forecasting. It examines how the economist Wesley Clair Mitchell (1874–1948) and the engineer and politician Herbert Hoover (1874–1964) attempted to harness the potential of economic forecasting not for private gain or personal advancement but for the benefit of American society. They believed that unexpected boom-bust cycles threatened the very future of the country's capitalist economy and they sought a remedy. "If we could foresee the business cycle, there would be none," said Mitchell.[1] Their work had lasting importance. Together, Mitchell and Hoover in the 1920s were among those who helped pave the way for the view that government should play a role in macroeconomic management. This change in thinking had great consequence for the forecasting field in the twentieth century, investing it with a new sense of power, prestige, and purpose.

The first figure discussed in the chapter, Wesley Mitchell, is like some of the others in the book: an economist who was fascinated by business cycles and devoted much of his life to studying them. Mitchell's *Business Cycles* (1913) was the most comprehensive survey of the subject of economic fluctuations of the time. He was the co-founder of the National Bureau of Economic Research, which became the nation's leading economic research institution and remains so today. In the 1910s and 1920s, Mitchell was as famous an economist as Irving Fisher, and he attracted scores of students to Columbia to study with him. He was not primarily a forecaster and the term is not often used to describe him, but his engagement with the subject of economic fluctuations made him a central figure among the forecasting crowd. Hoover referred to him as an "umpire" because of his sound judgment in weighing conflicting ideas.[2] The economist Joseph Schumpeter said of Mitchell in a eulogy: "Here was a man who had the courage to say, unlike the rest of us, that he had not all the answers; who went about his task without either haste or rest; who did not care to march along with flags and brass bands; who was full of sympathy with mankind's fate, yet kept aloof from the market place; who taught us, by example and not by phrase, what a scholar should be."[3]

The second person profiled in this chapter, Herbert Hoover, is unlike the other figures mentioned in the book. He was an international businessman and politician who served as head of the Department of Commerce for most of the 1920s and then as the thirty-first president of the United States from 1929 to 1933. The designation "odd man out" suits him. In many ways, Herbert Hoover was sui generis: at odds with other politicians of the time, conservatives and liberals alike. He, like many other businesspeople of the 1910s and 1920s, became fascinated by business cycles. He was not interested in the subject of economic prediction in a scholarly way but for political reasons. Hoover believed that the ebb and flow of economic cycles threatened the country by bringing unemployment, labor conflict, and violence. He wanted to find a way to eliminate severe economic fluctuations from the American economy by advising businesspeople of likely future economic trends. He believed that the forecasting industry could provide a vital service to keep business productive and avoid economic crisis. It was so important, in fact, that the job of predicting the economic future, in which business could flourish, could not be left entirely to enterprising entrepreneurs but had to be facilitated by the state.

Despite their different backgrounds and experiences, and occasionally conflicting views, Mitchell and Hoover shared a vision of improving society through the use of expert analysis, statistical investigation, and the reform of business methods. They were not partners in the sense of Charles Bullock and Warren Persons of the Harvard Economic Service, but Herbert Hoover relied on the advice and counsel of Wesley Mitchell. Hoover recruited Mitchell for the Department of Commerce's Business Cycle Committee in the early 1920s and the two men continued to collaborate on government matters for over a decade. Hoover sought to find a solution to the problems of unexpected economic crisis. Mitchell sought to unearth data that would help make the workings of the business cycles more understandable in the first place.

The public nature of Hoover and Mitchell's enterprise gave their effort a different goal than that of the entrepreneurs discussed in this book. Profit-oriented commercial forecasting firms issued reports to individual companies in order to give them a chance to secure themselves while their competitors failed in an unexpected downturn. Hoover and Mitchell instead proposed to provide guidance and data to all firms, and forecasting agencies, to help produce more accurate forecasts. They believed that through stewarding the distribution of scientifically objective data and through improved knowledge of the causes of fluctuations, government could entice business leaders to enact countercyclical policy that would flatten the swings of the business cycle. Managers and investors would hence improve national economic stability and create a balance of production and consumption.[4] If previously forecasting had aimed to help individuals find a lifeboat in an economic storm (to use a maritime analogy), the goal of the state was to use forecasts to calm the entire sea.

This was not the first time that government had been involved in forecasting endeavors, especially in the fields of meteorology and agriculture.[5] Ulysses Grant's administration founded the National Weather Service in 1870, placing it under the secretary of war, who gave it its first name: the Division of Telegrams and Reports for the Benefit of Commerce.[6] By 1891, as the memory of the Civil War receded, it moved to the Department of Agriculture, which played a role in preparing farmers for the future. Various levels of government also monitored agricultural production from its inception. The states, led by Massachusetts, held this role in the early part of the century, and the federal government took over in 1862 when Abraham Lincoln created the Department of Agriculture (USDA). From at least the 1890s, the USDA's statistical arm saw its mission as redressing information asymmetries in the market: commodity merchants, particularly in the four "speculative" crops of wheat, corn, oats, and particularly cotton, tended to have better information than the farmers they did business with. John Hyde, USDA chief statistician from 1897 to 1905, specifically dedicated himself to protecting U.S. producers from getting fleeced.[7] It was not until 1911, however, that the USDA regularly produced crop predictions. USDA officials felt that having a single official forecast would help stabilize the market.[8]

As secretary of commerce, Hoover hoped to do something similar for the world of business: he wanted government to provide data and conceptual insight and business to act. While head of the Commerce Department, Hoover initiated the Committee on Business Cycles, led by Mitchell, to improve knowledge of the causes of economic fluctuations and find ways to predict them. Hoover described the business cycle as "a constant recurrence of ir-regularly separated booms and slumps" that was due to "wastes, extravagance, speculation, inflation, over-expansion, and inefficiency in production."[9] In this way, Hoover approached the business cycle as he did many business and engineering problems—as an instance of inefficiency and waste that could be lessened through good management. Business leaders would reduce waste through careful consideration of facts and advice in the Department of Com-merce's *Survey of Current Business* and other government publications.

The plan for state involvement in forecasting led to opposition from both politicians and commercial forecasters, some of whom found Hoover and Mitchell's work redundant. Of Hoover's interest in state-run efforts to im-prove predictions of business cycles and spur businessmen to undertake coun-tercyclical action, one congressman said: "I would rather postpone a panic until the time when God brings it, than to have Hoover entrusted with this power, and get the panic a year sooner."[10]

But Hoover's intention was not to try to regulate the private forecasting industry or put it out of business. Instead, he and Mitchell hoped to rid the economy of the quack theories circulated by some forecasting agencies (such as those by Babson, from whom they continually kept their distance), im-prove the data on which forecasters relied, and to build an objective theory of business cycles—one not swayed by the profit motive.

They also hoped to popularize the idea that cycles *could* be modified through the voluntary association of government officials, philanthropic in-stitutions, and enlightened managers.[11] This was a somewhat utopian scheme at a time before Keynesian ideas of government fiscal policy—and the direct intervention of the state in managing cycles—took hold. For Hoover, a cos-mopolitan figure who had spent extensive time living in China, Australia, and Europe, business-cycle modification through research and education of-fered government a middle path between the two extremes of laissez-faire and centralized economic planning then in progress across the world, as a num-ber of governments turned to state ownership of key industries and other methods to control the economy. Hoover was not trying to *eliminate* uncer-tainty from the economy but to reduce it. He was not interested in direct state intervention in the economy but only in enabling other entities (like private firms) to forecast more correctly. For Hoover and Mitchell, the goal was to preserve American-style capitalism.

WESLEY MITCHELL

Wesley Clair Mitchell spent most of his youth in Decatur, Illinois, on a ten-acre farm called Leafland, where he collected butterflies, bugs, and beetles. His father, a Civil War veteran and physician, had recurrent health problems. The family seldom enjoyed financial security, but both parents encouraged their seven children to pursue an education.

Mitchell moved to Chicago to go to college. The city was a fast-growing metropolis in the late nineteenth century. It was the terminus of railroads from the farms and timberlands of Canada and the northern United States. It was the center of commodity trading, at the Chicago Board of Trade, and cattle butchering. Mitchell arrived there in fall 1892, just before the World's Columbian Exposition, celebrating four centuries since the arrival of Columbus, held its dedication ceremonies.[12]

Mitchell entered the first class of the University of Chicago. The school had been organized by the American Baptist Education Society and funded by oil magnate John D. Rockefeller. The university had fine new Gothic buildings and an outstanding faculty that had been lured away from other schools with high salaries and the promise of intellectual adventure.[13] Mitchell's teachers included philosopher and educational reformer John Dewey and economists J. Laurence Laughlin, who had come from Cornell to head the Chicago economics department, bringing with him the eccentric but dazzling Thorstein Veblen, formerly a fellow in Laughlin's department in Ithaca.[14]

Veblen had a doctorate in philosophy from Yale University (1884) and encouraged Mitchell to take a multidisciplinary approach to understanding how economies functioned, advising him to study psychology, ethnology, anthropology, and culture. At the time Mitchell arrived, Veblen was undertaking a statistical analysis of commodity prices—similar to the type of work Mitchell produced throughout his career.[15] This, however, was not something Veblen continued to pursue. While Veblen is known as a brilliant satirist, analyst, and phrasemaker, Mitchell is remembered as a quintessential observer and data gatherer.[16] While Mitchell was still at the University of

Chicago, Veblen published *The Theory of the Leisure Class (1899)*, his classic text on conspicuous consumption. The book offered a description of capitalist economies as complex phenomena, rife with envy, ornament, and display—worlds away from the rational marketplace of utility maximizers that Irving Fisher described in his dissertation.[17]

In many ways, Mitchell followed Veblen's lead. To him, economics was a science of human behavior rather than of timeless principles of wealth creation. Classical economists, such as Adam Smith and his followers, wrote as if their theories were permanently true. Mitchell thought instead that economic theories evolved over time and that economic "laws" depended on context. He was interested in developing the field of economics as one that took into account what human beings actually did.

For his doctoral thesis, Mitchell studied the printing of greenbacks by the federal government during the Civil War. In 1903 he published it as *A History of the Greenbacks with Special Reference to the Economic Consequences of Their Issue, 1862–1865*.[18] Mitchell reviewed the legislative acts of the greenback issuance and the impact this had on prices in a range of industries and on salaries. In this project, Mitchell linked careful theoretical discussion with detailed empirical observations. The book is nearly 600 pages long, with roughly 150 pages devoted to statistical tables covering gold prices, wages, cotton prices, salaries, and other data for 1860 to 1866. Mitchell disputed the idea, expressed in the Quantity Theory of Money, that changes in prices occur evenly throughout industries. Instead he gathered detailed evidence to see what actually happened to prices as new bills were introduced. Mitchell found that in some, but not all, industries, prices increased and that the effects of the new bills were unevenly distributed.

After completing the dissertation, Mitchell took a job with the U.S. Census Office in Washington, the first of many political appointments throughout his life. But he wanted to get back to his own research and so returned to the University of Chicago, taking a position as a lecturer.[19]

Business Cycles

In 1902, at age twenty-eight, Mitchell became an assistant professor of economics at the University of California at Berkeley, where he stayed for a decade.[20] He spent much of his time there researching economic fluctuations.

His eventual book on the subject, *Business Cycles* (1913), was a massive empirical and historical study. Mitchell looked at the evolution of thinking about the subject. He brought together and summarized the existing major studies and theories on business cycles and undertook a detailed statistical investigation to see how well theoretical approaches fit historical reality.

Mitchell did not use the term "economy" (which did not come into vogue until after World War II) but the term "business economy" or "money economy" to describe the entire economy and society; this terminology emphasized the logic of money-making.

Business Cycles succeeded on many levels. It criticized the notion that depressions or expansions were aberrations from some "normal" level of economic activity. Instead, Mitchell pointed out that business fluctuation was a constant process, a necessary consequence of a monetized capitalist economy.[21] Of the fourteen existing theories of business cycles that he describes, noting that they all are plausible, he is particularly approving of Fisher's monetarist explanation as set forth in *The Purchasing Power of Money* (1911).[22]

Mitchell's *Business Cycles* did not treat the ups and downs of the market as unconnected singular periods of "panic" and "crises" or as phenomena dependent on external events like sunspots (as William Stanley Jevons had thought) but as inherent to economic activity. Moreover, he used statistical series to reveal these cycles, studying numerous types of economic data to determine how cycles in one sector of the economy could affect fluctuations in another.[23] Though he regarded cycles as an intrinsic feature of capitalism, he did not from this conclude that they were inevitable or inalterable. The book embodied Mitchell's commitment to rigorous empiricism, but his approach was based on the premise that it was possible to control the extremes of the peaks and troughs of cycles—once enough was known about them.[24] Along these lines, he described as "ingenious" Fisher's proposal to tame the cycle by controlling price fluctuations, or "stabilizing the dollar."[25] He also argued for the need for measures of national incomes and of national product, two projects he would later pursue.

Mitchell likened the task of a social scientist trying to construct a theory of business cycles to a mechanical engineer trying to improve the design of an existing machine—say, a lamp. The engineer first had to understand the operation of all existing lamps and their flaws and then painstakingly design a new one, testing it over and over again to see that it was efficient. This described how Mitchell worked carefully through existing business-cycle theo-

Wesley Clair Mitchell, Mt. Tamalpais, California, c. 1915, at age forty-one. Source: Lucy Sprague Mitchell Papers, box 11, Rare Book & Manuscript Library, Columbia University, New York. Used by permission of the Rare Book & Manuscript Library.

ries. But, Mitchell conceded, his own work was more difficult than that of the engineer. "The social sciences give no such guidance to a social engineer as the physical sciences give to a mechanical engineer," he wrote. "Human beings are the most intractable of materials. Nor can an inventor experiment with them at will as he can with alloys and plastics; he has to persuade his fellows to experiment on themselves, which they are generally reluctant to do."[26] For Mitchell, as for Warren Persons, this was one of the fundamental challenges of economics and forecasting: the field was not like a natural science but required patient analysis of the realities of human experience.

Business Cycles brought Mitchell acclaim among economists. Years later, Mitchell's colleague Arthur Burns called it *the* key work between Alfred Marshall's *Principles of Economics* (1890) and Keynes's *General Theory of Employment, Interest, and Money* (1936)—a claim that has merit.[27] In a review of *Business Cycles*, Warren Persons wrote that the genius of the book lay in "the marshaling of the data, and the clear expositions and the combination of the ideas of various writers into a self-consistent theory of business cycles."[28]

A Rising Star

The Panic of 1907 raised public interest in business cycles. Mitchell, who published articles on the topic of economic fluctuations frequently in the *Quarterly Journal of Economics* and the *Journal of Political Economy* while working on his 1913 book on the subject, found himself in demand.[29]

In 1908–9 Mitchell lectured at Harvard, teaching courses on financial crises and on money. Edwin F. Gay, dean of the university's new business school, was impressed by Mitchell and tried to get him to join the Harvard faculty. Though Mitchell declined the offer, he and Gay became lifelong friends. In a letter to his wife, Lucy Sprague, Mitchell explained that Gay had wanted him to "take charge of organizing a really good statistical laboratory, for the use of both the department of economics and the graduate school of business administration." Had this happened, Mitchell would have created a statistics-gathering group at Harvard a full decade before the formation of the Harvard Economic Service. But Mitchell feared that the Harvard faculty was too obsessed with teaching to allow him sufficient time for research. "People here take their teaching with such desperate seriousness that I am becoming infected," he wrote.[30]

Irving Fisher brought Mitchell to New Haven in the hope of luring the economist to Yale, but to no avail.[31] In some ways Mitchell's background and interests paralleled Fisher's. Both came from families with little or no money, and both studied at elite institutions with famous minds of the day: Fisher with sociologist and political scientist William Graham Sumner and physicist Willard Gibbs at Yale, and Mitchell with Thorstein Veblen and John Dewey at Chicago.

Each advocated greater use of statistics in economics. In 1918, the American Economic Association and the American Statistical Association held a joint annual meeting in Richmond, Virginia—a short trip from Washington, D.C., where so many social scientists were then completing war work. Fisher was president of the economic society and Mitchell of the statistical one. Each gave keynote addresses and talked about the role that social sciences could play in government and of their desire to form a national statistical organization.[32]

Both Mitchell and Fisher argued that the postwar years offered a great opportunity for statisticians and economists. Out of the catastrophe of war, Mitchell argued, great advances could come. "Anthropologists have come to recognize that catastrophes have played a leading role in advancing culture." It was time, he argued, to take "a definite stand upon the continuation of the new statistical activities begun during the war" and continue the work of the Central Bureau of Planning and Statistics.[33] Fisher, too, saw a special opportunity for the use of economics in directing public policy. "The war has kindly lifted us, for a time, out of the old rut," he wrote. But this open-mindedness would not last. More rigorous, mathematical approaches to economics could help inform policy, he thought.

Yet the two men also had radically different conceptions of the economic world. Fisher used a series of terms borrowed from physics, writing of "equilibrium," "friction," and "stability" in his descriptions of the economy, and he believed that much could be discerned from the mathematical relationship $MV = PT$.[34] Mitchell opposed Fisher's deductive reasoning and instead gathered a colossal amount of empirical data about economic realities in order to draw inductive generalizations.[35]

Rather than Harvard or Yale, Mitchell chose to join Columbia, moving to New York City in 1913. He enjoyed being near the nation's financial center and compared the buildings around Wall Street to the cliffs he had seen while in California. "Now I feel as if I were just back from the mountains," he wrote to his wife humorously. "The stupendous buildings of lower Broadway and Wall Street, the wind whistling through the narrow canyons, and the vague shadowy cliffs give me the same impression of power as the high Sierra."[36] The move also suited Lucy Sprague Mitchell, who was the former dean of women at Berkeley. Both became active in New York's intellectual life. Wesley Mitchell offered many public talks at the Women's Political Union, Household Arts Economics Club, the Junior League, and the Division of Engineering and Industrial Research of the National Research Council. Lucy Sprague Mitchell founded Bank Street College, originally the Bureau of Educational Experiments, to study childhood development.

Like his wife, Mitchell was an institution builder. In New York he was instrumental in the founding of three important economic institutions, all of which today are important elite international organizations: the New School for Social Research, founded in 1919; the Social Science Research Council, founded 1922–23; and, the most important for the subject of forecasting, the National Bureau of Economic Research (NBER), established in 1920.

The NBER became the nation's preeminent center of economic data. Mitchell and Edwin Gay had originally conceived of the idea of creating such an organization during World War I, when both of them worked for the Central Bureau of Planning and Statistics. They had envisioned turning the Central Bureau into a peacetime organization. But Woodrow Wilson was opposed to this and the bureau came to a close in June 1919.

Mitchell and Gay then decided to pursue the formation of a private bureau. Malcolm Rorty, a statistician from AT&T, joined them and helped secure $20,000 in funding from the Commonwealth Fund, a philanthropy founded by Anna Harkness following the death of her husband, Stephen, a Standard Oil executive. Rorty had long had an interest in the subject of forecasting and helped produce AT&T's newsletters on business conditions.[37] In February 1921, the NBER was incorporated. Mitchell served as the research director from the NBER's founding to 1945 and was its intellectual leader. The Bureau's first project led to the two-volume report *Income in the United States, Its Amount, and Distribution, 1909–1919* (1921).[38]

The idea of a scientific research center was largely new in economics, a field still dominated by nonquantitative methods.[39] The organization had a clear mandate from the outset to provide practical information. Mitchell's goal at NBER was not only tracking historical business cycles but also taking the pulse of the current phase.[40]

The organization, which is now headquartered near the Harvard University campus, was originally based in New York City. It became the government's official recorder of business cycles and their peaks and troughs, and its figures became the most widely accepted throughout the United States and abroad. Today, no other economic research organization enjoys such prestige. Over the course of the twentieth century, virtually every well-known economist has been associated with the Bureau. Many of the Nobel laureates of the twentieth century were members, including Simon Kuznets, Milton Friedman, George Stigler, Robert Fogel, Robert Merton, Joseph Stiglitz, and Paul Krugman.

Mitchell combined his historical approach to understanding cycles, which he saw as a global phenomenon, with an urgent call for more data collection from around the world. The NBER was central to this data collection effort. His main point was that history served as a guide to general trends. He wrote,

> "Business Cycles" is merely a vivid term for this recurrent ebb and flow of business activity which past experience has taught the wary to expect. Depressions pave the way for business revivals, revivals develop into "booms," booms breed crises, and crises run out into depressions. A tolerably regular repetition of such cycles can be traced in American experience for at least a century. Similar cycles run their round in all countries of highly developed business organization. They have a long history in the Netherlands and England, a shorter history in France, Germany, Austria, Italy, and the Scandinavian countries, they have made their appearance in Russia, Canada, Australia, South Africa, Chile, the Argentine, British India, and Japan.[41]

Businessmen scarcely recognized the cycle, he noted, and tended to see their own successes or failures as entirely of their own making.

The safest guide to the future was detailed empirical analysis of the past that would reveal the workings of the capitalist economy and to educate businesspeople about the findings. In this way, Mitchell was quite like Warren Persons. While Persons sought to build a representation of the economy in the form of the ABC curves, Mitchell was more interested in gathering extensive details on what business cycles were and building an international institution to measure and observe current economic phenomena unfolding.

In the early 1920s, however, the NBER was still small. It lacked a promise of continuing funds and did not have the prestige or the ability to market its research. Herbert Hoover would help the NBER gain all of these things.

HERBERT HOOVER

Herbert Hoover is chiefly remembered as a failed president. "I am well aware that uninformed persons recollect my term as President solely as the period of the Great Depression," he wrote in his 1951 memoirs. "That was indeed the nightmare of my years in the White House."[42] But Hoover's association with the Depression masks the dynamic nature of his early career.

Hoover was a deeply ambitious person who came from poverty and was an orphan. He was a native of West Branch, Iowa—the first U.S. president to have been born west of the Mississippi River. Both his parents died before he reached the age of ten. In 1885 he was sent to Oregon to live with his aunt and uncle. Hoover entered Stanford's first class in 1891 (a year before Mitchell entered the University of Chicago's first class) and studied geology. There, he met his wife, Lou Henry, another geology major.

After graduation, Hoover began a twenty-year career as a mining engineer. He traveled to Western Australia and then to China for a British mine-engineering firm (Bewick, Moreing and Company), where he worked from 1897 to 1908. He gained a reputation as a tough manager and aggressive cost-cutter, with little tolerance for organized labor. He became a partner in the firm in 1901 and, working in London, became deeply involved in the financial dealings involved in mining, rather than mining itself. In 1908 he went into business for himself, forming a consulting firm based largely on mine valuation. His time in London coincided with large investments by London firms in mining regions around the world. He became fantastically rich before the start of World War I, with a fortune of $4 million (about $82 million today). His reputation, particularly during his time working on his own, came from his financial and promotional skill rather than his engineering expertise.[43]

In 1914, at age forty, Hoover entered public life when he assumed leadership of the Commission for Relief in Belgium, an institution funded by a combination of U.S. government grants and private philanthropy and dedicated to provisioning German-occupied Belgium. Hoover showed great skill in negotiations with German, Belgian, and British officials. During the U.S. involvement in the war, he went on to serve as Wilson's U.S. Food Administrator (1917–19), trying to persuade firms and consumers to conserve food and fuel. He then became director-general of the American Relief Administration in Europe (1919–20). Hoover supervised the distribution of food throughout Europe, overseeing the prices of commodities, checking distribution channels, clearing transportation routes, and coordinating shipments. In all of these tasks, Hoover emphasized the importance of efficient operations and technical planning.

Hoover's administration of American food relief in Europe during and after the war brought him favorable publicity and set him up for further advancement on the public stage.[44] "I now found myself in a burst of popular-

Herbert Hoover in London, 1915. Source: Yale University, Manuscripts & Archives, Image no. 46138, box 20.

ity," he later wrote of his return to the United States in 1919. "The newspapers dubbed me, falsely, a 'leading American.' In fact, the *New York Times* poll to select the ten most important living Americans placed my name on the list."[45] President Woodrow Wilson invited him to attend conferences on problems in industry and on the growing conflicts between management and labor.[46] The year 1919 was indeed a bitter one, with a citywide strike in

Seattle in February, a strike by the Boston police in September, and a drawn-out national steel strike that began in the fall and lasted four months.

THE DEPARTMENT OF COMMERCE

Shortly after Hoover returned to the United States, the country entered one of the most severe slumps in its history. The high prices of the war years dropped precipitously in 1920, followed by a period of depression in which unemployment climbed to well over 10 percent and nearly half a million farmers lost their farms.[47] Most of this downturn occurred during President Wilson's term of office, but he did little to address the situation. Wilson had suffered a stroke in October 1919 that left him nearly incapacitated for much of his remaining term—that is, for the eighteen months until Warren Harding entered office in March 1921.

After winning the presidential election, Harding invited Hoover to join his cabinet, offering him either the Department of the Interior or the Department of Commerce. Hoover's choice of Commerce—a department he headed from spring 1921 until mid-1928, when he began his successful campaign for president—was unexpected. When he joined, the department consisted of the Bureaus of Foreign and Domestic Commerce, Lighthouses, Navigation, Coast and Geodetic Survey, Census, Standards, and Fisheries, and the Steamboats Inspection Service. One of his predecessors at Commerce told him that the job required no more than two hours of work per day: "Putting the fish to bed at night and turning on the lights around the coast were possibly the major concepts of the office," as Hoover later characterized the responsibilities of the post when he entered the office.[48]

Hoover built the department into one of the most influential organizations in the federal government. He became deeply involved in a number of issues, including war debts, reparations, tariffs, foreign loans, and domestic economic growth.[49] Hoover represented the interests of American export-oriented businesses and received an enormous amount of favorable publicity for directing relief efforts after the Mississippi River flood of 1927.[50] Hoover replaced former political appointees with men with technical backgrounds. He also expanded the department by bringing over the Bureau of Mines and the Patent Office from the Department of the Interior. During his tenure, the department's annual appropriations rose from $24 million to $38 million.[51]

More than any other politician up to that point, Hoover focused attention on the business cycle and unemployment. The idea of a "business cycle" was still catching on just after World War I, though it would soon come to be the central issue among economists and politicians. The predominant sense among businessmen in the early 1920s was that there were simply periods of bad business and unpredictable events. There was little belief that economic events were cyclical or an appreciation that government intervention might help end panics or increase employment during downturns.[52] Hoover and Mitchell helped change these views.

GOVERNMENT AS FORECASTER

In the 1920s, Herbert Hoover hoped to develop a government-led program that would provide business leaders and analysts with information that would enable them to improve their ability to forecast economic conditions. He aimed to educate business leaders on economic affairs so that they would make their businesses more efficient and more attuned to economic conditions. Business leaders who recognized whether they were in the midst of a boom or bust cycle, he thought, would enact countercyclical policy.

To achieve his goals, Hoover had the Department of Commerce issue a series of publications for managers and businessmen, including the *Survey of Current Business*. Most of these were available at no charge and covered subjects such as foreign demand for American goods, the consumption of meats and crops, and the use of business statistics.[53]

Though Hoover and his experts preferred to use the more neutral sounding term "trend analysis," they moved the U.S. Department of Commerce into the realm of business forecasting. Hoover later recalled, "We hoped the business world might better detect the approach of booms and slumps."[54] Such warnings of impending economic change, Hoover thought, would be especially helpful to smaller firms that could not afford to hire statisticians and were more likely to be unaware of general economic conditions.

Hoover was insistent that the actual work of tempering cycles come from the voluntary acts of business managers. He did not want the government to directly intervene in the economy with countercyclical monetary or fiscal policy but with helpful and illuminating information. Proper, objective fore-casting information coming from reliable, state-sponsored publications would ensure the sustainability of American-style capitalism, which had lately been too subjected to booms and busts.

Hoover's concern for finding a way to combat economic volatility stemmed from his experiences in Europe. In the wake of the Bolshevik Revolution in Russia, politicians throughout Europe and the Americas saw class revolution as a genuine threat. "We have witnessed in this last eight years the spread of revolution over one-third of the world," Hoover wrote in the first sentence of his book *American Individualism* (1922).[55] He wanted to eliminate the "hallucinations transported from Europe" of rosy ideas about socialism.[56] Hoover's national interest helped change the meaning of forecasting, giving the discipline relevance on a broad public stage.

The commerce secretary hoped to establish a uniquely American solution to the problem of economic crises. His overriding idea was that the New World was separated from the Old by the American sense of individualism. An earlier generation of pioneers had surveyed and explored the American West; new ones would shape the country's economic and social future. They would explore the "continent" of science. The goal was not to overturn capi-talism with a new system but to encourage individuals to act in ways that would alleviate its cyclical extremes and avoid its bottlenecks.

Hoover thus believed the work of forecasting was central to healthy, stable economies. He also promoted the idea that governments need to have a deep engagement with the business cycle. His work helped set up the modern forecasting market, in which government plays a major role in supplying data to industry and in which many forecasters compete to predict the effects of policy.

The plan depended on three interested parties: the Department of Com-merce, which would circulate ideas and information; economists and statisti-cians (at the NBER), who would provide objective data and analysis; and private philanthropies, which would fund these efforts. The number of philan-thropies interested in improving society through expert-led research increased substantially in the early twentieth century: the Carnegie Foundation (1905), the (Julius) Rosenwald Fund (1917), the Rockefeller Foundation (1913), and many others were formed during this time.

THE BUSINESS CYCLE COMMITTEE

Essential to Herbert Hoover's plan was an improved understanding of the nature of the business cycle.[57] He was suspicious of popular investment theories that seemed to abound on Wall Street. To gain knowledge and to draft policy, Hoover believed in holding conferences of experts from diverse backgrounds. He set about creating an extraordinary network of businesspeople, scholars, and philanthropists to assist him. Among the experts were: Harvard Business School (HBS) dean Edwin Gay; Arch Shaw (1876–1957), a Chicago office supplier and HBS instructor; John J. Raskob (1879–1950), an executive at DuPont and General Motors; Henry S. Dennison (1877–1952), a leading paper goods manufacturer and an advocate of business-cycle planning; Clarence Woolley (1863–1956), the head of one of the nation's largest plumbing companies; and Owen D. Young (1874–1962), an industrialist, lawyer, diplomat, and chairman of General Electric. Several in this group had written on the subject of forecasting and business planning. Dennison, in particular, promoted the idea of business-cycle forecasting.[58]

Hoover spared no superlative in his efforts to induce Mitchell to join his group. He wrote: "I feel that you are the one man in the country who could adequately take care of this job."[59] Mitchell played a major role in Hoover's efforts for the entire span of Hoover's political career, though Mitchell often did so without an official title, most of the time shuttling between Washington and the offices of the NBER in New York.

As secretary of commerce, Hoover held three major business-cycle conferences, each of which produced a major report: *Business Cycles and Unemployment* (1923); *Recent Economic Changes in the United States* (1929); and *Recent Society Trends of the United States* (1933). Mitchell, as research director at the NBER, contributed significant essays to each of these reports and supervised the collection of articles for all of them.

Mitchell wrote four of twenty-one chapters for *Business Cycles and Unemployment* (1923), the report of the first meeting. The book advanced several recommendations to reduce the extremes of business cycles. It emphasized the importance of the dissemination of statistical information and encouraged the active role of the Federal Reserve in moderating cyclical fluctuations. The report also called for "informed action by individual businessmen in periods of rising markets in order that excessive expansion may be prevented and the extent of the decline reduced."[60]

The central idea was that forecasting needed to be supported and facilitated by objective administrators without financial ambition or ideological leanings. Hoover and Mitchell did not invite John Moody or Roger Babson to join their team, although Irving Fisher and members of the Harvard Economic Service (including Charles Bullock and Warren Persons) played advisory roles. Feeling somewhat locked out of the Business Cycle Committee, Babson sent Hoover a report of his own accomplishments "in the hope of being of some service at this time when statistical organization is under consideration."[61] But neither Hoover nor Mitchell accommodated the Wellesley oracle's request to become part of their group. Instead they wished to distance themselves from those they considered dubious financial gurus.

The Business Cycle Committee's distrust of the current state of the forecasting industry was evident in the critical remarks about private agencies found in committee reports. "If the work of applying statistics to the guiding of business affairs were easy and obvious, it would long ago have been undertaken as universally as bookkeeping," wrote Oswald Knauth, one the report's coauthors.[62] Only the careful research of the economists and statisticians at the NBER was capable of unlocking the mysteries of the business cycle and providing objective facts to businesspeople and analysts.

The concern with private forecasting agencies went deeper than the complexity of the task. Hoover and Mitchell were troubled by the incentives of the industry, which were oriented toward profit making rather than accuracy. Hoover and Mitchell feared that forecasters were more interested in pleasing clients with optimistic and simplistic predictions than with objective analysis.[63] One academic, who studied the forecasting industry, concluded as much, writing that forecasters were careful not to anger clients with dire predictions. "A warning of trouble ahead, if given, is likely to be more delicately phrased than is an assurance of continued or increasing prosperity," wrote a professor at the University of Chicago, Mitchell's alma mater, in 1929.[64]

Hoover and Mitchell were worried that the commercial forecasting agencies gave the mistaken impression that cycles were entirely predictable. This cultivated a false sense of security among businesspeople and investors, as well as a good deal of "misunderstandings and exaggerations" in popular discussion. "Many a businessman is developing the precipitate zeal of a new convert and talking about cycles as if they came around with the regularity of presidential elections," wrote Mitchell in a 1923 article in the *Journal of Accountancy*. "Not a few forecasting agencies are publishing prophecies as if they had the certainty of history." Mitchell and Hoover feared that investors and businessmen had begun to have blind faith in entrepreneurial forecasters, who hoped to prosper from boom-and-bust calls. There was a need, wrote Mitchell, for "clear and sober thinking ... by men of trained minds."[65]

Educated Intuition

In the early 1920s, Mitchell completed a series of forecasts in the *New York Evening Post*, where his friend Edwin Gay was then working as editor.[66] These are important writings because they show Mitchell's practical and pragmatic approach to solving economic problems. He viewed forecasting as an indispensible part of the effort to lessen the extremes of the business cycle. Moreover, it could be approached scientifically. Forecasting allowed economists to learn by their mistakes, in cases where forecasts failed to come true, and to see what new knowledge was needed to predict where the economy was headed.[67]

The forecasting undertaken by Mitchell was of a different character than that of others in this book in the sense that it was more circumspect and more historical. In his own forecasts, Mitchell looked at a great number of indicators, including factors that would affect demand for crops, and economic conditions overseas. To these he added his view of the expectations of investors and myriad other statistical and nonstatistical conditions.[68]

His method of forecasting depended on a knowledgeable expert reviewing a mass of data, some of it conflicting, and coming to a reasoned judgment. Unlike Irving Fisher and the economists at the Harvard Economic Service, Mitchell did not believe that he had solved the problem of forecasting by formulating good theory. Instead Mitchell viewed the task of understanding business cycles as one of incessant observation of past and present economic activity. More and more data, and more measurement, would make the contours of economic cycles visible; but the process would not have an end point, only continuing observation.

Mitchell argued that the process of analyzing business cycles, as he did for his 1913 book *Business Cycles*, was unlike the effort to forecast. The former required economists to examine the commonalities of business cycles, while the latter (prediction) required that analysts study what made one cycle *different* from the previous ones.

Mitchell presented no single model of prediction. In his forecasting, he considered, for instance, whether the structure of prices in one line of commodities was way out of line with those in other lines, which could be a sign something was wrong. He looked to see if there were unusually large bank reserves, which would indicate that a period of contraction was coming to an end. Mitchell also looked into crop conditions that would affect farmers' demand for goods; into conditions abroad, which would affect foreign demand for American goods; and into construction activity, which affected demand for investment.

The idea was to pay careful attention to indicators and make a reasoned assessment. He warned that the idea of business cycles provided only a rough guide; the term "cycles" suggested a regularity that was not apparent. It was essential not to oversimplify the rules of forecasting. Mitchell recognized the tendency to build models but suggested that they were misleading. The "business cycle" was not a fixed law but a working hypothesis. He especially noted that past experience was not much help in determining how long cycles lasted. The key was not to look to history as a model but to look at history as a way to understand complex signals of when things were changing.

Though Mitchell did not believe the business cycle would be eradicated, he thought there was no proof that taking measures to curb the cycle were useless. What kinds of things could be tried? Long-range planning of public works, a change in the policy of banks regarding credit ratios, and establishing new forms of unemployment insurance.[69]

Nor did he believe in the perfectibility of knowledge about cycles; he thought that the search would be ongoing. But he also believed that there was no need to wait until more knowledge had been gained before acting. It was important to press ahead to try to curb unemployment. "Social experimentation, based on clearly thought-out hypotheses and accompanied by careful record-keeping, is one of the essential processes in increasing social knowledge and gaining social control," wrote Mitchell.[70] In this way his thinking was parallel to that of his teacher John Dewey as it pertained to solving social problems. Ideas needed to be tested through experimentation; this separated economics from other sciences.[71] It was impossible to produce a fully formed model of forecasting and expect it to work without practical experimentation; it was also unrealistic to expect that the same model would continue to perform well forever.

Mitchell expressed this approach of "educated intuition" toward forecasting in *Business Cycles and Unemployment*. The volume was published with great publicity. Editorials, many written by Mitchell, were sent to ten thousand newspapers. Other articles summarizing the findings of the Business Cycle Committee were published in popular periodicals, such as *The Nation's Business*, *Colliers*, and *World's Work*.[72]

The report enjoyed a wide circulation among businessmen. Part of the reception no doubt came from a class of businesspeople who still had the fear of 1920–21 in their minds and were cautiously eyeing the uptick in securities prices of 1922–23. One of the biggest critics of Hoover and Mitchell's work, however, was Wallace B. Donham, a board member of the Harvard Economic Service who had replaced Edwin Gay as dean at the Harvard Business School when Gay left the university. Donham was appalled at the Business Cycle Committee reports, which he found too theoretical and believed called for too much of a role for government. It was "incoherent" and not as clear a guide as the Harvard Economic Service's ABC curves. He was upset that Hoover turned to the NBER but did not consult with either the faculty at Harvard Business School or Harvard's own business-cycle experts in the Harvard Economic Service. Indeed, outside of Gay, who had been an advisor to the Harvard Economic Service, there was little connection between the Hoover-Mitchell group and the Harvard-based forecasting team.

Donham believed that the Business Cycle Committee should have relied more on his colleague Charles Bullock, whom he called "the best authority in the United States" on business cycles.[73] He found it a radical proposal for a government organization to supply business managers and the forecasting industry with statistics and to provide instructions on how to respond to economic trends. Donham wrote, "I still get back to my very firm belief that you will not successfully control the business cycle through governmental activities."[74]

A WINNING FORMULA

Despite these contentions, Hoover continued his approach to economic management (involving government committees, independent research organizations, and philanthropies) with great optimism. And why not? To him and many others in the Business Cycle Committee, the collaboration between social science and management seemed to be accounting for the success of the 1920s.[75]

Hoover believed that there was nothing like the prosperity of the United States in mid-1920s in all of economic history. With each booming year, the United States gained greater distance from European countries, which were experiencing general strikes and depressions. As he saw it, American managers, analysts, and investors were more informed, more aware, and better trained.[76] Hoover and his colleagues took credit for controlling the business cycle of 1923–24; that is, the committee took credit for an event that did *not* happen—an economic panic.

By 1927, America had become what Hoover called the "world's marvel." He and his group thought they deserved credit for much of the stability that had brought this about: low inflation, continuous production, and no inventory gluts. "The past five years have been remarkable for generally sustained prosperity, without the violent fluctuations which have characterized most of the previous periods of great activity," he wrote in 1928. "In large measure this has been due to greater knowledge of the current facts of business and a growing experience in utilizing this knowledge."[77]

Hoover escalated his efforts to create macroeconomic stability through improved information-gathering systems. In January 1928, the committee on Recent Economic Changes began its work. The group was a similar stellar mix of academics, politicians, and businessmen as the Business Cycle Committee.[78] Its goal was to make a critical appraisal of the factors of stability and instability and explain the causes of the prosperity that flourished for much of the 1920s. The Carnegie Corporation funded the study.[79] Hoover contacted Gay and Mitchell about working on the new project, and both were enthusiastic about it. Such a study would place Hoover's efforts in front of the public even more.

The launching of the committee coincided with Hoover's campaign for the presidency and served as a way to publicize the nation's economic progress since he joined the Commerce Department. Hoover campaigned against the Democratic candidate, Governor Alfred E. Smith of New York, who faced an uphill battle because of the booming economy and Hoover's popularity but also because Smith was a Catholic and favored repeal of Prohibition. Hoover won the election with 444 electoral votes to Smith's 87.[80]

When the committee on Recent Economic Change published its report, in May 1929, it seemed to confirm Hoover's campaign slogans. *Recent Eco-*

nomic Changes in the United States was a descriptive overview of economic changes from 1922 to 1927 in the U.S. economy. Much of the research and writing had been done by members or affiliates of the NBER. Edwin Gay wrote the report's introduction and Wesley Mitchell wrote the conclusion. It documented how, during the period 1922–28, the standard of living rose, credit was abundant, and strikes were few. Mitchell credited the use of science and intelligent reflection and research for these trends—the most important of which was improved awareness of the business cycle.[81]

CAPITALISM UNDER THREAT

In the years 1929–33, however, Herbert Hoover's and Wesley Mitchell's plan for economic stability through a managerial elite unraveled. The same period that washed away many individual forecasting agencies also devastated Hoover. Ironically, the politician who had devoted so much of his career to flattening the business cycle entered the White House shortly before the start of the worst economic period in the country's history. Ironically, too, the politician who had put so much faith in numbers and lobbied for the production and publication of statistics on a grand scale misread the booming figures of the late 1920s. The Depression years saw a rejection of the work of the expert committees, and business executives failed to create stable economic expansion.

The idea of an enlightened managerial elite curbing business cycles gave way to a reliance on government policy to intervene in economic affairs. Direct government intervention to temper the business cycle began under President Hoover and continued far more aggressively under Hoover's successor, Franklin D. Roosevelt. The theoretical justification for fiscal intervention came with the 1936 publication of John Maynard Keynes's *General Theory*, though countercyclical public spending on construction and other projects had been going on for some time.

As the foremost authority on business cycles, Mitchell found himself in demand, but he was not greeted as an economic savior. His history-oriented approach to forecasting, which emphasized sorting out alternatives, won fewer devotees than either the simple prophecies of Roger Babson in 1930 or the far more serious and compelling policy recommendations of Keynes. Still, the work of Hoover and Mitchell heralded the idea that the federal government had an obligation to temper the extremes of the business cycle and to help grow national output according to a statistical aggregate, which after 1936 was measured by the new formulation of gross national product.

* * *

Hoover had begun his presidency in 1929 thinking, like most Americans, that prosperity would continue into the future. He was right for the first six months of his term, during which he continued to promote "cooperative individualism" as he had done as secretary of commerce.[82] For Hoover, the goal was to preserve the American system of capitalism, as he defined it, while also fighting severe swings of the business cycle. He failed at both: the 1930s brought the Great Depression, followed by Roosevelt's New Deal.

The Depression unfolded slowly. In the months after the stock market crash, nearly everyone assumed the market would soon rebound. Hoover was indifferent to stock market losses, which he considered the fault of speculators—just as Irving Fisher had dismissed the "lunatic fringe" of investors who had pushed up securities prices. Hoover was far more troubled by falling commodity prices and declining automobile, steel, and coal output.

Hoover held conferences to restore business confidence, as he had done as commerce secretary. In November 1929 Hoover convened business leaders, including Henry Ford, Alfred Sloan, Owen D. Young (of General Electric), Walter Gifford (of AT&T) and his former treasury secretary Andrew Mellon, all of whom were optimistic about the future.[83] Hoover pushed key businessmen to promise not to cut production or to lay off workers. He also asked labor leaders to resist striking for higher wages or better hours.

Believing that there was a link between economic performance and presidential rhetoric, Hoover went on what writer Frederick Lewis Allen described as a "campaign of optimism."[84] He made a succession of optimistic statements, including one in March 1930 that predicted recovery in sixty days. As the stock market and some production indexes seemed to rebound that spring, Hoover declared in May that the worst was over.

Hoover stepped up his promotion of optimistic forecasts and encouraged others, including representatives in business and in academia, to join him in such reassurances. Standard Statistics noted in spring 1930 that government publications tended "to point out whatever is bright in the picture." Hoover's frequent predictions of prosperity became increasingly jarring as economic conditions remained dire, ultimately undermining confidence rather than restoring it—and challenging his claim that government would be an objective steward of economic information. As economist Christina Romer concluded, "It seems quite possible that Hoover's prosperity propaganda program contributed to the uncertainty of consumers in 1930 by generating forecasts that were so at odds with actual economic conditions."[85]

Private sector forecasters kept seeing recovery just around the corner throughout the early 1930s too, and their pronouncements were greeted as ritual; the academic forecasters of Harvard and Yale were jeered for their optimism. Hoover's sunny predictions for the future were viewed far more critically, as part of a calculated policy of propaganda.[86]

Hoover eventually used government spending to fight the Depression, increasing the federal budget from $3.1 billion in 1929 to $4.6 billion in 1932, nearly a 50 percent increase. But it hardly seemed to make a difference; it was not nearly enough.

The presidential campaign of 1932 was particularly bitter for Hoover. He believed that his greatest fears about the future of capitalism were being realized, with a rising interest in increased state intervention in economic affairs. His challenges were both the dire economy and the powerful political skills of his opponent, Franklin Delano Roosevelt. Hoover lost the election, receiving just 59 electoral votes to Roosevelt's 472.

After the election, Hoover departed for Palo Alto and later moved to New York, all the while remaining staunchly opposed to the New Deal. Hoover continued to be involved in politics for much of the rest of his life, however, serving on government commissions under Truman and Eisenhower, and founding the Hoover Institution on War, Revolution, and Peace at Stanford.[87]

Hoover's 1951 memoir was one of his many efforts to redeem his image. He addressed the role "optimism" had played in bringing about the October 1929 stock market crash, an event he felt had been exacerbated by the worst sort of commercial forecasters and by members of the press. He cited scripture and the "little cloud out of the sea" (1 Kings 18:44) that warned Ahab to "prepare thy chariot, and get thee down, that the rain stop thee not." The quote evoked the idea that one had to prepare for inclement weather, heeding the smallest warnings almost out of faith. Hoover then wrote that "[o]ne of these clouds was an American wave of optimism, born of continued progress over the decade, which the Federal Reserve Board transformed into the stock-exchange Mississippi Bubble." Hoover blamed the relatively steady increase of prosperity from World War I onward for inculcating a sense of economic invulnerability. It "gave birth to a foolish idea called 'the New Economic Era.' That notion spread over the whole country. We were assured that we were in a new period where the old laws of economics no longer applied."[88]

But Hoover must have realized his own role in helping create a sense that the rules of business had changed for the better. This had been his major emphasis at the Department of Commerce, from publication of the *Survey of Current Business to* the creation of the Business Cycle Committee. The problem Hoover described in his memoir was indeed a central challenge for state-sponsored forecasting in capitalist economies: How could one promote a reasonable sense of optimism without creating a zealous overconfidence?

MITCHELL AND THE NBER

Mitchell never regarded the stock market crash and the ensuing Depression as a repudiation of his work for Hoover. Instead he thought it signaled the need for even greater research.[89]

Many institutions and organizations (including the NBER) active during Hoover's administration continued under Roosevelt, but the ideological context of the times shifted. The aim was not to lead managers and firms to action but rather to stimulate consumption. Roosevelt's New Deal brought a transition from forecasting to planning.

As the nation's premier expert on business cycles, Mitchell was highly regarded during this time of great interest in the economy. But despite the press of circumstance, Mitchell did not become an advocate of a particular policy to end the Depression. He remained the embodiment of the idea that economic research was nonpartisan and above politics. After Mitchell died in 1948, Hoover remembered him as one of "those who searched patiently and objectively for the truth, recognized the obvious falsity of a single cause for a highly complex phenomenon, and were unwilling to compromise devotion to scientific truth for the sake of some temporary political advantages."[90] In a request to be included at a dinner in Mitchell's honor at Columbia, Hoover telegraphed, "It is my belief that he has contributed as much as any one man during the last generation to pour the truth into the American stream of thought."[91]

Despite their many setbacks in the 1930s, including the failure of business leaders to revive the economy, the decade was a triumph for much of Mitchell and Hoover's work. Mitchell and Hoover promoted the idea that it was the government's role to track economic cycles, collect and publish economic data, endorse a standard measure of economic prosperity (NBER's measure), and attempt to flatten the extremes of boom-and-bust periods. The federal government continued all of these activities under Roosevelt and every president since. That is not to say, of course, that presidents used the same means to curb economic cycles. President Roosevelt's direct fiscal involvement in the economy was far different than Hoover's ideal, for example. But it was in the 1930s that the presidential office took on responsibility for these activities.

In the late 1930s, economists and researchers at the NBER created a new measure of total output: gross national product (GNP). GNP eventually became the international standard for measuring a country's prosperity. The figure was developed by one of Mitchell's students, Simon Kuznets, who later won the Nobel Prize in economics. It was a major innovation in the history of economics and forecasting because it provided an accepted baseline from which to measure change over time. GNP came to replace other measures, such as Babson's "business activity" and the Harvard Economic Service's index of industrial production. GNP differed from the Harvard group's index because it emphasized consumption rather than production, and it was far better than Babson's in its statistical sophistication and in avoiding double counting. It also provided a clear way to compare different national economies; the British economist Colin G. Clark was among those who recognized the use of GNP for this purpose.[92]

The impact of these legacies of Mitchell and Hoover's can hardly be overstated. No president since Franklin D. Roosevelt has failed to make a promise to improve GNP and promote steady economic growth. The consequences of these goals have engaged thousands of government personnel, have been the focus of elections, and have been a measure of success of presidential administrations.

Hoover and Mitchell shaped the forecasting industry, too, popularizing the idea that the role of the state was to provide objective data to supplement the forecasting activities of private firms. They promoted the idea that government should take an active part in researching economic phenomena and that the Department of Commerce would be central to these efforts. In the process, they helped create acceptance for the idea that forecasting could be a public good.

CHAPTER 6

Visions of the Future
||||||||||||||||||||||||||||||||||||||||

Entrepreneurs created the modern economic forecasting industry in the early decades of the twentieth century, a time when everyone was familiar with economic crises and feared the next "panic." Forecasting newsletters appealed to those who sought to safeguard their money but also those who sought comfort amid uncertainty. Others, like Herbert Hoover, promoted forecasting as an important step in reducing national inefficiency and unemployment from unanticipated downturns.

During the 1920s, the field matured as individual forecasters, including academic economists, gained converts for their predictions and their views of how the economy worked. By the end of the decade, the forecasting industry had earned such a following that Wesley Mitchell feared that many businessmen had become convinced that cycles were now predictable and that unexpected financial panics were a thing of the past.

How had forecasting become so successful? Forecasters popularized one of the greatest inventions of the century: the idea of an autonomous "economy" that followed decipherable rules. Seldom after 1920 was there talk of "panic"; instead, the less fearsome-sounding terms "recession" or "depression" became popular. Forecasters did not originate the idea, for it stretched back to Adam Smith, at least, but they did popularize it, gave the "economy" a visual form, and pushed people to think about it in generally positive terms.[1]

The pioneer forecasters were great communicators who provided readers with the reassuring message that the future was discernible. Behind each prediction was a vision of how the economy worked. These visions were very powerful, for they also shaped a sense of what was possible. They offered a vocabulary with which to talk about the future and, when expressed as charts and diagrams, a set of images for conceptualizing abstract economic ideas. These were also inherently political visions that implicitly (and sometimes explicitly) outlined the purpose of the state and its capacity to control cyclical swings. This history has highlighted five of these worldviews:

1. A view of the future as discernible through the study of past patterns, including numeric sequences. This was Roger Babson's view. It was not the same as the worldview of today's free marketeers, who believe the marketplace, with little government regulation, leads to improved societies and lives. Rather it was (in Babson's terms) an Old Testament–inspired idea of the inevitability of cycles of loss and gain, brought on by fear and greed, and inalterable by man—and only mitigated, perhaps, by improved morality and temperance. The enormity of the economy led to a comparison with the atmosphere and the use of meteorological terms like "barometer" and "cycles." This analogy provided a great sense of comfort because it made the future seem, if not entirely predictable, at least recognizable. It also gave followers, who could trace historical patterns on a chart, a sense of control and clarity in a way that obscure econometric calculations, intelligible only to experts, did not.

2. A view of the future as perceivable through mathematical insight and reason. Irving Fisher wrote that historians compiled unconditional facts ("*A is true*" or "*B is true*"), while scientists, including mathematicians and economists, uncovered conditional relationships ("*if A is true, then B is true*"). Mathematical analysis could help make sense of the precise nature of economic relationships and the timing and consequences of economic change. In terms of an analogy, the economy was like a great machine that could be improved through pushing the right levers or, rather, enacting correct policy. This view provided comfort to those who believed that national economic performance could be improved by academic experts, good policy, and by the innovations (including, for instance, patented inventions and new managerial styles) of enlightened business leaders.

3. A view that the future is graspable with detailed knowledge of the motivations and resources of the leading economic actors, as well as the financial health of the firms they headed. The economy, in this understanding, was like a beehive of activity—with the distinction that the

"bees" were the decision makers of Wall Street and the heads of large manufacturing firms, with all the mortal vices and virtues. John Moody's systems of forecasting required a massive collection of current data of all sorts—news, annual reports, gossip, and everything in between. It depended on transparency: the more information and financial news, the better. It was not so much a theoretical approach to understanding economies and markets as it was an effort to anticipate moves by big players and find bargains for investments.

4. A view of upcoming trends as discernible through the study of analogous past episodes with similar characteristics. This was the mode of operation of the Harvard Economic Service. The Harvard group claimed to have uncovered the internal sequence of capitalist movements through the use of leading indicators—and looked for similar ups and downs in past crises. It was like saying, "the last time we had a fire in Chicago, it took two years before we recovered; now another fire has broken out and we expect a similar recovery time."[2] Such an approach appeals to the idea that the economy has alarm bells (indicators) that will sound when something is amiss. The Harvard group claimed to be merely making empirical observations without theoretical bias and established "observatories" around the world to collect economic data.

5. A view that forecasting requires a multidisciplinary approach, making use of leading indicators, mathematical models, and knowledge of leading firms, and entails a high degree of judgment and even intuition. This view, that of Wesley Mitchell, tended to favor the empirical and historical approach of the Harvard Economic Society but also acknowledged the careful testing of theory undertaken by Fisher and his colleagues. Mitchell also believed governments had an obligation to try to temper swings in unemployment and downturns in production. He emphasized the idea that forecasts only exist within the context of a specific political system; no two crises are alike. This made a formulaic approach to forecasting impossible.

These visions, seldom written about directly in weekly forecasts, were nonetheless behind the predictions forecasters made. Their careers, the companies and organizations they built, and their very sense of self were dependent on them.

A WILL TO BELIEVE

Readers took forecasts on faith; there were no systematic tests of accuracy for much of the 1920s. Only at the end of the decade did a major study of forecasting accuracy appear—and it seemed to confirm the optimistic assessment. Garfield Cox (1894–1970), a professor of economics at Mitchell's alma mater, the University of Chicago, sought to determine whether forecasters were any good at what they claimed to do: predict.[3] Cox constructed an elaborate quantitative metric to assess six different agencies, including Babson's, the Harvard Economic Service, and Moody's Investors Service, over the period 1919 to 1928.[4]

He found that testing for accuracy was an unexpectedly difficult task. Forecasts of the business cycle—that is, of the "real" economy rather than the stock market—tended to be imprecise. Forecasters often wrote only generally about whether "business activity" would continue in the direction it was headed or whether some turning point was imminent.[5] Few services ever committed to a specific time when the events they forecast would take place. But Cox and a team of his graduate students persisted, reading nearly a thousand predictions from the 1920s and assessing their accuracy on a scale from −1 (harmful) to +1 (helpful), in .25 increments.[6]

After tabulating his data, Cox concluded that the most reliable service belonged to Babson, who scored a .45 on his scale, followed by the Harvard Economic Service, at .31, and Moody's, at .21.[7] The scores were all greater than 0, which Cox found impressive. A score of 0 would have meant that a forecaster was "neither helpful nor harmful"; any positive number was better than that. Cox noted that Babson had been "slightly helpful" in predicting all significant ups and downs of the decade and "helpful" in predicting the downturn of 1920. The Harvard Economic Service, meanwhile, had been "helpful" in predicting both the 1920 downturn and the 1921 upturn but downright "misleading" in its advice just before the 1923 downturn. Moody was found to be "slightly misleading" in failing to foresee the upturn of 1919 and only "neutral" in the boom economy starting in 1927.[8]

But Cox's big message was not about any single forecaster. Instead he made a positive appraisal of the industry overall: each forecaster proved better than guessing, he reasoned. He reassured subscribers that they could expect that forecasting services "will be right considerably oftener than they will be wrong." Over the long run, dependence upon the advice of one or more forecasting experts "would prove much better than dependence upon luck."[9]

Despite the scale of Cox's effort, the study lacked rigor. He did not, for instance, adequately test how a randomly picked forecast would perform against his agencies but assumed random forecasts would achieve a score of 0. Nor did he question why the group failed, over the decade, to improve its performance, as one would expect with a scientific endeavor.

Moreover, Cox barely mentioned his most interesting finding: that fore-casters had far less success predicting downturns than upturns. He believed that this did not have to do with a lack of insight or an inherently sunny dis-position. Rather, it stemmed from a fear of antagonizing clients or, as he put it, a fear of "the resentment which many business men, in a time of active business, feel against anyone who gives publicity to doubts concerning the foundations of the current prosperity."[10] Customers wanted forecasters to provide reassurance about the future—and some forecasters, at least accord-ing to Cox's data, were inclined to give them that reassurance.

In many ways, Cox's book is a testament to this same phenomenon: a de-sire to see forecasts in a positive light. The biggest problem for Cox's book, however, was not in the execution of his study or his own bias but in the tim-ing of his publication. He submitted the manuscript just prior to the stock market crash of 1929. When his largely favorable account of the forecasting industry (*An Appraisal of American Business Forecasts*) came out in the winter immediately following the crash, it received almost no attention. Cox quickly sought to publish a revision.[11]

The Unforecastable Age

For the pioneer forecasters, the 1930s brought unprecedented challenges. The 1929 stock market crash was not immediately fatal for the forecasters who had been taken unawares. Most focused on predicting the overall, or "real," economy rather than the stock market. At first, many forecasters (Fisher, C. J. Bullock, and Moody among them) offered a reassuring account of good times to come. But the weeks, months, and eventually years of lingering re-cession tested their models of the economy.

This was an economic context unlike anything they had seen. Unemploy-ment rose from 3 percent in 1929 to 25 percent in 1933. Financial institutions once thought safe revealed previously unimagined vulnerabilities. About 9,000 banks failed from 1930 to 1933, with total losses to depositors and shareholders of $2.5 billion. The Consumer Price Index fell 24 percent from 1929 to 1933.[12] In the context of such uncertainty, consumers postponed expensive purchases based on a lack of knowledge about future income. This led to a decline in spending, especially on durable goods, like automobiles and pianos (a popular purchase at the time), which required an ongoing financial commitment to pay off installment loans. Business investment plummeted to an even greater degree. From 1929 to 1933, consumption dropped 19 percent and business investment fell by a staggering 87 percent. Business executives in many industries decided to let inventories fall and ceased investments in new plants and products.[13]

As forecasters failed time and time again in their predictions of a recovery, they were faced with the choice of abandoning the field, blaming an external cause, or altering their long-held methods and changing their mind-set as to how the economy functioned. Of these, the third was the most difficult—and really only Irving Fisher tried to do this.

Fisher had built an intricate method of forecasting based on faith in the nation's enormous manufacturing capacities, technological innovations, and patents. But while he grasped the potential of the country's productive capacities (which became fully evident during and after World War II), he paid little attention to the problem of lagging aggregate demand in his book, *The Stock Market Crash and After* (1930). Fisher went back to the drawing board. In 1933 he formulated his "debt-deflation" theory to explain depressions—a theory that was initially ignored but has gained popularity since the 1980s and has become one of his most cited contributions.

John Moody and Charles Bullock both left the forecasting field. Moody, who had based his forecasts on the plans and expectations of business leaders, and on the financial strength of their firms, found little to guide him as business confidence dropped and investment plummeted. He retired from forecasting and moved to California, leaving Moody's Investors Service to executives he had placed in charge. The Harvard Economic Society, which had neatly charted the historic sequences of speculation, business, and banking, saw, by the early 1930s, new ABC patterns arise that were not analogous to anything in their archives. Still clinging to the Harvard Economic Society model, but finding no clients, Bullock ceased publication of the *Weekly Letter* at the end of 1931.

Even Roger Babson ran afoul. Babson was, to all appearances, the forecaster who had best anticipated the market collapse. He spent the fall of 1929 appearing on magazine covers, disparaging his competitors in the press, and directing an advertising campaign that urged subscribers to "Be Right with Babson." These messages brought new attention to the Babsonchart at a time when people were desperate for advice. But Babson's triumph was based on the simplest model—that for each action there would be a reaction, after each bust would come a boom. Even that model, stretched or spun by a guru like Babson, eventually failed to convince readers when, year after year, a boom never came. In the mid-1930s Babson moved largely into the self-help industry and mounted his unsuccessful bid for the U.S. presidency on the Prohibition Platform.

In a final effort to reassure subscribers, several forecasters looked backward to the most recent past crisis. Shortly after the stock market crash, the Harvard Economic Service's *Weekly Letter* reported that "a serious and prolonged business depression, like that of 1920–21, is out of the question."[14] In May 1930, Fisher made a comparison to the 1920 depression and argued that the former crisis had been far worse. He noted, "It seems manifest that thus far the difference between the present comparatively mild business recession and the severe depression of 1920–21 is like that between a thunder-shower and a tornado."[15]

The 1920–21 crisis served as a baseline of sorts: most of the forecasters thought that things could not be worse than they had been then. They assumed that the Federal Reserve, policymakers, and businesspeople were savvier than they were a decade before and thus the economy would not get as out of hand. As long as they could make comparisons to the events of 1920–21, forecasters had something to offer their readers. By 1931, however, even this scant comfort was denied them. By then, the current depression—the "Great Depression"—had persisted longer than the previous one.

The result of the failure of their methods, the loss of their audiences, and the inability to even maintain a worst-case scenario brought the decline of many of the pioneering forecasters. They had flourished for much of the 1920s, a decade in which economic change looked familiar; they floundered in the 1930s. Here the distinction made in 1921 by economist Frank Knight between "risk" and "uncertainty" is relevant.[16] In the first period, forecasters, like many of their customers, had come to perceive the future as a world of "risk"—that is, they believed that judging the trends of economic events was susceptible to rules and was largely calculable. But in the 1930s, they began to perceive that the future was, instead, entirely uncertain and followed no discernible patterns.

In such a climate, a Babson salesman wrote to headquarters, faith in experts had evaporated. "All across the country, everyone with whom I talked was uncertain," he began. "The feeling is that there are so many uncertainties in the air today that 'no one can forecast what is going to happen' and that 'one person's guess is as good as another's.'"[17]

A well-publicized study on forecaster accuracy produced at the depths of the Depression seemed to confirm this idea that the pioneering forecasters had no insight into the future. In 1933, Alfred Cowles offered an appraisal of forecasting that was as well matched to the mood of the times as was Garfield Cox's optimistic assessment of the late 1920s—and far more sophisticated in its methodology. Cowles was a Chicago native, whose family had made a fortune from the *Chicago Tribune* and the American Radiator Company. He graduated from Yale in 1913, having studied with Irving Fisher. Like Fisher, Warren Persons, and Roger Babson, Cowles moved to Colorado Springs after contracting tuberculosis; unlike them, he remained there most of his life. He started a stock-advisory service there in the 1920s, but after failing to foresee the 1929 stock market crash, he became interested in understanding why he, like so many others, had failed so badly.

Cowles undertook a study that analyzed advice from twenty-four financial publications between January 1, 1928, and June 1, 1932.[18] He asked a panel of readers to examine the recommendations of each publication and make "investments" accordingly. Cowles also created a set of twenty-four random forecasts by selecting from predictions written on a deck of playing cards.[19]

Cowles's research revealed no evidence that forecasters were accurate. Simply shuffling cards and randomly drawing one, he found, brought about a better record of stock market prediction than following the professionals' advice.[20] Random guesses, he concluded, were as accurate as carefully calculated predictions.[21] Cowles answered his own question, "Can Stock Market Forecasters Forecast?" with a resounding no. The results made headlines in newspapers in Chicago, New York, and other cities. The reign of the first group of forecasters, with their oversized aspirations, was over.[22]

The Next Generation

Cowles's 1933 assessment of forecasting was prescient in more than one way. True, Cowles helped shape the perception that the pioneering forecasters were primitive and unhelpful. But this judgment did not lead him to conclude that the whole endeavor was useless or impossible: just the opposite. Cowles argued that forecasting was merely in its infancy but had great promise. As he and other observers recognized, forecasting, by the 1930s, was well entrenched in government and international agencies, financial institutions, investment houses, and virtually every division of corporations large and small.

In 1938, *Fortune* magazine noted that forecasting had become as required as "breathing" in the operation of a firm: "Business can no more do without forecasting than it can do without capital. From birth to death a business is the moving sum total of its adjustments to the future."[23] In that decade, for instance, Sears, Macy's, and other firms employed professional economists to predict future demands.[24] By the post–World War II period, a large firm like IBM would have dozens of economists on staff, all engaged in producing forecasts and other projections for the use of senior management.[25] Not only did forecasting itself continue, but the specific models, methods, and approaches of the first generation of forecasters saw new life in the revised and refined methods of the next generation.

In 1931, the *New York Times* reported that a wide variety of "investment counselors" were selling predictions of all different types throughout the city. Numerology had the most adherents among street-corner investment advisors: "There are hundreds of amateur numerologists, more than 1,000 professionals."[26] Forecasts were regularly featured in the news. In February 1933, the *Wall Street Journal* reported that in an old school desk in Philadelphia, a piece of yellowed paper from the nineteenth century had been found showing a graph that seemed to predict the current depression. It turned out, however, to be a spiky chart from none other than Samuel Benner, the long-deceased market prophet whose work had inspired Roger Babson to enter the field.[27] The chart seemed to reignite interest in Benner, whom the *Journal* now called "Wall Street's earliest 'market counselor' of renown."[28] The paper even ran a forecast by Benner's grandson, Ralph Benner, who predicted that the country was "in a normal natural decline that will end prior to 1942."[29]

New schools of investing and forecasting blossomed in the 1930s, sometimes building on the earlier generation. The Columbia economist and playwright Benjamin Graham (1894–1976) helped bring Moody's disregard for business cycles, and his focus on firms, into the postwar period. Graham produced what became the bible of "fundamental" analysis, *Security Analysis* (1934), and a more accessible version, *The Intelligent Investor* (1949).[30] Like Moody, Graham distrusted the business cycle and thought it was simply a distraction from serious analysis of investment opportunities. He argued that investing was a "businesslike" proposition in which a specific security must be researched using all available information. If securities were thought to be underpriced, they should be purchased. Then the investor had simply to wait until the market uncovered their real value and then sell. Graham's student, Warren Buffett, used insight from Graham to begin his career as one of the United States' most famous investors—and, incidentally, a leading shareholder of Moody's Investors Service.

Roger Babson's interest in historical patterns was echoed in another popular investment advisor who emerged in the 1930s, Ralph Nelson Elliott (1871–1948), a statistician who began to study historic price data in the 1930s, mostly of U.S. stocks. In 1938 Elliott published, with Charles J. Collins, *The Wave Principle*. Elliott argued that stock market prices were not random but followed predictable patterns of mass optimism and pessimism that could be understood by using Fibonacci numbers—a numeric sequence beginning with 0, 1, and with each subsequent number the sum of the previous two. Elliott detailed his findings in twelve articles for *Financial World*. In 1946 he expanded his "wave" theory to a broader range of activities in his book, *Nature's Law—The Secret of the Universe*. Elliott's ideas did not initially receive much attention, but they came to prominence during the market crisis of the 1970s and especially following the publication of Robert R. Prechter Jr.'s popular book *The Elliott Wave Theory* (1978).[31]

ECONOMETRIC FORECASTING

Although the writings of popular experts gained a wide following, the far more influential work in the field of economic forecasting, as Alfred Cowles had recognized, moved, by the 1930s, from entrepreneurs to the academy—

and the forecasting industry eventually became dominated by mathematical and statistical models.

The greatest postwar movements that changed the intellectual and theoretical context of economic forecasting were the rise of Keynesian economics and the development of econometrics. Keynes had a fundamentally different view of the inevitability of business cycles than did promoters of "business barometers." He had said as much in his 1925 letter to Charles Bullock, in which he had criticized the work of the Harvard Economic Service, suggesting that their model treated business cycles as natural phenomena like the ocean's tide. He implied, further, that such a belief was socially inimical, for it meant that forecasters would have a vested interest in seeing cycles continue—in order to profit by predicting the next one.

Instead, Keynes championed the idea that government fiscal policy could flatten cycles. He shifted much of the focus of the next generation of economists to questions of policy and to the role of consumption in the economy. In advocating policy, he proposed a different vision than Herbert Hoover, who had advocated the idea of an "associationalist" state in which business leaders played an essential part in bringing stability to the economy and in which the Department of Commerce, and other government agencies, provided guidance and information. But, in a larger sense, the role of government in controlling cycles was not only reaffirmed but strengthened.

Like Irving Fisher, Keynes was an expert on monetary policy and an advocate of its use in stabilizing economies. But in the 1930s Keynes came to believe that monetary policy would not be enough to get the United States out of the Depression and advocated government spending and budget deficits. This would have a direct effect on the economy by stimulating consumption. Also, he argued, government spending would signal to investors and consumers that better times were ahead. Business managers in this scenario would welcome the increased demand by reopening their shops and factories, thus increasing production and employment.[32]

The Keynesian approach flourished in a mixed economy in which the scale of industry and the size of government spending had increased dramatically—as FDR had initiated the New Deal and, even more important, increased spending for wartime mobilization. In 1932, total federal government spending was $12.4 billion; in 1942, it had risen to $45.6 billion. In the immediate postwar years, it rose even higher—to $99.9 billion in 1952. Government obligations included Social Security, Medicare, and unemployment benefits.

The rise of the mixed economy was one reason why the business cycle was much flatter in the decades after World War II, from 1940 through the end of the twentieth century.

While Keynes was concerned with people's expectations of the future, he did not engage in producing commercial forecasts in the way others described in this book did.[33] Instead, the development of the next generation of commercial forecasting services developed, in time, through the field of econometrics.

In the early years of the Depression, the econometrics movement was still quite small, though it was backed by prominent scholars, including Irving Fisher and Harvard's Joseph Schumpeter. The field got a big boost when Alfred Cowles devoted a portion of his inherited wealth to founding the Cowles Commission for Research on Economics. The Cowles Commission, based near Cowles's home in Colorado Springs, became the country's leading center for econometrics. Cowles also aided the Econometric Society (which had been started in 1930 by Fisher, Ragnar Frisch, and Charles Roos) by underwriting their journal *Econometrica* and providing other funds.[34]

Colorado Springs, that remote mountain town that had been a temporary home to many forecasting pioneers seeking treatment for tuberculosis, became the nation's center for econometrics, as members of the Econometric Society and the Cowles Commission traveled there for conferences. Among the people journeying to the Rocky Mountains were Irving Fisher, the English statistician R. A. Fisher, Corrado Gini of the University of Rome, and economist Elmer J. Working of the University of Illinois. The Cowles Commission continued to hold summer conferences in Colorado Springs from 1935 to 1939, at which point the society moved to the University of Chicago. The closeness of the group of econometricians in Colorado, and later Chicago, helped bring energy to the new field.

Despite the interest of major scholars, the econometric approach remained outside the mainstream of the field of economics for many years. The controversial nature of this work was evidenced in Keynes's hostile reaction to the first macroeconomic model of the U.S. economy, which was constructed by Jan Tinbergen and published in the League of Nations' report as *Business Cycles in the United States of America, 1919–1932* (1939). The model included seventy-one variables and forty-eight equations.[35] Keynes criticized Tinbergen's effort as merely "a piece of historical curve-fitting and description."[36]

While the founder of the Cowles Commission, Alfred Cowles, had a great interest in economic prediction, the organization was not focused on developing forecasting models.[37] The economists and mathematicians at the commission worked instead to differentiate themselves from economic statisticians and develop a theoretical and conceptual approach to their new field rather than focusing on applied problems. The organization eventually flourished under the direction of Jacob Marschak (director from 1943 to 1948) and Tjalling C. Koopmans, who moved the Cowles group to Yale in 1955. Because of their work and that of other Cowles members, notably the Norwegian Trygve Haavelmo, econometrics eventually became the primary approach of applied economics after 1950.[38]

The interest in forecasting developed slowly and came in the second generation of econometricians, with the arrival of Lawrence Klein.[39] It was really only with Klein that a member of the Cowles Commission became chiefly interested in the problem of applying econometrics to forecasting and in forming a forecasting agency. The econometricians at the Cowles Commission, who were great admirers of Tinbergen's work, recruited Klein to develop a similar econometric model, which he did. Klein described his model in his book *Economic Fluctuations in the United States, 1921–41* (1950) and used it to predict America's postwar prosperity. Klein moved to the University of Pennsylvania in 1958 and Penn's Wharton School in 1968.[40] In 1969 he helped create Wharton Econometric Forecasting Associates (WEFA), whose aim was to produce a working econometric forecasting model that would advise firms and governments. In 1980 Klein won the Nobel Prize in Economic Sciences for his work.

With the application of econometrics to the problems of prediction, the next age of great optimism in forecasting finally began—optimism that was equal to that of the pioneer forecasters. A new group of forecasters competed for business and acclaim. In 1969, the same year WEFA was incorporated, the Harvard economist Otto Eckstein founded, with financier Donald Marron, Data Resources, Inc., in Lexington, Massachusetts; around the same time, Michael K. Evans started Chase Econometrics in Bala Cynwyd, Pennsylvania. Each of these organizations, great cathedrals of econometrics, developed massive forecasting models and sold their predictions, and reams of economic data, through computer time-sharing devices. The computers running their forecasting models, developed by IBM and Burroughs, were in a sense the great-grandchildren of Fisher's 1898 hydrostatic machine. This new group of forecasters, like the pioneering generation, would eventually confront harsh economic realities not foreseen by the models, in this case the stagflation of the 1970s. But by that time they, again like the pioneers, had come to enjoy great influence on economic institutions and ideas.

* * *

In these ways, the pioneer forecasters were succeeded by the next generation in the post–World War II period and beyond. Each generation of forecasters asked different questions; each had a different sense of the *possibilities* of the future. In the Keynesian-inspired forecasting of the post-Depression years, statistical and mathematical tools once used merely to predict business cycles were employed in flattening them and anticipating policy outcomes. But more broadly, the pioneering group of forecasters had helped launch an industry that afterward only trended up, growing in size and centrality to business, government, and American life.

POSTSCRIPT
||||||||||||||||||||||||||||

This book was written in a period that evokes earlier crises. When I started it, prior to the 2008 recession, an editor told me that the history of economic forecasting was unlikely to resonate with modern audiences. That seems less of a problem today, given the enduring climate of uncertainty and the wealth of excellent studies bearing on predictions, including, for instance, Nassim Nicholas Taleb's *The Black Swan*, Nouriel Roubini and Stephen Mihm's *Crisis Economics*, and Andrew Ross Sorkin's *Too Big to Fail*—to name only a few books on the current crisis.[1]

Fortune Tellers is a book about a different time. Today's global economy is immensely more complex. There are far more individual investors, many of whom own mutual funds. There is also sophisticated automated trading done by computers and colossal pension funds and other government obligations. Business managers have, at their fingertips, access to vastly more information about financial markets than their ancestors of the 1920s would have had if they combed through every periodical, regional newspaper, and stock ticker, and summoned every Wall Street news-deliverer and shoe-shiner to their office. Over the course of the 1920s, the Dow Jones Industrial Average (DJIA) increased from about 64 to 380; even in the boom years of 1928 and 1929, an active day on the New York Stock Exchange consisted of about 4 million trades.[2] Since 2011, the DJIA has consistently been above 10,000, and automated stock trading programs, which operate according to preset algorithms, make the number of trades almost unimaginably large.[3]

But reading today's headlines and the crop of new books on investing, we can see echoes of the earlier time. When the stock market dropped catastrophically in the fall of 2008 and the recession began, newspapers recalled scenes of the most memorable recent catastrophe. In 1929 it was 1920–21; in 2008, it was the Great Depression. The cast of characters in 2008 reads like a musical chairs version of 1929. The constellation of commentators included a Yale professor (Robert Schiller this time, who predicted calamity, instead of Irving Fisher, who did not) and a Wall Street prophet (TV's Jim Cramer, instead of, for instance, John Moody or Roger Babson). Among the individuals and institutions blamed for the crisis were securities ratings agencies (Moody's, in particular), which had erroneously valued assets, handing out high ratings to undeserving securities. Indeed, there is great irony that rating services, of minor influence in the late 1920s, were now a central *cause* of the crisis rather than part of the solution.

Elite institutions were also part of the story. A *Financial Times* article in the autumn of 2008, titled "Blame It on Harvard," listed the number of the school's graduates involved in the crisis, just as a 1930 headline blamed the Harvard Economic Society for promoting false optimism.[4] There were also doomsayers who, like New York University professor Nouriel Roubini, claimed to have foreseen the impending meltdown, as Babson had in 1929. Commentators highlighted a number of factors that contributed to the 2008 catastrophe, all of which hearkened back to 1929: overexuberance in the securities markets, ballooning consumer credit, exotic new financial instruments, and a mortgage crisis.

Moreover, in the recent crisis, the pioneer methods of prediction—using historical patterns, mathematical models, expectations, and empirical analogies—each continue to have purveyors and believers. Fundamental analysis is a vibrant field, embodied, for example, in the sage of Omaha, Warren Buffett, whose followers travel in droves to the annual shareholders meeting of Berkshire Hathaway. And technical analysis, the study of past trends in prices in order to make predictions, has been given new life by practitioners of behavioral finance, who seek patterns in irrational behavior.[5] Today Big Data seems to claim an approach to prediction that is beyond theory, much like the Harvard Economic Society did when it built economic observatories around the world.

The one method that dominates, of course, and has been implicated in the crisis, is mathematical models. The continuing appeal of these approaches to making sense of the marketplace is not surprising. This is the method that (as the economist Frank Knight might have said) most aggressively seeks to make future uncertainty look like manageable risk. In the recent crisis, quantitative analysts at investment firms and other financial institutions promoted an immense faith in the power of these models to describe reality. The belief in a rational and efficient marketplace yielded a range of new investment products, including types of derivatives and subprime mortgages. These sophisticated products had distant origins in Fisher's mathematical approach to economics. But they had far greater real-world impact and were promoted via marketing skills and technology that make Roger Babson seem like a town crier. In 2008, the Bank for International Settlements in Switzerland estimated the face value of all derivatives contracts worldwide to be an astonishing $680 trillion.[6] These products, intended to reduce risk, were very hard to value and yet were all over the world's financial markets—and they were the ones that left people blindsided when the crisis hit.

In addition to seeing the echoes of these earlier models, the recent crisis also recalled for me three of the themes of the earlier period covered in this book. The first theme is that the unsettling nature of future uncertainty, and the desire of people to avoid ambiguity, helps illuminate much about modern economies. It helps us understand, for instance, the range of institutions that have been developed to combat uncertainty, such as the evolving insurance industry and the growing economic-data gathering centers that collect unprecedented volumes of information. It provides insight into the behavior of firms, whose leaders try to protect themselves from unexpected events, and of consumers, who quickly curb purchases during turbulent times. It also, of course, helps explain the centrality of forecasting practices and the endless variety of predictions that are so much a part of our economy and life.

The second theme is the seductive belief, held by many, that today we live in a smarter and less risky era than our ancestors and that calamity will not happen to us. This is another way of saying what economists Carmen Reinhart and Kenneth Rogoff noted when they wrote that investors continually fool themselves into thinking that "this time is different."[7] The events leading up to 2008 revealed a similar account of the mistaken hubris of investors in the 1920s, who believed uncertainty had largely been removed from the marketplace. Both episodes, then and now, emphasize the important role that skepticism should play in evaluating rosy economic scenarios and the promises of market gurus.

The third theme is that in periods of unexpected calamity old worldviews shatter and new ones arise. The idea of "business barometers" grew following the 1920 crisis and declined in the uncertain economy of the 1930s. In the current crisis, former Federal Reserve chairman Alan Greenspan (the most powerful forecaster in the world during his tenure at the helm of the Federal Reserve between 1987 and 2006) explained his failure to foresee the subprime crisis of 2008 in dramatic terms. His belief in the efficiency of markets to accurately price investment products and the "self-interest of lending institutions to protect shareholders' equity" was based on his faith in mistaken economics. "The whole intellectual edifice ... collapsed in the summer of last year," he told Congress in October 2008.[8] The collapse brought confusion to politicians, bankers, and individual investors around the globe.[9]

It is too early to tell what will emerge as the next dominant paradigm for understanding our economic world. But it is a reasonable bet that forecasts and forecasters will continue to play a role in shaping that worldview. The debates over how to make predictions, and over which forecasts should command authority, are not narrowly about investment strategy or public policy, but about how we envision economies and what drives them.

ACKNOWLEDGMENTS
|||||||||||||||||||||||||||||||||||||||||||||||||||

I started this book shortly after a discussion with Thomas K. McCraw, the Pulitzer Prize–winning historian and longtime head of the group of historians at Harvard Business School. After I finished my last book, I gave Tom a list of new projects that I was thinking about working on. On the list was the subject of economic forecasting, but so were numerous others. As we talked, we kept returning to the possibilities of the subject of forecasting. The topic seemed to open a trunkful of ways to think about the nature of capitalism and its endless capacity for change. Tom helped me throughout the project, suggesting resources, commenting on drafts, and even editing my text. I was deeply saddened by his death in 2012. He was a great historian and a great human being who took time out from his own writing and teaching to mentor a generation of students and colleagues throughout his career.

I am also indebted to the creative scholars who helped me research and think about this book, including Caitlin Anderson, Oona Ceder, and Anastasia Kolendo. I want to thank Marcel Boumans, Peter Eisenstadt, Jeff Fear, Per Hansen, David Hendry, Daniel Horowitz, Richard R. John, Chris McKenna, Stephen Mihm, Susie Pak, Vicky Solan, Jason Scott Smith, Jeff Strabone, and Dick Sylla for reading and commenting on large portions of the manuscript.

Throughout the project, Harvard Business School (HBS) has been supportive, and for that I would like to thank Valerie Porciello, Toni Wegner, and Steve O'Donnell of the Division of Research. Geoff Jones, the current Isidor Straus Professor of Business History, has provided a wonderful environment for history to flourish at the school. In 2012, he worked to establish the Business History Initiative to support and promote research and teaching. David Moss helped me enormously by asking me to write a case on forecasting for his financial history class. David's comments, and the ability to hear him teach the case, enabled me to sharpen the book's themes. Sven Beckert, of the History Department, asked me to present a portion of my book in his seminar on the history of capitalism, where I benefited from his comments and from those of his insightful students. Felice Whittum helped me in innumerable ways by finding sources, answering queries, and providing thoughtful suggestions throughout. Many other colleagues at HBS commented on the manuscript, offering advice and suggesting improvements, including Frank Cespedes, Rakesh Khurana, Joseph Lassiter, Noel Maurer, Aldo Musacchio, Tom Nicholas, Julio Rotemberg, Richard Tedlow, and Gunnar Trumbull. The book was also helped by the creativity and resourcefulness of the staff of Baker Library, including the director of historical collections, Laura Linard, and Christine Riggle, Katherine Fox, Erin Wise, and Rachel Wise. I also benefited from those who made research materials available to me, including Jackie Kilberg of the Corporate Archives, McGraw-Hill Companies, Inc., and by Ron (Rip) Rybnikar of Babson College. I received valuable research materials from the archivists at the Harvard University Archives; the Rare Book & Manuscript Room at Butler Library, Columbia University; the Herbert Hoover Papers at the Herbert Hoover Presidential Library-Museum; the Franklin D. Roosevelt Presidential Library and Museum; and the Library of Congress. The New York Public Library remains a favorite place to do research and to write and contains an amazing range of books, periodicals, and ephemera that cannot be found elsewhere.

I would like to acknowledge the help of scholars and friends who discussed the project with me and offered their suggestions and comments: Edward Balleisen, Hartmut Berghoff, Ludovic Cailluet, Francesca Carnevali, David Chambers, Barry Cohen, Andrea Colli, Francis Diebold, David Engerman, Giovanni Favero, Gelina Harlaftis, Meg Jacobs, Chris Kobrak, Ken Kolber, Pamela Laird, Ken Lipartito, Deirdre McCloskey, Paul Miranti, Mary Morgan, Charles O'Hay, Rowena Olegario, Julia Ott, Laura Phillips, Kim Phillips-Fein, Jamie Pietruska, Tobias Roetheli, Mark Rose, Caitlin Rosenthal, Bruce Sandys, Andrea Schneider, Bruce Schulman, Jonathan Silvers, Hans Sjögren, George Smith, Christian Stadler, Marc Stern, Dick Sylla, and Julian Zelizer. I am grateful to have had the chance to present portions of this book at the Business History Conference, the European Business History Conference, and the Association of Business Historians. Sections of my chapter on the Harvard Economic Service appeared previously in "The Harvard Economic Service and the Problems of Forecasting," *History of Political Economy* 41:1 (2009): 57–88, and I would like to thank

Duke University Press for their permission to include them here. Isabelle Lewis made the map of New York City that appears in the book.

I would also like to thank Seth Ditchik, who took an interest in the project and acquired the book for Princeton University Press, and to Beth Clevenger and Leslie Grundfest, also of the Press, who helped me get the manuscript in shape. Jennifer Backer made many improvements to the prose.

Writing a book begins as an entrepreneurial act but soon becomes a family business. I am grateful for the support of my family, including my father, Carl, who, before his death in 2010, passed along relevant articles and frequently checked in to see how I was doing. He and my mother, Marjorie, always encouraged me to investigate the things I became curious about—even things like the genius of a good direct mail campaign, sales pitch, or business barometer. Finally, my greatest joy comes in thanking my wife, Susan, to whom the book is dedicated, and our daughter, Orli, both of whom keep me optimistic about the future.

NOTES
||||||||||||||||||||||||||||||

Preface

1. See *Webster's Third New International Dictionary of the English Language Unabridged* (Springfield, MA: Merriam-Webster, 1993), 888, which defines the verb "forecast" as to "anticipate, calculate, or predict (some future event or condition) usually as a result of rational study and analysis of available pertinent data." Some definitions in this paragraph are from the *Oxford English Dictionary*, 2nd ed. (New York: Oxford University Press, 1989). See also the *Pocket Oxford American Thesaurus*, 2nd ed. (New York: Oxford University Press, 2008), 645, for distinctions between alternative terms for "predict." David F. Hendry and Neil R. Ericsson's *Understanding Economic Forecasts* (Cambridge, MA: MIT Press, 2001), 17–20, contains an excellent discussion of forecasting terminology and includes remarks on the history of "cast."

2. Henry Newton Dickson, *Meteorology: The Elements of Weather and Climate* (London: Methuen & Co., 1893), 156.

Introduction

1. See Adams's obituary in the *New York Times*, November 11, 1932, p. 19. Adams's best-known book is *The Bowl of Heaven* (New York: Dodd, Mead & Company, 1926). For a general biography, see Karen Christino, *Foreseeing the Future: Evangeline Adams and Astrology in America* (Amherst, MA: One Reed Publications, 2002). Adams claimed to have advised J. P. Morgan. But a note from the Pierpont Morgan Library, New York, to the author, dated January 31, 2006, denies any link between the two. The library acknowledges no correspondence between the two and no notes in any datebooks. The library noted, however, that Morgan was a member of Zodiac Club (a men's dining club) and had zodiacal symbols incorporated into the design of his library.

2. Adams was arrested at least three times in the 1910s and 1920s under the fortune-telling laws then in force in New York State for "pretending to tell fortunes." See Christino, *Foreseeing the Future*, 85–100. On one such incident, see "Fortune Teller Is Held," *New York Times*, January 25, 1923, p. 16. According to the report, "She was accused of having accepted $10 from Mrs. Helen B. Osnato, a policewoman, for telling Mrs. Osnato's fortune."

3. For a discussion of the future-orientation of capitalism, see the introduction to Thomas K. McCraw, ed., *Creating Modern Capitalism: How Entrepreneurs, Companies, and Countries Triumphed in Three Industrial Revolutions* (Cambridge, MA: Harvard University Press, 1995), 1–16.

4. Melvin T. Copeland, "Statistical Indices of Business Conditions," *Quarterly Journal of Economics* 29:3 (May 1915): 523.

5. Walter Lippmann, *Drift and Mastery: An Attempt to Diagnose the Current Unrest* (New York: M. Kennerley, 1914).

6. Frank H. Knight, *Risk, Uncertainty, and Profit* (Boston: Houghton Mifflin, 1921), 237, 238; italics in the original. I am grateful to David Moss for pointing out this passage to me.

7. Irving Fisher, "Our Unstable Dollar and the So-Called Business Cycle," *Journal of the American Statistical Association* 20:150 (June 1925): 180. Many of these are listed in an unpublished booklet by the Illinois Chamber of Commerce (Research Dept.), *Commercial Services* (Chicago, 1927), available in Baker Library, Harvard Business School.

8. In part through such rulings and through cultural references, forecasters came to be defined as men, rather than women, who made use of statistical series and made a clear distinction between analysis and investment, on the one hand, and speculation and gambling, on the other.

9. *The People of the State of New York, Respondent, v. Alice I. Ashley, Appellant*, Supreme Court of New York, Appellate Division, Second Department, 184 A.D. 520; 172 N.Y.S. 282; 1918 N.Y. App. Div. Lexis 6590, October 25, 1918; italics added.

10. For "disenchantment of the world," see Max Weber, "Science as a Vocation," in Hans H. Gerth and C. Wright Mills, eds., *From Max Weber: Essays in Sociology* (New York: Oxford University Press, 1946), 139. See also Keith Thomas, *Religion and the Decline of Magic: Studies in Popular Beliefs in Sixteenth and Seventeenth Century England* (Oxford: Oxford University Press, 1997); and Jackson Lears, *Fables of Abundance: A Cultural History of Advertising in America* (New York: Basic Books, 1995).

11. Katherine Anderson, *Predicting the Weather: Victorians and the Science of Meteorology* (Chicago: University of Chicago Press, 2005), 1. On the influence of meteorology on economic prediction generally, see Jamie Pietruska, "Propheteering: A Cultural History of Prediction in the Gilded Age" (Ph.D. diss., MIT, 2009) and "U.S. Weather Bureau Chief Willis Moore and the Reimagination of Uncertainty in Long-Range Forecasting," *Environment and History* 17 (2011): 79–105.

12. Robert Marc Friedman, *Appropriating the Weather: Vilhelm Bjerknes and the Construction of a Modern Meteorology* (Ithaca: Cornell University Press, 1989).

13. Anderson, *Predicting the Weather*, 5.

14. The term "barometer," meaning a statistical aggregate series used to predict fluctuations of business and industrial activity, was used by Roger Babson, James Brookmire, and the Harvard Economic Service. See Roger Ward Babson, *Business Barometers Used in the Accumulation of Money* (Babson Park, MA: Babson's Reports, Inc., 1909); James H. Brookmire, *The Brookmire Economic Charts: A Graphic Record of Fundamental, Political and Industrial Conditions as a Barometer to the Financial and Business Situation* ... (St. Louis: Brookmire Economic Chart Co., 1913); and Warren Persons, "Construction of a Business Barometer Based upon Annual Data," *American Economic Review* 6:4 (December 1916): 739–69.

15. Judy L. Klein, *Statistical Visions in Time: A History of Time Series Analysis, 1662–1938* (Cambridge: Cambridge University Press, 1997), 73–101.

16. Copeland, "Statistical Indices of Business Conditions," 522–62, discusses various sources for statistics.

17. Klein, *Statistical Visions in Time*, 26.

18. William Stanley Jevons, "Commercial Crises and Sun-Spots," *Nature* 19 (14 November 1878): 33–37.

19. Irving Fisher, "Mathematical Investigations in the Theory of Value and Prices" (Ph.D. diss., Yale University, 1892), 3.

20. With the coming of big business at the very end of the nineteenth century, wrote historian Alfred D. Chandler Jr., "the leading entrepreneurs of the period, men like Rockefeller, Carnegie, Swift, Duke, Preston, Clark, and the DuPonts, had to become, as had the railroad executives of an earlier generation, experts in reading and interpreting business statistics." Alfred D. Chandler Jr., "The Beginnings of 'Big Business' in American Industry," *Business History Review* 33:1 (Spring 1959): 26–27.

21. Lawrence Chamberlain, *The Work of the Bond House* (New York: Moody Magazine and Book Co., 1913), 9.

22. Thomas K. McCraw, *American Business since 1920: How It Worked*, 2nd ed. (Wheeling, IL: Harlan Davidson, 2009), 190. See also Julia Ott, *When Wall Street Met Main Street* (Cambridge, MA: Harvard University Press, 2011), 2, for some further figures. Ott writes that less than 1 percent of the U.S. population owned stocks or bonds in 1899 but that nearly one-third of the population bought some form of federal bond during World War I.

23. Sven Beckert addresses efforts to justify and rationalize capitalism in "Capitalism," in Eric Foner and Lisa McGirr, *American History Now* (Philadelphia: Temple University Press, 2011), 314–35. Philip Mirowski's *More Heat than Light: Economics as a Social Physics, Physics as Nature's Economics* (Cambridge: Cambridge University Press, 1989) analyzes the ways in which economists drew inspiration from physicists in their efforts to make their field scientific.

24. On the idea that the era of capitalism was waning, see Howard Brick, *Transcending Capitalism: Visions of a New Society in Modern American Thought* (Ithaca: Cornell University Press, 2006). Michael A. Bernstein, *A Perilous Progress: Economists and Public Purpose in Twentieth-Century America* (Princeton: Princeton University Press, 2001), discusses the formation of the economics profession in the context of the crisis.

25. These ideas are discussed in Thomas K. McCraw's introduction to Joseph Schumpeter, *Capitalism, Socialism and Democracy* (New York: Harper Perennial Modern Classics, 2008), esp. xviii, xix.

26. On the more theoretical developments of the field, see Mary S. Morgan, *The History of Econometric Ideas* (Cambridge: Cambridge University Press, 1990); Francis X. Diebold, "The Past, Present, and Future of Macroeconomic Forecasting," *Journal of Economic Perspectives* 12:2 (Spring 1998): 175–92; and Terence C. Mills, ed., *Economic Forecasting* (Cheltenham: Edward Elgar, 1999).

27. Sherwood Anderson, *Winesburg, Ohio: A Group of Tales of Ohio Small Town Life* (New York: Modern Library, 1919).

Chapter 1. Roger W. Babson: The Rule of Past Patterns

1. John Kenneth Galbraith, *The Great Crash, 1929* (1954; Boston: Houghton Mifflin, 1988), 84–85. The best sources on Babson are his own autobiography, *Actions and Reactions: An Autobiography of Roger W. Babson* (1935; New York: Harper & Bros., 1950); a biography of Babson quite similar to the autobiography, Earl L. Smith, *Yankee Genius: A Biography of Roger W. Babson: Pioneer in Investment Counseling and Business Forecasting Who Capitalized on Investment Patience* (New York: Harper, 1954); and a dissertation by Horace R. Givens, "Roger Babson and His Major Contemporaries" (Ph.D. diss., New York University, 1975). There are also mocking accounts, such as Martin Gardner, "Sir Isaac Babson," in *Fads and Fallacies in the Name of Science* (New York: G. P. Putnam's Sons, 1952), 92–100. Babson's papers are found in the Roger W. Babson Collection, Babson College Archives and Special

Collections, Horn Library, Babson College, Wellesley, Massachusetts (hereafter Babson Collection).

2. George W. Coleman, "The Babson Statistical Organization, 1904–1929," 13, found in section of Babson Collection labeled "Babson Business: Babson Statistical Organization, box 1, folder 1, "25th Anniversary Celebration, 1929."

3. Babson, *Actions and Reactions*, 341, 2. "Thousands of attempts have been made by earnest inventors to develop a machine to operate by gravity without the aide [*sic*] of any fuel or other power," wrote Babson. Yet none had been satisfactory. Babson was aware of the skepticism the Gravity Research Foundation would provoke: "Those who have been interested in the study and harnessing of gravity have been disappointed with the attitude taken by many college professors and engineers in connection with it. The mention of gravity too often brings a smile as if the inquiry were not taken seriously."

4. Ann Fabian, "Speculation on Distress: The Popular Discourse of the Panics of 1837 and 1857," *Yale Journal of Criticism* 3:1 (1989): 127–42; Joseph Dorfman, *The Economic Mind in American Civilization, 1606–1933*, 5 vols. (New York: Viking, 1946–59), especially volume 3, which covers 1865–1918. See also David A. Zimmerman, *Panic! Markets, Crises & Crowds in American Fiction* (Chapel Hill: University of North Carolina Press, 2006) for cultural interpretations of panics.

5. Babson, *Actions and Reactions*, 56.

6. Ibid., 15. Shortly before this, around 1890, Babson underwent a religious conversion, joining the Gloucester Methodist Church. The conversion remained important to him and he claimed to have carried his Sinner's Dedication Card with him for most of his life.

7. Samuel C. Prescott, *When M.I.T. Was "Boston Tech," 1861–1916* (Cambridge, MA: MIT Press, 1954).

8. Babson, *Actions and Reactions*, 41.

9. George F. Swain, *How to Study* (New York: McGraw-Hill, 1917). On his interest in statistics, see George F. Swain, "Statistics of Water Power Employed in Manufacturing in the United States," *Publications of the American Statistical Association* 1:1 (March 1888): 5–44.

10. Swain's work habits are recounted in William Hovgaard, "Biographical Memoir of George Fillmore Swain, 1857–1931," *National Academy of Sciences of the United States of America Biographical Memoirs* 17 (1936).

11. Babson and his wife were among the world's largest holders of Newtonia, owning many editions of his books and even floorboards and furniture from the great scientist's home. Ironically, Newton is reputed to have lost a fortune in the South Sea Bubble but was able to recover. For a discussion of Newton's investments, see Julian Hoppit, "The Myths of the South Sea Bubble," *Transactions of the Royal Historical Society*, 6th ser., 12 (2002): 141–65, esp. p. 149; and Milo Keynes, "The Personality of Isaac Newton," *Notes and Records of the Royal Society of London* 49:1 (January 1995), 1–56, esp. p. 51.

12. The tree was acquired from the Pennsylvania Historical Commission, according to the "Babson's Timeline" found on the Babson College website.

13. On the importance of bonds in the pre–World War I period, see Chamberlain, *The Work of the Bond House*.

14. Babson, *Actions and Reactions*, 77–80.

15. Ibid., 94. For an interesting account of contemporary efforts to finance utilities, see Peter Leininger, "Public Utility Financing, 1919–1927," *Journal of Land and Public Utility Economics* 6:2 (May 1930): 208–12.

16. Babson, *Actions and Reactions*, 68. He wrote, on that page, "I have come to believe that most great lawyers, physicians, surgeons, preachers, and even scientists and statisticians, are 'great' because of their salesmanship qualities rather than their real knowledge."

17. Chamberlain, *The Work of the Bond House*, 28–29. On the culture of Wall Street during this time, see Ott, *When Wall Street Met Main Street*.

18. On statistics of backgrounds of business leaders, see Neil Fligstein, *The Transformation of Corporate Capital* (Cambridge, MA: Harvard University Press, 1993); and Walter A. Friedman and Richard S. Tedlow, "Statistical Portraits of American Business Executives," *Business History* 45 (October 2003): 89–113.

19. On Grace Babson, see Henry Macomber, "Mrs. Roger W. Babson and Her Interesting Life," unpublished ms., April 1958, box 1: "Obits/memorials/testimonial," folder "Macomber," Papers of Grace Knight Babson, Horn Library, Babson College.

20. Babson, *Actions and Reactions*, 74.

21. Sheila Rothman, *Living in the Shadow of Death: Tuberculosis and the Social Experience of Illness in America* (New York: Basic Books, 1994), 15. On the history of tuberculosis in Colorado Springs, see Douglas R. McKay, *Asylum of the Gilded Pill: The Story of Cragmor Sanatorium* (Colorado: State Historical Society of Colorado, 1983).

22. Babson, *Actions and Reactions*, 98.

23. On Poor, see Alfred D. Chandler Jr., *Henry Varnum Poor: Business Editor, Analyst, and Reformer* (Cambridge, MA: Harvard University Press, 1956).

24. Certificate of incorporation, "Office of Roger W. Babson Incorporated," Records of Office of Roger W. Babson Incorporated, bound books, Babson Collection.

25. See Roger Ward Babson, *Analyzing and Comparing Railroad Stocks; with Directions for Using the Stock Cards of the Babson System* (Wellesley Hills Station, MA: The Babson System, c. 1908), found in Widener Library, Harvard University.

26. Babson, *Actions and Reactions*, 84.

27. For figures, see Kim England and Kate Boyer, "Women's Work: The Feminization and Shifting Meanings of Clerical Work," *Journal of Social History* 43:2 (December 2009): 307–40; for a history of the period, see Margery W. Davies, *Woman's Place Is at the Typewriter: Office Work and Office Workers, 1870–1930* (Philadelphia: Temple University Press, 1982).

28. "Roger Babson to Rewed: Statistician Will Marry Miss Nona Dougherty, an Aide," *New York Times*, May 17, 1957, p. 18.

29. Babson, *Actions and Reactions*, 101.

30. This rough figure is calculated using the Consumer Price Index available on the website "How Much Is That?" for the years 1920 and 2011, http://eh.net/hmit/.

31. See Roger W. Babson, *Bond Offerings* (Wellesley Hills, MA: R. W. Babson, 1908). This publication, for the years 1906 to 1913, can be found in Baker Library, Harvard Business School.

32. Babson, *Actions and Reactions*, 203. He started the correspondence course in bond selling with his hometown friend Gus Linnekin. The two later created courses in economics and distribution that were similarly offered through the mail.

33. Jon Moen and Ellis W. Tallman, "The Bank Panic of 1907: The Role of Trust Companies," *Journal of Economic History* 52:3 (September 1992): 611–30; Robert Bruner and Sean Carr, *The Panic of 1907: Lessons Learned from the Market's Perfect Storm* (Hoboken, NJ: John Wiley and Sons, 2007).

34. Babson, *Business Barometers Used in the Accumulation of Money*, 192–94.

35. Alexander D. Noyes, "A Year after the Panic of 1907," *Quarterly Journal of Economics* 23:2 (February 1909): 186.

36. On the history of the Federal Reserve System, see Allan H. Meltzer, *A History of the Federal Reserve, Vol. I, 1913–1951* (Chicago: University of Chicago Press, 2003). On fears of Morgan's control over the banking industry, see p. 66.

37. Babson, *Actions and Reactions*, 107.

38. "macroeconomics, n.," *OED*, http://www.oed.com.ezp-prod1.hul.harvard.edu/view/ Entry/111940?redirectedFrom=macroeconomics.

39. See Babson, *Business Barometers Used in the Accumulation of Money*. See especially chapter 1, pp. 13–29, in which Babson differentiates between what he calls "comparative" statistics concerning the debt, earnings, and the financial and physical condition of specific firms or properties and "fundamental" statistics that related to the underlying conditions of economic prosperity that Babson relied on to forecast the business cycle.

40. Babson, *Business Barometers Used in the Accumulation of Money*, 15.

41. Roger W. Babson, "Barometric Indices of the Condition of Trade," *Annals of the American Academy of Political and Social Science* 35:3 (May 1910): 113. "Fundamental" statistics, rather than "comparative" ones, would help determine the current phase of the cycle. On this idea from Babson, see Givens, "Roger Babson," 185; Givens discusses Babson's emphasis on picking trends rather than individual stocks.

42. Stephen J. Brown, William N. Goetzmann, and Alok Kumar, "The Dow Theory: William Peter Hamilton's Track Record Reconsidered," *Journal of Finance* 53:4 (1998): 1311–33. See also Justin Fox, *The Myth of the Rational Market: A History of Risk, Reward, and Delusion on Wall Street* (New York: Harper, 2009); Fox compares Babson and Dow on pp. 16–19.

43. Samuel Benner, *Benner's Prophecies of Future Ups and Downs in Prices* (Cincinnati: Robert Clarke Company, c. 1897; edition used, 1907), iv. These words served as an epigraph to the book and Babson included the quote on p. 108 of *Actions and Reactions*, misquoting Benner slightly. On Benner's philosophy and meteorological origins, see Peter Eisenstadt, "The Origins and Development of Technical Market Analysis," *Essays in Economic and Business History* (East Lansing: Michigan State University Press, 1997), 15:335–51.

44. Roger W. Babson, *Business Barometers and Investment* (New York: Harper & Brothers, 1940), 33–34.

45. "Rumor Mongers Exercise Optimism without Restraint," *Washington Post*, May 8, 1925, p. 17. The article quotes the recollections from a salesman at the bookstore of Robert Clarke & Co., Cincinnati, Ohio.

46. Samuel Benner, *Benner's Prophecies of Future Ups and Downs in Prices: What Years to Make Money on Pig Iron, Hogs, Corn, and Provisions* (Cincinnati: Published by the author, 1875).

47. Ibid., 13–15. The same prophecies were reprinted in every edition of the book, even editions that were printed *after* the year being predicted. Benner simply added new forecasts to the end of the volume with each edition.

48. "By-the-Bye," *Wall Street Journal*, September 19, 1933, p. 6; Benner, *Prophecies*, 149.

49. Benner, *Prophecies*, 108–9.

50. Ibid., 117.

51. Ibid., 28.

52. For discussion of the influence of meteorology on Benner, see Eisenstadt, "The Origins and Development of Technical Market Analysis," esp. p. 339. See also Pietruska, "Propheteering."

53. Eisenstadt, "The Origins and Development of Technical Market Analysis," 339.

54. Samuel Crowther, *John H. Patterson: Pioneer in Industrial Welfare* (New York: Doubleday, 1923), 78.

55. On Smith, see Henry Clews, *Fifty Years in Wall Street* (1908; New York: John Wiley and Sons, 2006). See also "Stock Gambling," *Chicago Tribune*, October 6, 1885, p. 7, and "The Stock-Gamblers' Failure," *Chicago Tribune*, October 4, 1885, p. 4.

56. "By-the-Bye," 6.

57. "The Financial Markets," *New York Times*, January 3, 1898, p. 8.

58. N. S. B. Gras, *Business and Capitalism: An Introduction to Business History* (New York: F. S. Crofts and Co., 1939), 297–98. For other mentions of Benner in academic literature, see Henry W. Broude, "Bottleneck Phenomena and Cyclical Change: The Role of the Iron and Steel Industry," *Quarterly Journal of Economics* 68:3 (August 1954): 437–60; Samuel Rezneck, "Distress, Relief, and Discontent in the United States during the Depression of 1873–78," *Journal of Political Economy* 58:6 (December 1950): 492–512, mentions Benner's work in footnote 12, as an "early attempt to advance 'the science of price cycles' by relating it to a Jupiter cycle of magnetic storms, mixed with a naïve venture in forecasting" (498); Arthur H. Cole, "Conspectus for a History of Economic and Business Literature," *Journal of Economic History* 17:2 (September 1957): 333–38; Harold F. Breimyer, "Emerging Phenomenon: A Cycle in Hogs," *Journal of Farm Economics* 41:4 (November 1959): 760–68; Harold F. Breimyer, "Nature's Felicity in Supply Response Analyses: Comment," *American Journal of Agricultural Economics* 52:1 (February 1970): 146–47.

59. Joseph A. Schumpeter, *History of Economic Analysis* (1954; New York: Oxford University Press, 1994), 1134n30.

60. Arthur H. Cole, "A Note on Continuity of Enterprise," *Business History Review* 35:1 (Spring 1961): 77.

61. Babson, *Actions and Reactions*, 108.

62. Babson, *Business Barometers Used in the Accumulation of Money*, chapter 4, pp. 102–40, is titled "Law of Equal and Opposite Reaction, Theory of the Compositplot." See also Charles O. Hardy and Garfield V. Cox, *Forecasting Business Conditions* (New York: Macmillan, 1927), chapter on the Babson Service, beginning on p. 41. Babson also described his barometer in other articles. See, for instance, Babson, "Barometric Indices of the Condition of Trade," 111–34; and Roger W. Babson, "Factors Affecting Commodity Prices," *Annals of the American Academy of Political and Social Science* 38:2 (September 1911): 155–88.

63. Babson, *Actions and Reactions*, 109; Babson, *Business Barometers Used in the Accumulation of Money*, 105–6.

64. Persons, "Construction of a Business Barometer Based upon Annual Data," 743.

65. Criticism of Babson's methods, including his placement of the normal line, can be found in James H. Brookmire, "Methods of Business Forecasting Based on Fundamental Statistics," *American Economic Review* 3:1 (March 1913): 49–51; Copeland, "Statistical Indices of Business Conditions," 543–52; and Persons, "Construction of a Business Barometer Based upon Annual Data," 740–44, quoted in Copeland, "Statistical Indices of Business Conditions," 546.

66. Hardy and Cox, *Forecasting Business Conditions*, 48.

67. Babson, *Business Barometers Used in the Accumulation of Money*, 111.

68. Ibid., 116.

69. Babson therefore believed that psychology played a big role in market behavior. He thought he could rationally predict the irrational and, in his mind, immoral behavior of the herd. He never explained his view of psychology in theoretical terms, but he viewed market behavior as substantially a matter of psychology—and saw economics as a study of the psychology of economic actors. For others, such as Irving Fisher (discussed in chapter 2), mass psychology was mass error; in the 1929 stock market crash, for instance, Fisher described the "shaking out of the lunatic fringe" and felt that such "lunacy" had only temporary effect. Irving Fisher quoted in Galbraith, *The Great Crash, 1929*, 97.

70. Herbert Hoover, *Memoirs of Herbert Hoover*, vol. 3, *The Great Depression, 1929–1933* (New York: Macmillan, 1951), 30.

71. Roger W. Babson, "Ascertaining and Forecasting Business Conditions by the Study of Statistics," *Publications of the American Statistical Association* 13:97 (March 1912): 41.

72. Ibid., 36.

73. David Logan Scott, *Wall Street Words: An A to Z Guide to Investment Terms for Today's Investor* (Boston: Houghton Mifflin, 2003), 242.

74. Babson had previously sold the card service to two of his former employees but had retained substantial interest in the firm. Babson, *Actions and Reactions*, 102–3.

75. Babson, *Actions and Reactions*, 135.

76. Diaries of Roger Babson, box 1, 1910, Babson Collection. The "diaries" are a series of vest-pocket calendars detailing Babson's daily activities.

77. Babson, *Actions and Reactions*, 135.

78. Babson to Edison, December 7, 1910, Digital Collection, Thomas Edison Papers, Rutgers University. Thanks to David Hochfelder for showing this to me.

79. *New York Times*, February 10, 1910, p. 6, provides a description of one such talk.

80. See Babson to Lorimer, September 28, 1931, Correspondence, box 4, file: "Lorimer, George H.—Correspondence with RWB," Babson Collection. For articles, see Roger W. Babson, "Mining Securities," *Saturday Evening Post*, February 3, 1912, p. 28 (telling readers to keep out of mining ventures altogether); "A Message from Edison to the Man Who Pays the Bills," *Saturday Evening Post*, March 16, 1912, p. 6; "Defaulted Bonds," *Saturday Evening Post*, March 30, 1912, p. 31; "The Cost of Living: An Interview with Senator Burton," *Saturday Evening Post*, March 2, 1912, p. 6 (in which Babson claimed that Ohio senator Theodore E. Burton was America's leading authority on prices, aside from Irving Fisher); "Water Power Bonds," *Saturday Evening Post*, April 20, 1912, p. 30; and "America's Great Industries: Iron," *Saturday Evening Post*, June 1, 1912, p. 32.

81. "Administrative, Royalties—Roger W. Babson" folder, box "Babson Statistical Organization," Babson Collection.

82. "The Country Needs a Period of Rest and Readjustment," *New York Times*, July 31, 1910, p. SM1.

83. The article for *American Magazine* (February 1920) was by Mary B. Mullett and was reprinted in Babson, *Actions and Reactions*, 81–85.

84. Roger Babson, "Recoveries from the Famous Panics of America," *New York Times*, December 25, 1910, p. SM9. Babson's capitalization.

85. Historian Bob Cuff noted that at the outset of this period "U.S. federal administration lagged behind administrative developments abroad and innovations in corporate enter-

prise at home." Robert Cuff, "Creating Control Systems: Edwin F. Gay and the Central Bureau of Planning and Statistics, 1917–1919," *Business History Review* 63:3 (Autumn 1989): 605.

86. See Guy Alchon, *The Invisible Hand of Planning: Capitalism, Social Science, and the State in the 1920s* (Princeton: Princeton University Press, 1985), 174; and William J. Breen, "Foundations, Statistics, and State-Building: Leonard P. Ayres, the Russell Sage Foundation, and U.S. Government Statistics in the First World War," *Business History Review* 68:4 (Winter 1994): 451–82. Breen wrote, "No adequate statistical information was available to policy makers as they struggled to mobilize the American economy" (455).

87. See Stephen Jay Gould, *The Mismeasure of Man* (1981; New York: Norton, 1996), esp. 222–55. See also Richard Von Mayrhauser, "The Manager, the Medic, and the Mediator: The Clash of Professional Psychological Styles and the Wartime Origins of Group Mental Testing," in Michael Sokal, *Psychological Testing and American Society, 1890–1930* (New Brunswick, NJ: Rutgers University Press, 1987).

88. Walter A. Friedman, *Birth of a Salesman: The Transformation of Selling in America* (Cambridge, MA: Harvard University Press, 2004), 172–89; Von Mayrhauser, "The Manager, the Medic, and the Mediator."

89. Breen, "Foundations, Statistics, and State-Building," 451–82; Cuff, "Creating Control Systems," 588–613. Ayres made organization charts for separate sections within the Council of National Defense: the Aircraft Production Board, the General Munitions Board, the Medical Section, and others. He also developed organization charts for the American Red Cross and for Herbert Hoover's Food Administration.

90. Wesley C. Mitchell, *The Backward Art of Spending Money* (New York: Augustus M. Kelley, 1950), 42, originally the presidential address to the Annual Meeting of the American Statistical Association in Richmond, Virginia, December 1918.

91. See Cuff, "Creating Control Systems."

92. Roger Babson, *W. B. Wilson and the Department of Labor* (New York: Brentano's, 1919), 220.

93. Babson, *Actions and Reactions*, 180–81. See also Gordon S. Watkins, "Labor Problems and Labor Administration in the United States during the World War," *University of Illinois Studies in the Social Sciences* 8:3 (September 1919): 211–13.

94. Quoted in Loren Baritz's introduction to Sinclair Lewis, *Babbitt* (1922; New York: Signet Classic, 1998), vii. Babson's account of his wartime experience is in *Actions and Reactions*, 179–88.

95. Howard Florence, "What Really Happened?" *Review of Reviews* 81 (January 1930): 116.

96. Kenneth Lipartito and Yumiko Morii, "Rethinking the Separation of Ownership from Management in American History," *Seattle University Law Review* 33:4 (Summer 2010): 1026.

97. "Business & Finance: Up or Down," *Time Magazine* 31:18 (April 25, 1938). The article claimed that the *Business Bulletin* was "the favorite economic reading of most U.S. tycoons."

98. Babson to Harding, January 12, 1922, Correspondence, box 4, "Harding," Babson Collection.

99. On Peavey, see obituary, "Leroy D. Peavey," *New York Times*, March 26, 1937, p. 22.

100. Babson, *Actions and Reactions*, 222.

101. Ibid., 187.

102. "Babson, Paul T.," Roger Babson to Paul Babson, October 25, 1934, Abell–Babson Park folder, box 1, Correspondence, Babson Collection.

103. Givens, "Roger Babson," 179.

104. *Log of the Crew* 4:1 (January–May 1920): 19. The *Log of the Crew* was the Babson Statistical Organization's in-house bulletin. It reported the total subscriptions for 1920: *Barometer Letter* (11,909); *Speculative Bulletin* (6,272); *Industries Bulletin* (5,291); *Commodity Bulletin* (5,749); and *Labor Bulletin* (3,475). *Log of the Crew* is found in the Babson Collection.

105. *Log of the Crew* 7:1 (Summer 1923): 26–27.

106. *Log of the Crew* 5:1 (Spring 1921): 20–21.

107. *Log of the Crew* 4:1 (January–May 1920): 12.

108. Babson, *Actions and Reactions*, 160, describes the formation of the syndicate.

109. Ibid., 209.

110. Ibid., 205.

111. Ibid., 206. Babson also cultivated an interest among students in forecasting in other ways. In 1924, for instance, he offered prizes to the two best essays on the subject of forecasting published in the *American Economic Review*. See Daniel V. Gordon and William A. Kerr, "Was the Babson Prize Deserved? An Enquiry into an Early Forecasting Model," *Economic Modelling* 14 (1997): 417–33.

112. Homer B. Vanderblue, "The Florida Land Boom," *Journal of Land & Public Utility Economics* 3:2 (May 1927): 113–31; quote from Hill is on p. 118. Note that Vanderblue became an important editor and promoter for the Harvard Economic Service, the forecasting agency profiled later in this book. On Florida, see William Frazer and John J. Guthrie Jr., *The Florida Land Boom: Speculation, Money, and the Banks* (Westport, CT: Quorum Books, 1995); and Raymond Vickers, *Panic in Paradise: Florida's Banking Crash of 1926* (Tuscaloosa: University of Alabama Press, 1994).

113. Vanderblue, "The Florida Land Boom," 123.

114. Babson, *Actions and Reactions*, 239.

115. Vanderblue, "The Florida Land Boom," 258.

116. Babson, *Actions and Reactions*, 237.

117. Ibid., 238.

118. Roger W. Babson, *Religion and Business* (New York: Macmillan, 1920).

119. "Barometer Letter and the BabsonChart," *Babson's Reports*, December 26, 1922, p. 1, for both quotes.

120. "Trust Started Civilization," *Washington Post*, January 30, 1922, p. 12.

121. *New York Times*, July 26, 1910, p. 6.

122. Babson, *Actions and Reactions*, 97, 101.

123. Givens, "Roger Babson," 181.

124. *New York Times*, September 6, 1929, p. 12.

125. Ibid., 1. See also Galbraith, *The Great Crash, 1929*, 86, for a mention of the "Babson break," and 85–89 for a highly critical account of Babson.

126. *New York Times*, October 24, 1929, p. 2. See also chapter 2.

127. *New York Times*, September 7, 1929, p. 5.

128. "Dow Jones Industrial Average All-Time Largest One Day Gains and Losses," http://online.wsj.com/mdc/public/page/2_3047-djia_alltime.html.

129. *New York Times*, November 9, 1929, p. 33.

130. See Givens, "Roger Babson," 349, for selections from Babson's newsletters.

131. "Babson Flays Congress for Business Ills," *Washington Post*, November 20, 1929, p. 1.

132. *New York Times*, November 21, 1929, p. 1.

133. *New York Times*, November 10, 1929, p. 21.

134. *New York Times*, November 17, 1929, p. 2.

135. Ralph West Robey, "Being Right with Babson," *The Nation* 130 (March 26, 1930): 359–61; the subway is mentioned on p. 360.

136. *Babson's Reports*, December 16, 1929.

137. Henry F. Pringle, "Profiles: Prophet of Doom," *The New Yorker* (February 15, 1930): 23–25.

138. Robey, "Being Right with Babson," 360.

139. Pringle, "Profiles: Prophet of Doom," 23–25.

140. Babson, *Actions and Reactions*, 116–18, 127–30.

141. Babson's newsletters for July 21, 1930, and November 24, 1930, are quoted in Givens, "Roger Babson," 350.

142. Babson's newsletters for May 11, 1931, and June 1, 1931, are quoted in Givens, "Roger Babson," 350–51.

143. Paul Bairoch, *Economics and World History: Myths and Paradoxes* (Chicago: University of Chicago Press, 1995), 6–9.

144. "U.S. Industrial Stocks Pass 1929 Peak," *London Times,* November 24, 1954, p. 12.

145. Roger Babson, *Cheer Up! Better Times Ahead!* (New York: Fleming H. Revell, 1932), 10.

146. Babson, *Actions and Reactions*, 133.

147. In 1944 *Babson's Reports* had sales of $80,343 for the month of August 1944 and a net monthly profit of $6,356. The company had total assets and liabilities of $817,532. Box "Babson Statistical Organization," folder "Administrative: Babson's Reports Inc., Profit and Loss Statement, 1944," Babson Collection. Babson also helped build an even greater financial information empire under the "Babson" name. He advised his cousin Paul T. Babson to purchase Poor's Publishing Company and move its operations to Babson Park in 1934. Paul also had gained control of the Standard Statistics Company after the New York–based company fell on hard times in the late 1930s, after launching a major expansion in 1929. The merger of Standard and Poor's brought together the oldest financial publishing company (Poor's Publishing) and the largest (Standard Statistics). The company employed about nine hundred people and operated out of 345 Hudson Street in Manhattan, which Standard Statistics had occupied for a decade, and out of the editorial and printing offices of Poor's Publishing in Wellesley, Massachusetts. *New York Times*, March 1, 1941, p. 19.

148. David L. Lewis uses this term in his book *The Public Image of Henry Ford: An American Folk Hero and His Company* (Detroit: Wayne State University Press, 1976), 93.

149. Eisenstadt, "The Origins and Development of Technical Market Analysis," 335–51.

150. Babson, *Actions and Reactions*, 303.

151. Ibid., 318.

152. Babson to Friend, December 23, 1929, "Friend, Elizabeth. California" folder, Correspondence, box 4, Babson Collection.

153. Babson, *Actions and Reactions*, 342.

154. *Washington Post*, June 14, 1968, p. D12.
155. Mitchell quoted in Givens, "Roger Babson," 82.

Chapter 2. Irving Fisher: The Economy as a Mathematical Model

1. In 1913, for instance, the forecaster James H. Brookmire included Fisher as one of the major forecasting theorists (along with Samuel Benner, William Stanley Jevons, and Roger Babson). See Brookmire, "Methods of Business Forecasting Based on Fundamental Statistics," 43–58, esp. 52–53. Three years later Warren Persons highlighted Fisher's work on the first page of his article on constructing "business barometers." See Persons, "Construction of a Business Barometer Based upon Annual Data," 739–69. Persons wrote, "Professor Irving Fisher bases his forecasts upon changes which take place in the series entering into his equation of exchange" (739).

2. The best sources on Irving Fisher are two biographies, one by his son, Irving Norton Fisher, *My Father, Irving Fisher* (New York: Comet Press Books, 1956); and one by Robert Loring Allen, *Irving Fisher: A Biography* (Oxford: Blackwell, 1993). Fisher's successor at Yale, economist James Tobin, surveyed Fisher's academic legacies in "Irving Fisher (1867–1947)," *American Journal of Economics and Sociology* 64:1 (January 2005): 19–42. The economist Robert W. Dimand has written many significant articles on Fisher, including "Irving Fisher's Debt-Deflation Theory of Great Depressions," *Review of Social Economy* 52:1 (Spring 1994): 92–107; "Irving Fisher and Modern Macroeconomics," *American Economic Review* 87:2 (May 1997): 442–44; "Fisher, Keynes, and the Corridor of Stability," *American Journal of Economics and Sociology* 64:1 (January 2005), 185–99; and, with coauthor John Geanakoplos, "Celebrating Irving Fisher: The Legacy of a Great Economist," *American Journal of Economics and Sociology* 64:1 (January 2005), iii–vi, 3–18. Irving Fisher's papers, housed at Yale University (hereafter Fisher Papers), are voluminous and contain letters, both personal and professional, and all his published works. On Fisher's Index Number Institute, the organization that oversaw Fisher's forecasting, see the Karl G. Karsten Papers, Manuscript Division, Library of Congress, Washington, DC (hereafter Karsten Papers). From 1928 to 1930 Karsten was president of the Index Number Institute. Two recent books make special mention of Fisher's interest in forecasting. See Justin Fox, *The Myth of the Rational Market: A History of Risk, Reward, and Delusion on Wall Street* (New York: Harper, 2009); and Sylvia Nasar, *Grand Pursuit: The Story of Economic Genius* (New York: Simon and Schuster, 2011). On Fisher's forecasting in comparison with that of the Harvard Economic Service, see Kathryn M. Dominguez, Ray C. Fair, and Matthew D. Shapiro, "Forecasting the Depression: Harvard versus Yale," *American Economic Review* 78 (September 1988): 595–612.

3. "Meaning of British Election," *Wall Street Journal*, November 1, 1924, p. 1.
4. Quoted in Allen, *Irving Fisher*, 11.
5. Tobin, "Irving Fisher," 19.
6. *New York Times*, March 12, 1937, p. 11.
7. Irving Fisher and Eugene Lyman Fisk, *How to Live: Rules for Healthful Living Based on Modern Science* (New York: Funk & Wagnalls, 1915). Dr. Fisk was a partner with Fisher in several of his endeavors, including the Life Extension Institute.
8. Irving Fisher and O. M. Miller, *World Maps and Globes* (New York: Essential Books, 1944).
9. Irving Fisher, *The Rate of Interest: Its Nature, Determination, and Relation to Economic Phenomena* (New York: Macmillan, 1907), 104.

10. For Fisher's early forecasting work, see Irving Fisher, "'The Equation of Exchange' for 1911, and Forecast," *American Economic Review* 2:2 (June 1912): 302–19; and Fisher, "'The Equation of Exchange' for 1912, and Forecast," *American Economic Review* 3:2 (June 1913): 341–45. See also Dominguez, Fair, and Shapiro, "Forecasting the Depression," 595–612, which discusses Fisher's forecasting methods.

11. Irving Fisher, *The Money Illusion* (New York: Adelphi, 1928), 109.

12. See Irving Fisher, "Statistics in the Service of Economics," *Journal of the American Statistical Association* 28:181 (March 1933): 5.

13. On the popular attitude toward Fisher after the stock market crash, see Frederick Lewis Allen, *Only Yesterday: An Informal History of the Nineteen-Twenties* (1931; New York: HarperCollins Perennial Classics editions, 2000), 281; and Galbraith, *The Great Crash, 1929*, 70. There is some dispute as to whether Fisher said this exact phrase, although he certainly made very similar statements and used the word "plateau" to describe stock price. In *Rainbow's End: The Crash of 1929* (Oxford: Oxford University Press, 2001), Maury Klein raised doubts about whether Fisher actually said this famous phrase. He wrote, "The only source given for that remark is Edward Angly, *Oh Yeah?* (New York, 1931), 38, a satirical volume 'Compiled from Newspapers and Public Records.' In most cases, Angly gave at least the source of the statement, but for this one he did not." In any case, Fisher's comments were very close.

14. Some argue that Fisher was right in his assessment that security prices in 1929 were not overvalued. See Ellen R. McGrattan and Edward C. Prescott, "The Stock Market Crash of 1929: Irving Fisher Was Right!" *NBER Working Paper Series* (working paper no. 8622, 2001), 1–33. See also Harold Bierman Jr., *The Causes of the 1929 Stock Market Crash: A Speculative Orgy or a New Era?* (Westport, CT: Greenwood Press, 1998). "The stock market, in general, was not unreasonably priced" (ix).

15. Allen, *Irving Fisher*, 25.

16. Fisher's family life is described in Fisher, *My Father, Irving Fisher*, esp. p. 9. When he was six years old, his nine-year-old sister Cora died of typhoid fever.

17. Fisher, *My Father, Irving Fisher*, 9, 10, 12. Fisher finished his studies there a few years after Frank William Taussig, who later headed the Harvard economics department for many years.

18. Fisher, *My Father, Irving Fisher*, 14–15.

19. Allen, *Irving Fisher*, 36.

20. Ibid., 34.

21. The *New York Times* announced the first, second, and third freshman prizes, June 17, 1885, p. 5, and the news that Fisher was valedictorian on June 5, 1888, p. 5.

22. Nasar, *Grand Pursuit*, 147–48, discusses Gibbs's influence on Fisher. See also Lynde Phelps Wheeler, *Josiah Willard Gibbs: The History of a Great Mind* (New Haven: Yale University Press, 1951) and Muriel Rukeyser, *Willard Gibbs* (Garden City, NY: Doubleday, Doran & Co., 1942). Ironically, given Babson's interest in Newton, Gibbs was known as "the American Sir Isaac Newton." See Annie L. Cot, "Breed Out the Unfit and Breed in the Fit," *American Journal of Economics and Sociology* 64:3 (July 2005): 793–826, esp. p. 794.

23. On the rise of new business magazines, see Frank Luther Mott, *A History of American Magazines* (Cambridge, MA: Harvard University Press, 1938–68). The literature on the rise of an engineering and efficiency-minded culture is voluminous, including Samuel P. Hayes, *Conservation and the Gospel of Efficiency: The Progressive Conservation Movement* (Cambridge, MA: Harvard University Press, 1959); Thomas Parke Hughes, ed., *Changing Attitudes toward American Technology* (New York: Harper and Row, 1975); and, on one of the main stars of the

efficiency movement, Robert Kanigel, *The One Best Way: Frederick Winslow Taylor and the Enigma of Efficiency* (New York: Viking, 1997). On the scientific impulse in psychology, see the remarkable book by William James, *Principles of Psychology* (New York: Henry Holt, 1890); and for historical accounts, see Gould, *The Mismeasure of Man*. Richard Gillespie, *Manufacturing Knowledge: A History of the Hawthorne Experiments* (New York: Cambridge University Press, 1991).

24. Richard Hofstadter is responsible for the most lasting characterization of Sumner as a social Darwinist; see *Social Darwinism in American Thought* (Philadelphia: University of Pennsylvania Press, 1944), but specialists have agreed for some time that the term does not adequately describe Sumner's brand of optimistic, laissez-faire evolutionism. Robert C. Bannister Jr., "William Graham Sumner's Social Darwinism: A Reconsideration," *History of Political Economy* 5:1 (Spring 1973): 89–109.

25. Fisher quoted in Fisher, *My Father, Irving Fisher*, 45; see also Allen, *Irving Fisher*, 37–38, on Fisher and Sumner; and Fox, *The Myth of the Rational Market*, 9–10. For biographies of Sumner, see Bruce Curtis, *William Graham Sumner* (Boston: Twayne, 1981) and John K. Dickinson, *William Graham Sumner, 1840–1910* (Marburg: Kleinoffsetdruck H. Görich, 1963).

26. Irving Fisher, "Mathematical Investigations in the Theory of Value and Prices," *Transactions of the Connecticut Academy* 9 (July 1892); reprint (Fairfield, NJ: Augustus M. Kelley, 1991).

27. Joseph A. Schumpeter, "Irving Fisher's Econometrics," *Econometrica* 16:3 (July 1948): 222. See also Ragnar Frisch, who called it of "monumental importance" in "Irving Fisher at Eighty," *Econometrica* 15:2 (April 1947): 72.

28. Quoted in Allen, *Irving Fisher*, 11. The original source is Paul Samuelson, "Irving Fisher and the Theory of Capital," in William Fellner et al., *The Economic Studies in the Tradition of Irving Fisher* (New York: John Wiley and Sons, 1967), 22.

29. The review of the French translation can be found here: Irving Fisher, review of *Recherches sur la théorie du prix* by Rudolf Auspitz and Richard Lieben, translated from German by Louis Suret, *American Economic Review* 5:1 (March 1915): 106–8.

30. For a good, general discussion of the history of the idea of marginal utility, see Thomas K. McCraw, *Profit of Innovation: Joseph Schumpeter and Creative Destruction* (Cambridge, MA: Harvard University Press, 2007), 40–55.

31. See Allen, *Irving Fisher*, 52–55, for a concise discussion of Fisher's dissertation and his view of marginal utility and equilibrium.

32. Fisher, "Theory of Value and Prices," 14–15.

33. Ibid., 32, 55. The eminent political economist Francis Ysidro Edgeworth's review of Fisher's "Mathematical Investigations in the Theory of Value and Prices" explores these quotes and the ideal of marginal utility; see *Economic Journal* 3:9 (March 1893): 108–12.

34. Edgeworth, review of "Mathematical Investigations in the Theory of Value and Prices," 109.

35. Fisher, "Mathematical Investigations in the Theory of Value and Prices," 24.

36. Ibid., 24–25. E. F. Sheppard called Fisher's device an "ingenious toy" in his review of Fisher's "Mathematical Investigations in the Theory of Value and Prices" in *Mathematical Gazette* 13:191 (December 1927): 466–67. See also Mary S. Morgan, "The Technology of Analogic Models: Irving Fisher's Monetary Worlds," *Philosophy of Science* 64, supplement (December 1997): S304–S314, on the use of analogies.

37. Allen, *Irving Fisher*, 52; he writes, "In 1890 and even later, much of the conventional wisdom in economic theory was still mainly classical economics, devoid of any significant mathematical touch, and innocent of any American contribution of note."

38. Fisher, "Mathematical Investigations in the Theory of Value and Prices," 3, initial page of preface.

39. See Fisher, *My Father, Irving Fisher*, 60–61, describes the wedding. The Hazard family has left many relevant papers; see, for instance, the Rowland Hazard Papers, University of Rhode Island Library, Special Collections and Archive; and the Rowland Hazard III Papers, Rhode Island Historical Society, Manuscript Division.

40. *New York Times*, June 18, 1893, p. 16.

41. Allen, *Irving Fisher*, 64–65. Unfortunately, Fisher missed the chance to ever meet William Stanley Jevons (1835–82), who died more than a decade before Fisher's trip at the young age of forty-six. Fisher credited Jevons's *Theory of Political Economy* (1871) with introducing mathematical economics. Jevons also pioneered the forecasting field, with a series of papers on the relationship between sunspots and trade cycles. Like Fisher, Jevons had an inventive mind and had created a mechanical device, the "logic piano," to embody his theoretical ideas, not entirely unlike Fisher's machine. On Jevons and econometrics, see Morgan, *History of Econometric Ideas*, 18–25.

42. The best source on the Fisher's domestic life is Fisher, *My Father, Irving Fisher*, 69; see also Allen, *Irving Fisher*, 67, and on Fisher's office there, 102, 136–37. Fisher and his family suffered a setback in March 1904 when the house at 460 was substantially damaged by fire. See *New York Times*, March 6, 1904, p. 2. It was subsequently rebuilt and expanded.

43. Douglas W. Steeples and David O. Whitten, *Democracy in Desperation: The Depression of 1893* (Westport, CT: Greenwood Press, 1998), 37.

44. See Andrew W. Phillips and Irving Fisher, *Elements of Geometry* (New York: Harper and Brothers, 1896); and Irving Fisher, *A Brief Introduction to the Infinitesimal Calculus, Designed Especially to Aid in Reading Mathematical Economics and Statistics* (New York: Macmillan, 1897).

45. Allen, *Irving Fisher*, 43. In addition to other efforts to promote mathematical economics, Fisher supervised a translation, and wrote an introduction to, an important article by the pioneering mathematical economist and pioneer of general equilibrium theory Léon Walras. See Irving Fisher and Léon Walras, "Geometrical Theory of the Determination of Prices," *Annals of the American Academy of Political and Social Science* 3 (July 1892): 45–64.

46. Irving Fisher, "Appreciation and Interest," *Publications of the American Economic Association* 11:4 (July 1896): 36.

47. Fisher, *The Rate of Interest*, 336.

48. Irving Fisher, "What Is Capital?" *Economic Journal* 6:24 (December 1896): 509–34; "Senses of 'Capital,'" *Economic Journal* 7:26 (June 1897): 199–213; and "The Role of Capital in Economic Theory," *Economic Journal* 7:28 (December 1897): 511–37.

49. Fisher, "What Is Capital?" 513.

50. Ibid., 514.

51. Fisher, "The Role of Capital in Economic Theory," esp. 511–12.

52. Fisher, *My Father, Irving Fisher*, 74–77. After Colorado Springs, Fisher went to Santa Barbara and then back to Colorado Springs. On Colorado Springs and tuberculosis, see McKay, *Asylum of the Gilded Pill* and Rothman, *Living in the Shadow of Death*.

53. Allen, *Irving Fisher*, 84–85, discusses the effects of tuberculosis on Fisher.

54. Fisher quoted in Cot, "Breed Out the Unfit and Breed in the Fit," 795.

55. Allen, *Irving Fisher*, 82; William J. Barber, "Irving Fisher of Yale," *American Journal of Economics and Sociology* 64:1 (January 2005): 48; *New York Times*, May 26, 1907, p. SM4, which reported, "To make outdoor sleeping easy and popular, Professor Fisher, a firm believer in the air cure has invented a cheap and convenient portable shack"; and *New York Times*, May 27, p. 6 on "The Fisher Health Tent."

56. Fisher, *My Father, Irving Fisher*, 108–9. See Edmund Morris, *The Rise of Theodore Roosevelt* (New York: Random House, 2001), 452. On Kellogg, see Gerald Carson, *Cornflake Crusade* (New York: Rinehart, 1957).

57. Fisher and Fisk, *How to Live*, 1, 2, 4.

58. Ibid., 5.

59. Allen, *Irving Fisher*, 140, indicates that more than ninety editions of the book had been published by 1993.

60. Lucy Sprague Mitchell, *Two Lives: The Story of Wesley Clair Mitchell and Myself* (New York: Simon and Schuster, 1953), 241–42.

61. See ad, "The Virtues of Thorough Mastication," *New York Times*, January 1907, p. 4.

62. *New York Times*, May 24, 1907, p. 8; George Rosen, "The Committee of One Hundred on National Health and the Campaign for a National Health Department, 1906–1912," *American Journal of Public Health* (February 1972): 261–63.

63. See the *Transactions of the Sixth International Congress on Tuberculosis* (Philadelphia: William F. Fell Company, 1908), five volumes; see volume 3, *Proceedings of Section V: Hygienic, Social, Industrial, and Economic Aspects of Tuberculosis*, p. 745, which mentions Fisher's dietary tests; and Michael E. Teller, *The Tuberculosis Movement: A Public Health Campaign in the Progressive Era* (Westport, CT: Greenwood Press, 1988), 34–35.

64. Fisher and Fisk, *How to Live*, 415.

65. Richard Conniff, "God and White Men at Yale," *Yale Alumni Magazine*, May/June 2012.

66. Cot, "Breed Out the Unfit and Breed in the Fit," 798, quoting the membership pledge.

67. Andrew Scull, *Madhouse: A Tragic Tale of Megalomania and Modern Science* (New Haven: Yale University Press, 2005), 81–85.

68. Nasar, *Grand Pursuit*, 164–70.

69. Irving Fisher, *The Purchasing Power of Money, Its Determination and Relation to Credit, Interest, and Crises* (New York: Macmillan 1911), vii; see also Irving Fisher, *Why Is the Dollar Shrinking? A Study in the High Cost of Living* (New York: Macmillan, 1914).

70. Fisher, *The Purchasing Power of Money*, 25n2, on Newcomb.

71. See Irving Fisher, " 'The Equation of Exchange,' 1896–1910," *American Economic Review* 1:2 (June 1911): 296–305. Fisher later expanded the equation to include variables for bank deposits. He believed that the general level of prices (P) was determined by five, and only five, factors: the volume of money in circulation (M); the velocity of its circulation through the economy (V); the volume of bank deposits in checking accounts (M′) and their velocity of circulation (V′); and the total volume of trade, or the amount of goods and services bought and sold (T). Fisher expressed the relationship as $P = (MV + M'V')/T$, or more commonly $PT = MV + M'V'$. See also Fisher, *The Purchasing Power of Money*, 27. The equation is discussed throughout the book; it is elaborated on in an appendix on 488–90, in which Fisher discusses M, M′, V, V′, P, and T.

72. Fisher, "'The Equation of Exchange,' 1896–1910," 297.

73. Fisher, *Why Is the Dollar Shrinking?* 35–36.

74. Ibid., 37 for "turned over," and 49–50 for more on velocity. For Fisher, the level of output (T) was determined by a great number of factors, including innovation, managerial reform, labor policies, and anything else that bore on the creative and efficient production of goods. The velocity of money (V) was constant over the long run. Hence the price level depended on the quantity of money in the economy.

75. Allen, *Irving Fisher*, 114–15.

76. See Fisher, "'The Equation of Exchange,' 1896–1910," 298–99, for a discussion of sources of data. M, the money in circulation, was taken from estimates by the Director of the Mint and Comptroller of the Currency. M' was based on reports of the Comptroller of the Currency for individual deposits. T, the volume of trade, was based on the statistics of internal commerce published by the Bureau of Statistics in the Department of Commerce and Labor and included statistics of quantities of commodities exported and imported, sales of stocks, railroad tons carried, and post office letters carried. P, the price level, was based on figures from the Bureau of Labor for the wholesale prices of 258 commodities and on prices of stocks and hourly wages. Finally, V and V' were worked out by a formula developed by Fisher in "A Practical Method of Estimating the Velocity of Circulation of the Currency," *Journal of the Royal Statistical Society* 72:3 (December 1909): 604–18.

77. Fisher, *Purchasing Power of Money*, 306.

78. Ibid., 270; see also Brookmire, "Methods of Business Forecasting Based on Fundamental Statistics," 52–53. There was some discrepancy: Des Essars argued that the greatest velocity of money from deposit accounts came the year the crisis arrived, rather than a year before, as Fisher indicated.

79. Fisher, "'The Equation of Exchange,' 1896–1910," 300. Writing in 1910, Fisher remarked on the high velocity of check deposits in that year: "The high velocity means that the average man in the United States is now keeping an extremely small bank balance relatively to the large expenditures he is making; that is, he is leaning toward a spendthrift policy."

80. Fisher, *Purchasing Power of Money*, 60; Fisher, *Why Is the Dollar Shrinking?* 77–87, esp. p. 81. Fisher explained the sequence by which an economic crisis could emerge in a few steps: (1) Suppose, for instance, that prices began to rise in the economy, perhaps following the finding of new gold (as had happened in California in the 1840s, for instance). (2) "Enterprisers"—persons who undertake business enterprises of various kinds—began to receive much higher prices than before, without having much greater expenses (for interest, rent, salaries, etc.), and therefore made greater profits. (3) Enterpriser-borrowers, encouraged by the large profits, increase their borrowings. (4) Deposit currency (M') expands relative to money (M). (5) Because of this expansion of deposit currency (M'), prices continue to rise; that is (1) is repeated. Then (2) is repeated and so on. Fisher argued that this escalation in prices could lead to a crisis. Trade (T) was stimulated by the increase in loans in the form of new constructions of buildings, machinery, and so on. This led to a broad feeling that "business is good" and "times are booming." But, Fisher noted, the "times" were only good for a specific segment of the population, the "enterpriser-borrower" and not necessarily the landlord, salary earner, or others. This latter group experienced only increased prices and would therefore scheme to improve their situation with a sudden "jump," either by raising rental prices or by demanding an increase in salary, for instance. These changes would encourage banks to become more conservative. Now, because of these conditions, new enterprises, which

sought to continue borrowing funds, found that they could not. Some of these businesses, which had grown dependent on loans to continue their operation or even to get started, would fail. The failure of these firms then created a sense of panic and a feeling that "bad times had arrived," even perhaps inciting a bank run. Some banks might call in their original loans, causing more distress. This culminated in the upward price movement and brought about the beginnings of a crisis, "a condition characterized by failures due to lack of cash when and where it is most needed." See J. M. Keynes's review of Fisher's *The Purchasing Power of Money, Its Determination and Relation to Credit, Interest, and Crisis* (1911), *Economic Journal* 21:83 (September 1911): 393–98, for a critique of this scenario.

81. W. G. Langworthy Taylor, "Fisher's 'The Purchasing Power of Money,' " *Annals of the American Academy of Political and Social Science* 42 (July 1912): 334.

82. Fisher, " 'The Equation of Exchange' for 1911, and Forecast," 310.

83. Ibid., 345.

84. For a general history of economic performance cast in terms of business cycle fluctuations, see Victor Zarnowitz, *Business Cycles: Theory, History, Indicators, and Forecasting* (Chicago: University of Chicago Press, 1992), 228.

85. Roger W. Babson, "Factors Affecting Commodity Prices," *Annals of the American Academy of Political and Social Science* 38:2 (September 1911): 155.

86. Brookmire, "Methods of Business Forecasting Based on Fundamental Statistics," 52–53.

87. Persons, "Construction of a Business Barometer Based upon Annual Data," 739.

88. Allen, *Irving Fisher*, 189–190.

89. It is useful to compare Fisher's investment strategy to Keynes's investing idea. On Keynes, see David Chambers and Elroy Dimson, "Keynes the Stock Market Investor" (unpublished paper on Society Science Research Network, posted March 5, 2012), http://papers .ssrn.com/sol3/papers.cfm?abstract_id=2023011.

90. Irving Fisher, *The Making of Index Numbers: A Study of Their Varieties, Tests, and Reliability* (Boston: Houghton Mifflin, 1922), 2–3.

91. Ibid., 330–31; italics in the original.

92. Ibid., 3; italics in the original.

93. Irving Fisher, assisted by Hans R. L. Cohrssen, *Stable Money: A History of the Movement* (New York: Adelphi, 1934), 385.

94. Allen, *Irving Fisher*, 173. The core group at the Index Number Institute included Royal Meeker (1873–1953), a statistician who had earned a Ph.D. in economics at Columbia and studied at the University of Leipzig, and the Austrian-born statistician Max Sasuly (1888–1971), who earned bachelor's and master's degrees from the University of Chicago. Obituary for Royal Meeker, *New York Times*, August 18, 1953, p. 23. Some of Meeker's personal beliefs and views are in Royal Meeker, "The Promise of American Life," *Political Science Quarterly* 25:4 (December 1910): 688–99. Obituary, Max Sasuly, *Washington Post*, November 18, 1971, p. B7. See also Max Sasuly, "Irving Fisher and Social Science," *Econometrica* 15:4 (October 1947): 255–78, which contains some personal reflection.

95. Some of Fisher's pieces in the *New York Times* include "Stabilizing Price Levels," September 2, 1923, p. 10; "Future Realty Values," December 21, 1919, p. 114; "Fisher Finds Substitutes," May 16, 1925, p. 16; "Fisher on Deflation," August 24, 1925, p. 12; and "What Prohibition Has Done," January 27, 1929, p. 4.

96. Allen, *Irving Fisher*, 189.

97. On Kardex, see Allen, *Irving Fisher*, 185–86, 188.

98. Fisher to his son Irving Norton Fisher, June 17, 1925, folder 78, box 6, series I, group 212, Fisher Papers.

99. Irving Fisher to Rev. William G. Eliot Jr., November 24, 1925, folder 86, box 6, series I, group 212, Fisher Papers.

100. Karl G. Karsten, *Charts and Graphs: An Introduction to Graphic Methods in the Analysis of Statistics* (New York: Prentice-Hall, 1923). Karsten's obituary is in the *New York Times*, May 26, 1968, p. 84.

101. See Karl G. Karsten, "The Harvard Business Indexes: A New Interpretation," *Journal of the American Statistical Association* 21:156 (December 1926): 399–418.

102. See "Plan to Sell the Karsten Statistical Laboratory," Karl G. Karsten Papers, Library of Congress, box 1, folder 1, dated May 15, 1929.

103. Nasar, *Grand Pursuit*, 303.

104. Undated Index Number Institute pamphlets, MUDD Stacks, Yale University Library.

105. Salesman Wheeler, report February 15, 1928, "INI Policies" folder, box 5, Karsten Papers.

106. "Newdick, Edwin" folder, box 4, and "INI Policies" folder, box 5, Karsten Papers. The company found a group of advertisers, including General Electric, Remington Rand, Cunard Line, Metropolitan Life, and Phoenix Mutual, who placed ads on Fisher's page.

107. See Edwin Newdick, "How to Use Fisher Indexes," Index Number Institute, New Haven (c. 1929), Index Number Institute pamphlets, MUDD Stacks, Yale University Library.

108. "INI Policies" folder, box 5, Karsten Papers. "The capital involved in meeting the losses of business until it is self-supporting varied between $25,000 and $120,000 with the majority around $50,000," Karsten reported.

109. "Newdick, Edwin" folder, box 5, Karsten Papers. Fisher also explored joining his business with Luther Blake's at Standard Statistics. See Fisher to Luther Blake, March 25, 1929, "INI plans" folder, box 5, Karsten Papers.

110. Allen, *Irving Fisher*, 210.

111. See Carl F. Christ, "A History of the Cowles Commission, 1932–1952," *Economic Theory and Measurement: A Twenty Year Research Report* (Chicago: Cowles Commission for Research in Economics, 1952), 3–65.

112. *New York Times*, September 6, 1929, p. 12.

113. *New York Times*, October 16, 1929, p. 8.

114. Fisher, *The Stock Market Crash—And After* (New York: Macmillan, 1930), 257–69.

115. *New York Times*, October 22, 1929, p. 24.

116. Fisher quoted in Galbraith, *The Great Crash, 1929*, 97, 146.

117. Fisher, *The Stock Market Crash—And After*, 38.

118. "The Trend of Events," *Outlook and Independent* 153 (December 4, 1929): 532.

119. Babson Press release. November 1, 1929, Babson Collection, Babson College.

120. Fishers Business Page for January 29, 1930, quoted in Dominguez, Fair, and Shapiro, "Forecasting the Depression," 607. The date of the quote is January 29, 1930.

121. Fisher's Business Page for December 1, 1930, quoted in Dominguez, Fair, and Shapiro, "Forecasting the Depression," 607.

122. Fisher's Business Page for February 23, 1931, quoted in Dominguez, Fair, and Shapiro, "Forecasting the Depression," 607.

123. Fisher's Business Page for October 17, 1931; quoted in Dominguez, Fair, and Shapiro, "Forecasting the Depression," 607.

124. Irving Fisher, "Steadying the Dollar," *New York Times*, December 13, 1931, p. XX4. Fisher echoed these monetary themes in his *Booms and Depressions: Some First Principles* (New York: Adelphi, 1932). Fisher argued that the severity of the depression was due to the remaining indebtedness from the previous speculative boom and to the subsequent depreciation brought on by it. He revisited his view that the business cycle was largely a monetary phenomenon and devoted sections of the work to the role of interest rates, the volume and velocity of currency, the price level, psychological factors, and production.

125. Irving Fisher, "The Debt-Deflation Theory of the Great Depression," *Econometrica* 1:4 (October 1933): 337–57. Decades later, Fisher's theory began to gather many supporters. See Allen, *Fisher*, 253; and Nasar, *Grand Pursuit*, 314–15.

126. Advertisement, *New York Times*, January 25, 1931, p. RE9. Fisher tried to promote his views with several new publications and periodicals. None of these endeavors, introduced to make money in the early 1930s, succeeded. The periodical *Financial News Service*, founded in 1930 went out of business after about one year. This company was quickly succeeded by two short-lived enterprises, the *Trade and Money Index* and *Market Indicators*, neither of which lasted beyond 1934. Dominguez, Fair, and Shapiro, "Forecasting the Depression," 596n2.

127. Fisher sold the Index Number Institute in August 1936. Allen, *Irving Fisher*, 264.

128. See Allen, *Irving Fisher*, 236, on tax payment. For returns on selected stocks, see Exhibit 5, in Tom Nicholas, "Trouble with a Bubble: The Great Crash of 1929," Harvard Business School Case Number 808067-PDF-ENG.

129. Fisher's books on Prohibition: *The "Noble Experiment"* (with the assistance of H. Bruce Brougham) (New York: Alcohol Information Committee, 1930); *Prohibition at Its Worst* (New York: Macmillan, 1926) and *Prohibition Still at Its Worst* (New York: Alcohol Information Committee, 1928).

130. Allen, *Irving Fisher*, 269.

131. Fisher, *My Father, Irving Fisher*, 331–33. Fisher was suffering from cancer of the colon and was under the influence of Dr. Max Gerson, who advocated a diet consisting largely of fruit and vegetables cooked in their own juices. Fisher's last talk was titled "The Inflations and Deflations of My Eighty Years."

132. Christ, "History of the Cowles Commission, 1932–1952." As opposed to the Cleveland meeting, which was largely organizational, the first official meeting of the Econometric Society was held September 1931 at the University of Lausanne, Switzerland. Wassily Leontief, "Joseph A. Schumpeter, 1883–1950," *Econometrica* 18:2 (April 1950): 109. There were indications that mathematical economics would flourish. For one thing, the field was attracting some of the greatest economists of the day. Fisher's friend and near-contemporary Joseph Schumpeter (1883–1950) also supported his crusading interest in mathematical economics. Schumpeter, who was originally from Austria-Hungary but had joined the Harvard faculty for good starting in 1932, was one of the twentieth century's great economists. He joined with Fisher in forming the Econometric Society and served as its fifth president in 1940–41.

133. Fisher quoted in Fisher, *My Father, Irving Fisher*, 268.

134. Milton Friedman and Anna Jacobson Schwartz, *A Monetary History of the United States, 1867–1960* (Princeton: Princeton University Press, 1963).

135. See, for instance, Ellen R. McGrattan and Edward C. Prescott, "The 1929 Stock Market: Irving Fisher Was Right," Federal Reserve Bank of Minneapolis, revised December 2003.

136. Fox, *The Myth of the Rational Market*, 3–26, on Fisher as pioneer of rational market hypothesis.

137. Allen, *Irving Fisher*, 301.

Chapter 3. John Moody: The Bright Light of Transparency

1. Moody's Corporation, the parent company of Moody's Investors Service, had revenue of $2.3 billion in 2011 and employed 6,500 people worldwide. The best sources on the early history of the company and on John Moody are Moody's own article, "A Fifty Year Review of Moody's Investors Service," McGraw-Hill Archives, Record Group 7, series 2, subseries C, box 4, folder "Moody Manual Company—History," New York; and David Stimson with Christopher Mahoney, *Moody's: The First Hundred Years* (New York: Moody's Investors Service, 2008). Moody also wrote two autobiographies, *The Long Road Home* (New York: Macmillan, 1933) and *Fast by the Road* (New York: Macmillan, 1942); these chiefly concern Moody's literary and religious interests, though the first contains some information on his business career. On Moody's career as a forecaster, see Hardy and Cox, *Forecasting Business Conditions*, 96–107, and Givens, "Roger Babson." There is some archival material about the original *Moody's Manual*, from 1900 to 1907, in the Corporate Archives, McGraw-Hill Companies, New York. My thanks to research associate Jackie Kilberg for making this material available to me.

2. John Moody, *Moody's Analyses of Railroad Investments* (New York: Analyses Publishing Co., 1909), 12. The full subtitle of Moody's publication is worth noting, as it indicates his effort to separate himself from the heard-on-the-street type of newsletter then common on Wall Street: *Moody's Analyses of Railroad Investments Containing in Detailed Form an Expert Comparative Analysis of Each of the Railroad Systems of the United States, with Careful Deductions, Enabling the Banker and Investor to Ascertain the True Values of Securities, By a Method Based on Scientific Principles Properly Applied to Facts.*

3. On bucket shops, see Ann Fabian, *Card Sharps, Dream Books, and Bucket Shops: Gambling in 19th Century America* (Ithaca: Cornell University Press, 1990) and Ott, *When Wall Street Met Main Street*, which discusses Wall Street terms for investors.

4. Moody, *The Long Road Home*, 203–4.

5. John Moody, *The Railroad Builders: A Chronicle of the Welding of the States* (New Haven: Yale University Press, 1919) and *The Masters of Capital: A Chronicle of Wall Street* (New Haven: Yale University Press, 1921).

6. See David Moss, *A Concise Guide to Macroeconomics: What Managers, Executives, and Students Need to Know* (Boston: Harvard Business School Press, 2007), 67–86. See also Roman Frydman and Edmund S. Phelps, eds., *Individual Forecasting and Aggregate Outcomes: "Rational Expectations" Examined* (Ithaca: Cornell University Press, 1983); and Michael P. Clements and David F. Hendry, *The Oxford Handbook of Economic Forecasting* (Oxford: Oxford University Press, 2011).

7. The author of the article, Paul Clay, economist at Moody's Investors Service, continued: "The popular belief that the stock market discounts or anticipates has no basis in fact. The belief itself doubtless arises from the fact that trade conditions are so complex that very few people realize changes therein until months after these changes have occurred." Clay, "Forecasting Security Prices," *Journal of the American Statistical Association* 20:150 (June 1925): 245. This is also quoted and mentioned in Givens, "Roger Babson," 238, 246.

8. Moody, *The Long Road Home*, 6.

9. Ibid., 8. Moody recalls, on p. 4 of the book, a story in which his grandfather loaned P. T. Barnum $500—most probably never repaid—to start his circus (now Ringling Bros. & Barnum, Bailey) but turned down a full partnership in the enterprise.

10. Moody, *The Long Road Home*, 33.

11. Ibid., 52. On Chautauqua, see *The Chautauqua Moment: Protestants, Progressives, and the Culture of Modern Liberalism* (New York: Columbia University Press, 2003).

12. Moody, *The Long Road Home*, 42–43.

13. Ibid., 56–59. See also Eugene J. Koop, *History of Spencer Trask & Co.* (New York: Spencer Trask & Co., 1941).

14. Moody, *The Long Road Home*, 88.

15. Ibid., 66–67.

16. John Moody, *The Art of Wall Street Investing* (New York: The Moody Corporation, 1906), p. 147.

17. Their wedding announcement is in the *New York Times*, April 7, 1899, p. 7. They had two sons, one of whom died of typhoid in 1927. Anna Moody, who was born in Nice, France, was mentioned in Agnes de Mille, *Where the Wings Grow* (New York: Doubleday, 1978), 85, 196, 272. De Mille, the dancer and choreographer, was a neighbor in Merriewold and enjoyed the Moodys' many social events there.

18. Moody, "A Fifty Year Review," 1.

19. Moody, *The Long Road Home*, 90.

20. Albro Martin, "John Moody," *Dictionary of American Biography* (New York: Charles Scribner's Sons, 1980), 26:458.

21. Moody, *The Long Road Home*, 92–93.

22. On Poor, see Chandler, *Henry Varnum Poor*. Analysts of credit and industry performed a certain type of forecasting in their work—focusing on the financial conditions and business plans of individual concerns. They studied the character and aspirations of business entrepreneurs and their capacities to realize these dreams. The credit-reporting agencies, Dun and Bradstreet, also produced newsletters. It is not surprising that four years after Moody's death in 1958, the Moody firm was sold to the credit-reporting giant Dun & Bradstreet. Moody's work and interest was never far from the field of credit analysis.

23. Chandler, *Henry Varnum Poor*, esp. 48–71.

24. Ibid., 255.

25. Givens, "Roger Babson," 59.

26. Moody, *The Long Road Home*, 91.

27. Ott, *When Wall Street Met Main Street*, 23–35.

28. Moody, "A Fifty Year Review," 2–3.

29. Givens, "Roger Babson," 59.

30. Moody, "A Fifty Year Review," 3.

31. Ibid., 2–4.

32. Sources on the history of Standard & Poor's include Roy Porter, unpublished memoir, p. 2, McGraw-Hill Archives; "Business: Statistics," *Time Magazine*, February 9, 1931; and "The 100-Year History of Standard & Poor's Mirrors Rise of Financial Information," *New York Times*, April 24, 1960.

33. Givens, "Roger Babson," 65.

34. Moody, *The First 100 Years*, 29–30.

35. Moody, *The Truth about the Trusts: A Description and Analysis of the American Trust Movement* (New York: Moody Publishing Company, 1904), 494; italics in original.

36. Moody, *The Long Road Home*, 129.

37. Ibid., 151.

38. Moody, *The First 100 Years*, 38–39.

39. Moody, *The Long Road Home*, 154–55.

40. Ibid., 130.

41. Babson, *Actions and Reactions*, 104.

42. Roy Porter, unpublished memoir, 3–4, McGraw-Hill Archives, Record Group 7, series 2, subseries C, box 4, folder "Moody Manual Company—History"; Timothy Sinclair, *The New Masters of Capital: American Bond Ratings Agencies and the Politics of Creditworthiness* (Ithaca: Cornell University Press, 2005), 24–25. In 1914, Roy Porter purchased the *Manual* from Babson, although Babson seems to have remained deeply involved in its operation. Porter later merged Moody Manual Company with Poor's Railroad Manual Company to form Poor's Publishing Company. In 1924 Moody purchased back the rights to use the name "Moody's Manual" from Roy Porter. When Moody started his ratings service, Porter wanted to take legal action against John Moody. Porter recalled, "[Moody] had contracted to stay out of the business and a temporary injunction was taken out by the Moody Manual Co. to restrain him from publishing. Unfortunately, as I saw it then, and as I know it now, the Directors would not go through with a permanent injunction and John was allowed to start again." Roger Babson and Eliphalet Potter decided to be lenient on Moody. "Messrs. Babson and Potter are on record as casting the votes to 'let John alone.'"

43. Moody, "A Fifty Year Review," 9–10.

44. Ibid., 9.

45. Morton B. Parks to Dennis Jensen, Standard & Poor's, July 25, 1983, McGraw-Hill Archives, Record Group 7, series 2, subseries C, box 4, folder "Moody Manual Company—History." Moody "had sold the *Magazine* to Augustin Ferrin but held on to the subscription lists without Ferrin realizing Moody kept a copy. Moody gained back the majority of subscribers and within a few years caused Ferris to fold *Moody's Magazine!*"

46. Moody, *The First 100 Years*, 54.

47. On the credit-reporting agencies, see Rowena Olegario, *A Culture of Credit: Embedding Trust and Transparency in American Business* (Cambridge, MA: Harvard University Press, 2006); and Barry Cohen, "Constructing an Uncertain Economy: Credit Reporting and Credit Rating in the Nineteenth Century United States" (Ph.D. diss., Northwestern, 2012).

48. On the evolution of the ratings system, see Olegario, *Culture of Credit*, 119–39. The National Association of Credit Men, which was founded around the same time as the Chicago World's Fair, became a strong advocate for transparency. Both Dun and Bradstreet published regular articles in magazines and their own circulars on economic conditions that served as forerunners of Moody's forecasting periodicals. Starting in the late 1850s or 1860s, and more regularly by the late 1860s, Tappan's Mercantile Agency issued newsletters that were intended for subscribers but were often reproduced in major daily newspapers starting in the late 1850s. They centered on failure statistics but often included summaries of the various trades, regional economies, and business in general. In 1878 or 1879, Bradstreet's came out with a weekly (or twice-weekly) financial and business journal called *Bradstreet's*. Dun came out with an equivalent sometime in the 1890s titled *Dun's Bulletin*.

49. *Analyses of Railroad Investments*, 140. The quote appeared frequently in Moody's manuals from this period.

50. On ratings, see Richard S. Wilson, *Corporate Senior Securities: Analysis and Evaluation of Bonds, Convertibles, and Preferreds* (Chicago: Probus Pub. Co., 1987), 323–25. Note that Moody's original ratings were not credit ratings, as today, but investment quality ratings. (During the years of the Great Depression, investment grade securities were those rated Baa and above; speculative were those rated Ba and below).

51. Moody, *The First 100 Years*, 51.

52. See Wilson, *Corporate Senior Securities*.

53. It is unclear whether Moody devised the practice of evaluating securities by comparing their price to their earnings, but it appears to have emerged in the second half of the 1920s, and he was one of its earliest practitioners. The term first came into general usage around 1928 or 1929, with indications that it had "become very popular in recent years." George B. Roberts, "The Price-Earnings Ratio as an Index of Stock Prices," *Journal of the American Statistical Association* 24:165, supplement: Proceedings of the American Statistical Association (March 1929): 21–26, quote p. 21.

54. Moody, *The Long Road Home*, 168–69. He remembered the trip beginning with three quiet days of sail. But it was not to last: "[A]bout nine o'clock in the evening of the third day out (July 30th), all deck lights were suddenly extinguished, window curtains were drawn and every porthole on the ship was darkened. The great world war was on!"

55. Moody, *The First 100 Years*, 54–59.

56. Babson, *Actions and Reactions*, 103.

57. Moody, "A Fifty Year Review," 13–14.

58. Ibid., 14.

59. Ibid.

60. Moody, *The First 100 Years*, 60.

61. Moody, "A Fifty Year Review," 15.

62. John Moody, "The Remaking of Europe," *Saturday Evening Post*, October 22, 1921, beginning page 3.

63. John Moody, "Why I Think the Stage Is Set for a Constructive Period in Business," *American Magazine* (September 1922): 14–16.

64. Moody, "A Fifty Year Review," 21.

65. I thank Richard Sylla for these observations. On the rise of Wall Street, see Steve Fraser, *Every Man a Speculator: A History of Wall Street in American Life* (New York: HarperCollins, 2005); and Ott, *When Wall Street Met Main Street: The Quest for an Investors' Democracy* (Cambridge, MA: Harvard University Press, 2011).

66. Moody, "Why I Think the Stage Is Set for a Constructive Period in Business," 14–16.

67. See Richard Sylla, "Investment Banking," in Jackson, *Encyclopedia of New York City*.

68. Porter, unpublished memoir, 6–7; also Moody, "A Fifty Year Review," 20.

69. Moody, "A Fifty Year Review," 19.

70. Ibid., 19.

71. Hardy and Cox, *Forecasting Business Conditions*, 96–107; Givens, "Roger Babson," 235–37.

72. Hardy and Cox, *Forecasting Business Conditions*, 97, quoting Moody.

73. "Technical analysts" are most famous for studying price charts—Benner is a classic example, believing that "God is in prices." The Dow Theory is considered part of technical

analysis. The idea is that since all relevant information is already contained in prices, there is no need to study economic news and business information; everything, all wisdom, is correctly reflected in market prices. Trend analysts also believe that history tends to repeat itself. The fundamental approach was evident in Moody's forecasting techniques, which avoided the use of charts, denied the importance of historical trends, and instead focused on the expectations of corporate executives for profits. On technical and fundamental approaches to investing, see Burton Malkiel, *A Random Walk Down Wall Street* (New York: W. W. Norton, 1973).

74. "Forecasting Security Prices," 244–49. The report, which is not credited to an author, is quoting Paul Clay, economist at Moody's.

75. Moody, *The Railroad Builders*, 1.

76. Moody, *Masters of Capital*, 2.

77. Hardy and Cox, *Forecasting Business Conditions*, 105, quoting Moody from 1925.

78. Garfield V. Cox, *An Appraisal of American Business Forecasts* (Chicago: University of Chicago Press, 1929; a revised edition appeared from the same press in 1930), 66–68, provides a summary of Moody's methods. Moody mentioned this index when making a forecast of the business recession of 1923–24. Moody's was the only major service to correctly predict this downturn.

79. Richard S. Tedlow, Courtney Purrington, and Kim Eric Bettcher, "The American CEO in the Twentieth Century: Demography and Career Path" (HBS working paper #03-097, 2003).

80. F. E. Richter, "The Statistical Study of General Business Conditions," *Bell Telephone Quarterly* 3:4 (October 1924): 248.

81. On Macy's, see "Cheap & Smart," *Fortune Magazine*, May 1930, p. 83; and Ralph Hower, *History of Macy's of New York, 1858–1919: Chapters in the Evolution of the Department Store* (Cambridge, MA: Harvard University Press, 1943).

82. Henry S. Dennison, "Management and the Business Cycle," *Journal of the American Statistical Association* 18:137 (March 1922): 20–31. The article preached the importance of countercyclical business management. "Above all things we do not fire our salesmen during times of depression," wrote Dennison. "The time to fire salesmen, if we are going to fire them at all, is during prosperity when we have more orders than we need. Depression is the time to take on more salesmen, if finances will in any way allow" (30).

83. "Floors Are Leased at 200 Varick Street," *New York Times,* May 20, 1927, p. 34.

84. On the importance of architecture to corporate function and identity in the early twentieth century, see Carol Willis, *Form Follows Finance: Skyscrapers and Skylines in New York and Chicago* (New York: Princeton Architectural Press, 1995); and Daniel Abramson, *Skyscraper Rivals: The AIG Building and the Architecture of Wall Street* (New York: Princeton Architectural Press, 2001).

85. Moody, *The Long Road Home*, 233.

86. Moody, "A Fifty Year Review," 26, 28.

87. Moody, *The Long Road Home*, 213.

88. Stimson, *Moody's: The First Hundred Years*, 108.

89. Moody, *The Long Road Home*, 164.

90. Moody's Investors Service, October 7, 1929, p. 1.

91. Moody, *Weekly Letter*, October 28, 1929, p. 1.

92. Moody, "A Fifty Year Review," 29–30.

93. Moody's Investors Service, *Monthly Analyses of Business Conditions*, November 18, 1929, p. I-241, quoted in Christina D. Romer, "The Great Crash and the Onset of the Great Depression," *Quarterly Journal of Economics* 105:3 (August 1990): 612.

94. Moody's Investors Service, *Monthly Analyses of Business Conditions*, April 24, 1930, p. I-172, quoted in Romer, "The Great Crash and the Onset of the Great Depression," 614.

95. Moody's Investors Service, *Monthly Analyses of Business Conditions*, July 24, 1930, p. I-303-4, quoted in Romer, "The Great Crash and the Onset of the Great Depression," 617.

96. Moody, "A Fifty Year Review," 29–30. "The foregoing figures indicate eloquently enough the dire state we were in by the end of 1931—due so largely to the mistaken policy of investing our surplus cash in 'marketable securities' at the inflated prices of 1929 and early 1930, and then selling most of them out near the bottom of the market in 1931 and 1932."

97. Stimson, *Moody's: The First Hundred Years*, 84.

98. Moody, *Fast by the Road*, 4–5.

99. John Moody, obituary, *New York Times*, February 17, 1958, p. 23.

100. Moody, *The Long Road Home*, 259.

Gallery of Business and Forecasting Charts

1. See Playfair's graphs in, for instance, William Playfair, *An Essay on the National Debt, with Copper Plate Charts, for Comparing Annuities with Perpetual Loans* (London: G.G.J. and J. Robertson, Paternoster-Row, 1787).

2. For Gantt's approach to charts, see his book, *Work, Wages, and Profits* (New York: Engineering Magazine, 1916).

3. Snyder quoted in Karl G. Karsten, *Charts and Graphs: An Introduction to Graphic Methods in the Control and Analysis of Statistics* (New York: Prentice Hall, 1923), p. xxxvii. For contemporary works on business graphs, see Irving Fisher, "The 'Ratio' Chart for Plotting Statistics," *Publications of the American Statistical Association* 15 (1916–17): 577–601; A. R. Palmer, *The Use of Graphs in Commerce & Industry* (London: G. Bell and Sons, 1921); R. P. Falkner, "Uses and Perils of Business Graphics," *Administration* 3 (1922): 52–56; Karsten, *Charts and Graphs*; and H. Gray Funkhouser, "Historical Development of the Graphical Representation of Statistical Data," *Osiris* 3 (1937): 269–404. Three important histories of graphs in this period are Susan Buck-Morss, "Envisioning Capital: Political Economy on Display," *Critical Inquiry* 21:2 (Winter 1995): 434–67; Morgan, "The Technology of Analogical Models," S304–S314; and Alex Preda, "Where Do Analysts Come From? The Case of Financial Chartism," *Sociological Review* (2007): 41–64. On the nature of graphs generally, see Edward R. Tufte, *The Visual Display of Quantitative Information*, 2nd ed. (Cheshire, CT: Graphics Press, 2001).

4. Karsten, *Charts and Graphs*, 684. His ideas took the importance of measurement to the extreme, as in his idea that charts were ways to express abstract ideas simply and cleanly without the emotion of artwork. In one example, Karsten wrote that whereas a painter, depicting a great and majestic battle scene of the Crimean War, might create dramatic canvases of soldiers riding twenty horses on one side, straining against thirty riders on the other, a chart maker would convey the same information in a bar chart, with two bars on one side and three on the other, each representing ten animals.

5. Copeland, "Statistical Indices of Business Conditions," 522–62, provides lists of available statistics.

6. Peter Eisenstadt, "How the Buttonwood Tree Grew: The Making of a New York Stock Exchange Legend," *Prospects* 19 (October 1994): 75–98.

7. On Brookmire, see Givens, "Roger Babson," esp. 80–175. The most important academic writing by James H. Brookmire includes: *The Brookmire Economic Chart Company*; the article on his methodology, "Methods of Business Forecasting Based on Fundamental Statistics," 43–58; and "Graphical Methods in Forecasting Business Conditions," *Magazine of Wall Street* 12:3 (July 1913): 178.

8. On meteorological influences generally, see Preda, "Where Do Analysts Come From?" 40–64.

9. Brookmire, "Methods of Business Forecasting," 44.

10. On Rorty, see Donald Belcher, "Malcolm Churchill Rorty," *Journal of the American Statistical Association* 31:195 (September 1936): 603–4; and "Malcolm Churchill Rorty," in *Biographical Dictionary of American Business Leaders*, ed. John N. Ingham (Westport, CT: Greenwood Press, 1983), 1204–6.

11. "Round Flow of Money Income and Expenditure," in Malcolm Churchill Rorty, *Some Problems in Current Economics* (Chicago: A. W. Shaw Co., 1922), 63.

12. The populations of Massachusetts and California were far more similar (around 4 million people) in 1925 than they are today.

13. On Schumpeter, see Thomas K. McCraw, "Schumpeter's 'Business Cycles' as Business History," *Business History Review* 80:2 (Summer 2006): 231–61. See also Dorfman, *The Economic Mind in American Civilization*, 5:551, in a footnote: "The earliest use of the term 'business cycle' that the author has been able to find before Wesley C. Mitchell's *Business Cycles* (1913) was in the prospectus of one of the first forecasting services, the Financial Graphics Company, New York. In *Description of the Financial Graphics Service* (1910), the term 'financial business cycle' was used. It was stated in terms of the traditional concept of the variation in the supply of gold, primarily in the long run; but more interesting is its glimpse of the real nature of 'a recurring financial business cycle, of clearly defined characteristics though varying somewhat as to time and intensity.'"

14. See also Susan Buck-Morss, "Envisioning Capital: Political Economy on Display," *Critical Inquiry* 21:2 (Winter 1995): 437.

Chapter 4. C. J. Bullock and Warren Persons: The Harvard ABC Chart

1. There is less written about the leaders of the Harvard Economic Service than the other forecasters profiled in this book. Givens, "Roger Babson," provides a discussion of the Harvard Economic Service itself. Morgan, *History of Econometric Ideas*, analyzes the contributions of Warren Persons to econometrics. Two recent articles on the methods of Harvard Economic Society are Giovanni Favero, "Weather Forecast or Rain Dance? Interwar Business Barometers" (working paper, Department of Economics University of Venice, 2007), 1–34 and Tobias F. Roetheli, "Business Forecasting and the Development of Business Cycle Theory," *History of Political Economy* 39:3 (Fall 2007): 481–510. My own article, "The Harvard Economic Service and the Problems of Forecasting," *History of Political Economy* 41:1 (spring 2009): 57–88 also traces the history of the agency. On the influence of the Harvard Economic Service overseas, especially in Germany, see J. Adam Tooze, *Statistics and the German State, 1900–1945: The Making of Modern Economic Knowledge* (Cambridge: Cambridge University Press, 2001). The history of the agency and its leaders is also found in three archival collections

at Harvard: Records of President Abbott Lawrence Lowell, UAI 5.160 (hereafter Lowell Papers) and the Charles J. Bullock Papers, HUG 4245 (hereafter Bullock Papers), both at the Harvard University Archives; and the Office of the Dean (Wallace Brett Donham, 1919–1942), Harvard Business School Archives, Baker Library (hereafter Donham Papers). Some archival material on Persons is found in "Dartmouth College Faculty Roll for General Catalogue," Dartmouth College Library, Rauner Special Collections Library, folder on Warren Persons.

2. Charles J. Bullock, "The Variation of Productive Forces," *Quarterly Journal of Economics* 16:4 (August 1902): 473–513. This article is singled out in Edwin S. Mason, "The Harvard Department of Economics from the Beginning to World War II," *Quarterly Journal of Economics* 97:3 (August 1982): 402, and in Schumpeter's *History of Economic Analysis*, 944, 1165, as Bullock's most significant contribution.

3. Morgan, *History of Econometric Ideas*, 56–63, devoted a section of her book to Persons.

4. This is the subject of McKenzie, *An Engine, Not a Camera*.

5. C. J. Bullock to Lowell, May 22, 1928, Call No. UIA5.160, folder 352, Lowell Papers.

6. Tjalling C. Koopmans, "Measurement without Theory," *Review of Economics and Statistics* 29:3 (August 1947): 161–72.

7. For a lucid account of the distinction between structural and nonstructural forecasting, see Diebold, "The Past, Present, and Future of Macroeconomic Forecasting."

8. Taussig's quote, from 1929, in Mason, "The Harvard Department of Economics from the Beginning to World War II," 415.

9. Mason, "The Harvard Department of Economics from the Beginning to World War II," 383–433. Aside from Frank Taussig, Harvard suffered from the lack of a world-famous economist for much of the 1920s. In 1923, Taussig wrote to Harvard president Abbott Lawrence Lowell: "The department sadly needs men of [high] quality. I am well past middle life, Carver and [Charles J.] Bullock have lost the freshness of their interest in academic work, the younger men are still uncertain." Taussig to Lowell, February 19, 1923, Call No. UIA5.160, folder 352, Lowell Papers.

10. For a discussion of the field of economics in this period, see McCraw, *Prophet of Innovation*, 38–56. See also Geoffrey M. Hodgson, *How Economics Forgot History: The Problem of Historical Specificity in Social Science* (London: Routledge, 2001).

11. Mason, "The Harvard Department of Economics from the Beginning to World War II," 422.

12. William Z. Ripley, *Trusts, Pools, and Corporations* (Boston: Ginn & Co., 1905), *Railroads: Rates and Regulation* (New York: Longmans, Green, 1912) and *Railroads: Finance and Organization* (New York: Longmans, Green, 1915). The interest in business among Harvard historians continued in the next decade. Thomas N. Carver wrote *The Present Economic Revolution in the United States* (Boston: Little, Brown, 1925) on the dramatic growth in stock ownership. There was also Ripley's *Main Street and Wall Street* (Boston: Little, Brown, 1927), which became a best seller. F. W. Taussig wrote *American Business Leaders* (New York: Macmillan, 1932), with C. S. Joslyn.

13. Mason, "The Harvard Department of Economics from the Beginning to World War II," 406–7. Gay had an extraordinary career, becoming the first dean of the Harvard Business School, president and editor of the *New York Evening Post*, and the first president of the National Bureau of Economic Research.

14. For a brief review of Donham's career, see Serge Elisséeff, "Wallace Brett Donham, 1877–1954," *Harvard Journal of Asiatic Studies* 18:1/2 (June 1955): vii–ix.

15. Paul Samuelson, "Paradise Lost and Refound: The Harvard ABC Barometers," *Journal of Portfolio Management* 13:3 (Spring 1987): 7.

16. Mason, "The Harvard Department of Economics from the Beginning to World War II," 407–8.

17. C. J. Bullock, "The Need for Endowment in Economic Research," *Harvard Graduate Magazine* 23:92 (June 1915): 601. Bullock quoted in Edward J. Adzigian, "A Study of the Harvard Economic Society" (master's thesis, Harvard University, 1932), 10.

18. Adzigian, "A Study of the Harvard Economic Society," 3–4.

19. The members of the Harvard Economic Service are listed in the annual reports of the organization, labeled "Report of the Work of the Harvard University Committee on Economic Research." The reports are located in the Lowell Papers, as follows: The annual reports for 1919–22 are in box "Series 1919–1922," folder 310; for 1922–25 are in box "Series 1922–1925," folder 211; and 1925–28 are in box "Series 1925–1928," folder 147 (hereafter cited as "Annual Report" with the date).

20. Mason, "The Harvard Department of Economics from the Beginning to World War II," 414; Adzigian, "A Study of the Harvard Economic Society," 3–4.

21. Annual Report, 1919–1920.

22. "Economic Research at Harvard Recently Aided by $150,000 Grant from the Rockefeller Foundation," *The Harvard Crimson* (January 28, 1930): 1.

23. William Trufant Foster, "Warren Milton Persons," *Journal of the American Statistical Association* 34:206 (June 1939): 412. See also "Dartmouth College Faculty Roll for General Catalogue," Dartmouth College Library, Rauner Special Collections Library, folder on Warren Persons. On the history of tuberculosis, see Katherine Ott, *Fevered Lives: Tuberculosis in American Culture since 1870* (Cambridge, MA: Harvard University Press, 1996).

24. Warren M. Persons, "The Variability in the Distribution of Wealth and Income" (Ph.D. diss., University of Wisconsin–Madison, 1916).

25. Mason, "The Harvard Department of Economics from the Beginning to World War II," 411.

26. Foster, "Warren Milton Persons," 413.

27. Warren M. Persons, "Some Fundamental Concepts of Statistics," *Journal of the American Statistical Association* 19:145 (March 1924): 1–2.

28. Mason, "The Harvard Department of Economics from the Beginning to World War II," 415.

29. Persons, "Construction of a Business Barometer Based upon Annual Data," 739.

30. For Persons's ideas about statistics and its potential contribution to economic theory, see Warren M. Persons, "Statistics and Economic Theory," *Review of Economics Statistics* 7:3 (July 1925): 179–97.

31. Persons, "Construction of a Business Barometer Based upon Annual Data," 739–69, includes comments on other forecasters. There were several differences between the work of Persons and Brookmire. The two used different statistical series in making their forecasts. Both included stock market indexes, commodity prices, banking statistics, deposits, interest rates, and bank loans. Brookmire included more variables, including those on railroads and pig-iron prices.

32. Annual Report, 1921–22, p. 3.

33. Arthur Harrison Cole, *The Vanderblue Collection of Smithiana* (Boston: Kress Library of Economic Literature, Harvard Business School, 1948).

34. Between 1919 and 1928, Persons published 34 articles in the *Review of Economic Statistics* (26 of which he was the sole author). In 1919 he published: "Outline of the Method," 1:1 (January 1919): 37; "The Index: A Statement of Results," 1:2 (April 1919): 111–17; "Title: II. The Method Used," 1:2 (April 1919): 117–39; "III. Application of the Method to the Data, (A) The Individual Series," 1:2 (April 1919): 139–81; and "IV. Application of the Method to the Data, (B) The Groups of Series," 1:2 (April 1919): 182–205. He also published "A Non-Technical Explanation of the Index of General Business Conditions," *Review of Economic Statistics* 2:2 (February 1920): 39-48.

35. The sources for these data included the *Commercial and Financial Chronicle, Iron Age, Bradstreet's, New York Journal of Commerce, Monthly Summary of Foreign Commerce of the US, Babson's Desk Sheet*, the *Federal Reserve Bulletin and Bulletin of Bureau of Labor Secretary*, and *Wall Street Journal*. See Persons, "Outline of Method," 37, and Persons, "A Non-Technical Explanation of the Index of General Business Conditions," 39–48.

36. Fisher, "Our Unstable Dollar and the So-Called Business Cycle," 181.

37. London and Cambridge Economic Service, *Monthly Bulletin*, Introductory Number (January 1923): 4.

38. Persons, "The Index: A Statement of Results," 111–14. See also Hardy and Cox, *Forecasting Business Conditions*, 75, and Givens, "Roger Babson," 143.

39. Persons, "II. The Method Used," 117–39. An image of the light box appears on p. 121.

40. Warren Persons, *Measuring and Forecasting General Business Conditions* (Boston: American Institute of Finance, 1922), 23–24. For further discussion, see Jacky Fayolle, "The Study of Cycles and Business Analysis in the History of Economic Thought," in *Monographs of Official Statistics: Papers and Proceedings of the Colloquium on the History of Business-Cycle Analysis* (Luxembourg: Office for Official Publications of the European Communities, 2003), 13–14.

41. Persons, "I. The Index: A Statement of Results," 114. Group A, an index of speculation, comprised four items: the yield of ten railroad bonds; prices of industrial stocks; prices of twenty railroad stocks; and New York bank clearings. Group B, an index of business activity, comprised five series: pig-iron production, bank clearings outside of New York, Bradstreet's prices, Bureau of Labor prices, and reserves of New York banks. Group C, an index of banking, included four series: the rate on four- to six-month paper, the rate on sixty- to ninety-day paper, loans made by New York banks, and deposits in New York banks.

42. Persons, "A Non-Technical Explanation of the Index of General Business Conditions," esp. p. 48. See also Hardy and Cox, *Forecasting Business Conditions*, 79.

43. Quoted in Givens, "Roger Babson," 224. Original source: Harvard University Committee on Economic Research, *Scientific Business Forecasting* (Cambridge, MA: Harvard University, 1923), 4–5.

44. Persons, "A Non-Technical Explanation of the Index of General Business Conditions," 40.

45. Mason, "The Harvard Department of Economics from the Beginning to World War II," 416; Persons, "A Non-Technical Explanation of the Index of General Business Conditions," 40.

46. To the extent that Persons did allude to causality, he invoked Fisher and pointed to the idea that cycles occurred due to fluctuations in short-term interest rates, as well as responses from speculators and businesspeople. Persons, "A Non-Technical Explanation of the Index of General Business Conditions," 39–48. See also Fayolle, "The Study of Cycles and Business Analysis in the History of Economic Thought," 13.

47. Persons, "A Non-Technical Explanation of the Index of General Business Conditions," 46.

48. Christina D. Romer, "World War I and the Postwar Depression: A Reinterpretation Based on Alternative Estimates of GNP," *Journal of Monetary Economics* 22:1 (1988): 91–115.

49. Annual Report, 1919–20, p. 1.

50. Samuelson, "Paradise Lost & Refound," 4–9.

51. Annual Report, 1921–22, p. 1.

52. Annual Report, 1919–20, p. 2.

53. Annual Report, 1923–24, 1–3, and 1924–25, 2–3.

54. Annual Report, 1921–22, 8–9.

55. Annual Report, 1921–22, inserted into annual report at end.

56. Bullock to Keynes, December 7, 1922, HUG 4245, March 31, 1923–Letter to Keynes, box "Corr. A–K," Bullock Papers.

57. Annual Reports, 1921–22 and 1923–24.

58. Annual Report, 1924–25, 3–5.

59. Annual Report, 1926–27, 4, 7–8.

60. Samuelson, "Paradise Lost & Refound," 5.

61. It was not the first or last time the school's students would be involved in entrepreneurial adventure, of course: one need only think of Mark Zuckerberg and Facebook, for instance, or of Bill Gates.

62. Babson, *Actions and Reactions*, 135, 189.

63. Moody, "A Fifty Year Review," 19.

64. Annual Report, 1919–20, 1–2.

65. See Marcel Boumans, "Tinbergen's Business Cycle Analysis," in *Monographs of Official Statistics: Papers and Proceedings of the Colloquium on the History of Business-Cycle Analysis* (Luxembourg: Office for Official Publications of the European Communities, 2003), 113.

66. Michel Armatte, "Cycles and Barometers: Historical Insights into the Relationship between an Object and Its Measurement," in *Monographs of Official Statistics: Papers and Proceedings of the Colloquium on the History of Business-Cycle Analysis* (Luxembourg: Office for Official Publications of the European Communities, 2003), 64. See also Tooze, *Statistics and the German State*, 107.

67. Both Lucien March and Ernst Wagemann varied the type of data used. See Mary S. Morgan, "Business Cycle: Representation and Measurement," in *Monographs of Official Statistics: Papers and Proceedings of the Colloquium on the History of Business-Cycle Analysis* (Luxembourg: Office for Official Publications of the European Communities, 2003), 178–79. See also Tooze, *Statistics and the German State*, 107–9.

68. Annual Report 1921–22, 2–3.

69. Robert Skidelsky, *John Maynard Keynes*, vol. 2, *The Economist as Savior, 1920–1937* (London: Macmillan, 1992), 102–6.

70. Annual Report, 1921–22, pp. 4–5 and Annual Report, 1923–24, p. 10.

71. Skidelsky, *Economist as Savior*, 106; J. Adam Tooze, "Macroeconomics Denied: German Business-Cycle Research, 1925–1945," in *Monographs of Official Statistics: Papers and Proceedings of the Colloquium on the History of Business-Cycle Analysis* (Luxembourg: Office for Official Publications of the European Communities, 2003), 195.

72. Keynes to Bullock, December 8, 1922, HUG 4245, box "Corr. A–K," folder "Keynes," Bullock Papers.

73. Annual Report, 1922–23, 5, 10.

74. London and Cambridge Economic Service, *Monthly Bulletin*, Introductory Number (January 1923): 4.

75. Bullock to Keynes, May 1, 1923, HUG 4245, box "Corr. A–K," folder "Keynes," Bullock Papers.

76. Keynes to Bullock, February 11, 1925, HUG 4245, box "Corr. A–K," folder "Keynes," Bullock Papers.

77. Bullock to Keynes, February 29, 1924, HUG 4245, box "Corr. A–K," folder "Keynes," Bullock Papers.

78. Bullock to Keynes, March 4, 1925, HUG 4245, box "Corr. A–K," folder "Keynes," Bullock Papers.

79. Bullock to Keynes, October 25, 1928, HUG 4245, box "Corr. A–K," folder "Keynes," Bullock Papers.

80. See Michel Armatte, "Lucien March (1859–1933): Une statistique mathématique sans probabilité?" *Journal Electronique d'Histoire des Probabilités et de la Statistique* 1:1 (March 2005): 2–4, 7–8. March's publication of the index and research was concurrent with his active advocacy of eugenics, which began in approximately 1912. In 1913, he participated in the foundation of the French Society for Eugenics and became the organization's treasurer.

81. Annual Report, 1922–23, p. 10; Bullock described his correspondence with March in a letter to Keynes, March 31, 1923, HUG 4245, box "Corr. A–K," folder "Keynes," Bullock Papers.

82. Annual Report, 1923–24, pp. 3, 7.

83. Ibid., 12; Ottolenghi mentioned in Annual Report, 1924–25, p. 8.

84. Annual Report, 1925–26, 6–7.

85. J. Adam Tooze, "Weimar's Statistical Economics: Ernst Wagemann, the Reich's Statistical Office, and the Institute for Business-Cycle Research, 1925–1933," *Economic History Review* 52:3 (August 1999): 523–43, p. 525.

86. Annual Report, 1924–25, 8–9.

87. Bullock to Keynes, March 27, 1930, HUG 4245, box "Corr. A–K," folder "Keynes," Bullock Papers.

88. On Wagemann, see Tooze, *Statistics and the German State*, esp. p. 111.

89. Bullock to Keynes, March 27, 1930.

90. Annual Report, 1925–26, p. 7. On German indexes done at Harvard, see Emerson Wirt Axe and Harold M. Flinn, "An Index of General Business Conditions for Germany, 1898–1914," *Review of Economics and Statistics* 7:4 (October 1925): 263–87.

91. Tooze, *Statistics and the German State*, 107. See also "Germans Adopt Harvard Plans in Trade Study," *Boston Transcript*, February 1927, n.p., HUG 4245, box "Corr. L–Z," folder "Wagemann," Bullock Papers.

92. Tooze, *Statistics and the German State*, 109.

93. Ibid., 126. See also Tooze, "Macroeconomics Denied."

94. Tooze, *Statistics and the German State*, 16.

95. G. R. Steele, *The Economics of Friedrich Hayek* (New York: St. Martin's Press, 1993), 3.

96. Alan Ebenstein, *Hayek's Journey: The Mind of Friedrich Hayek* (New York: Palgrave Macmillan, 2003), 49–50.

97. Von Hayek to Bullock, April 14, 1927, HUG 4245, box "Corr. A–K," folder H, Harvard University Archives.

98. Annual Report, 1926–27, p. 9.

99. In February 1928, Von Hayek expressed a desire for closer collaboration between Österreichisches of Vienna and the Harvard Economic Society. Von Hayek to Bullock, February 28, 1928, HUG 4245, box "Corr. A–K," folder H, Bullock Papers.

100. Vincent Barnett, *Kondratiev and the Dynamics of Economic Development: Long Cycles and Industrial Growth in Historical Context* (New York: St. Martin's Press, 1998), 88.

101. Ibid., 89–93. See correspondence between Taussig and Kondratiev: Taussig to Kondratiev, January 13, 1925, and March 9, 1927, Call No. 4823.5, box K, folder 1923–29, Lowell Archives. Also see letters from Harvard librarian T. Franklin Currier to Taussig, October 5, 1927, and September 20, 1927, thanking him for Russian books from Kondratiev (HUG 4823.5, box L, Lowell Archives).

102. "The Problem of Foresight," in *The Works of Nikolai D. Kondratiev*, vol. 3, ed. Natalia Makasheva, Warren J. Samuels, and Vincent Barnett, trans. Stephen S. Wilson (London: Pickering and Chatto, 1998), 249, 247.

103. Leonid Grinin, Tessaleno Devezas, and Andrey Korotayev, "Introduction: Kondratieff's Mystery," in *Kondratieff Waves: Dimensions and Prospects at the Dawn of the 21st Century* (Volgograd: Uchitel Publishing House, 2012), 5–22.

104. Annual Report, 1927–28, p. 6.

105. Ibid., 6–7.

106. Annual Report, 1928–1929, p. 8.

107. Nicholas Wapshott, *Keynes-Hayek: The Clash That Defined Economics* (New York: Norton, 2011), 76.

108. Ray Vance, *Business and Investment Forecasting: Forecasting Methods and Their Application in Practical Use* (New York: Brookmire Economic Service, 1922), 77–79.

109. Roger W. Babson, "Business Forecasting and Its Relation to Modern Selling," *Annals of the American Academy of Political and Social Science* 115 (September 1924): 147.

110. See Karsten, "The Harvard Business Indexes," 399–418.

111. Ibid., 407–8. Others interpreted the Harvard data in new ways. See, for instance, John A. Crabtree, *Thoughts on Business Forecasting: Being Reflections on the Practice of Business Forecasting and a Challenge to the Harvard University Committee on Economic Research* (Walsall, England: Lincoln Works, 1928), a twenty-page booklet giving the author's own ideas about Harvard's forecasting curves.

112. Karl Karsten to Abbott Lawrence Lowell, August 9, 1926, Call No. UIA5.160, Lowell Papers.

113. C. J. Bullock to All Members of the Harvard University Committee on Economic Research, January 21, 1927, box 36, folder 15, "Harvard University Economic Service, Sept. 1921–37," Donham Papers.

114. C. J. Bullock, W. M. Persons, and W. L. Crum, "The Construction and Interpretation of the Harvard Index of Business Conditions," *Review of Economics and Statistics* 19:2 (April 1927): 74–92. That fall, Alvin Hansen, a prominent economist at the University of Wisconsin–Madison who came to Harvard in 1937 and popularized Keynesianism in the United States, also published a rebuke of Karsten's interpretation. Alvin H. Hansen, "Karsten's Interpretation of the Harvard Business Indexes," *Journal of the American Statistical Association* 22:159 (September 1927): 367–69. Subsequent articles pointed to a "quadrature hoax." See Sasuly, "Irving Fisher and Social Science," 255–78, who wrote, "Even the Edge-Karsten 'Quadrature' correlation hoax rendered some service to science." See Joseph Schumpeter, *Business Cycles: A Theoretical, Historical, and Statistical Analysis of the Capitalist Process* (New

York: McGraw-Hill, 1939), 1:181; and Karl G. Karsten, "The Theory of Quadrature in Economics," *Journal of the American Statistical Association* 19 (March 1924): 14–29. For more on the quadrature hoax, see Milton Friedman and Max Sasuly, review of Edward R. Dewey and Edwin F. Dakin, *Cycles: The Science of Prediction* in *Journal of American Statistical Association* 43:241 (March 1948): 139–45.

115. On Karsten, see also Boumans, "Tinbergen's Business Cycle Analysis," 109–26.

116. Oskar Morgenstern, "The Collaboration between Oskar Morgenstern and John von Neumann on the Theory of Games," *Journal of Economic Literature* 14:3 (September 1976): 805–16, quotes 805–6.

117. Quote from *Studies in Business Administration* 1:1 (University of Chicago, 1929), 6. Summary of Morgenstern's book based on Robert J. Leonard, "From Parlor Games to Social Science: Von Neumann, Morgenstern, and the Creation of Game Theory, 1928–1944," *Journal of Economic Literature* 33: 2 (June 1995): 730–61. See also Arthur W. Marget, "Morgenstern on the Methodology of Economic Forecasting," *Journal of Political Economy* 37: 3 (June 1929): 312–39. Despite Morgenstern's skepticism about the entire enterprise of business forecasting, he and his Instituts für Konjunkturforschung in Vienna were part of Harvard Economic Service's consortium of international partners and correspondents. See Harvard Economic Society, Annual Report, 1926–1927, p. 9.

118. Oskar Morgenstern, "Perfect Foresight and Economic Equilibrium," originally published in *Zeitschrift für Nationalökonomie*, vol. 6, part 3 (1935), trans. Frank H. Knight, reprinted in *Selected Economic Writings of Oskar Morgenstern*, ed. Andrew Schotter (New York: New York University Press, 1975), 169–83, quotes 173–74.

119. Martin Shubik, "Morgenstern, Oskar (1902–1977)," in Steven N. Durlauf and Lawrence E. Blume, eds., *The New Palgrave: A Dictionary of Economics* (London: Palgrave Macmillan, 1987).

120. Lowell was a complex personality. While promoting a more democratic environment in some ways, he also tried to limit the number of Jewish students enrolled at the school and bar African Americans from the freshman halls.

121. A. Lawrence Lowell to Harvard alumnus B. H. Dibblee, October 29, 1923, UAI 5.160, box "Series 1922–25," folder 211, Lowell Papers.

122. Letter to members, January 13, 1928, series 1928–1930, folder 148, Lowell Papers.

123. Lowell to Bullock, June 12, 1928, series 1925–1928, folder 147, Lowell Papers.

124. Annual Report, 1927–28, p. 3.

125. "Warren Persons, Statistics Expert," *New York Times*, October 14, 1937, p. 25.

126. *New York Times*, April 26, 1929, p. 8.

127. Annual Report, Harvard Economic Society, 1928, 1–2.

128. First Annual Report, Harvard Economic Society, 1928, 1–4.

129. Second Annual Report of the President of the Harvard Economic Society, 1929, folder "Second Annual Report of the President of the Harvard Economic Society," series 1928–1930, folder 148, Lowell Papers.

130. Harvard Economic Society, *Weekly Letter*, November 16, 1929, quoted in Romer, "The Great Crash and the Onset of the Great Depression," 612. After the October 1929 crash, the society continued to rely on its forecasting model, the three-curve "Index of General Business Conditions," to forecast business conditions. The three charts had been simplified over the years and since 1927 comprised fewer data series, as follows: (A, speculation) price of industrial stocks, price of railroad stocks; (B, business) bank debits, selected cities outside New York; wholesale commodity prices; and (C, money) rates on short-term money.

131. Harvard Economic Society, *Weekly Letter*, November 30, 1929, p. 281.

132. Harvard Economic Society, *Weekly Letter*, December 21, 1929, p. 308.

133. Harvard Economic Society, *Weekly Letter*, September 20, 1930, p. 233. See also Givens, "Roger Babson," 359.

134. Harvard Economic Service, *Weekly Letter*, November 15, 1930, p. 279. See also Givens, "Roger Babson," 359.

135. Letter from William P. Everts, '00, *Harvard Alumni Bulletin*, January 8, 1931, 463–64.

136. Ibid.

137. Press release in series 1930–1933, folder 265, Lowell Papers.

138. "Harvard Denies Onus for Trade Predictions," *New York Times*, January 11, 1931, p. 52. See also "Harvard on Forecasts," *Wall Street Journal*, January 13, 1931, p. 10.

139. Bullock to Lowell, January 14, 1931, series 1930–1933, folder 265, Lowell Papers.

140. Harvard Economic Society, *Weekly Letter*, August 22, 1931, p. 152.

141. Letter to Members and Subscribers, November 1931, series 1930–1933, folder 265, Lowell Papers.

142. Bullock to Lowell, November 16, 1931, series 1930–1933, folder 265, Lowell Papers.

143. Mason, "The Harvard Department of Economics from the Beginning to World War II," 418.

144. C. J. Bullock and W. L. Crum, "The Harvard Index of Economic Conditions: Interpretation and Performance, 1919–1931," *Review of Economics and Statistics* 14:3 (August 1932): 137.

145. Bullock to Hugh Bullock, February 8, 1934, "Corr. A–K," folder "Bullock, Hugh," Bullock Papers.

146. Foster, "Warren Milton Persons," 412.

147. Bullock to Charles Bullock, February 19, 1927, Corr. A–K, folder "Bullock, Charles," Bullock Papers.

148. Bullock to Wagenfuhr, October 23, 1934, box "Corr. L–Z," file "Wagenfuhr," Bullock Papers.

149. Bullock to F. L. Lipman, Chairman of Wells Fargo, March 26, 1935, box "Corr. L–Z," file "Lipman," Bullock Papers.

150. See obituary in *Review of Economics and Statistics* 57:1 (February 1975): vi–vii, by John Kenneth Galbraith.

151. Mason, "The Harvard Department of Economics from the Beginning to World War II," 418.

152. Bullock to Lipman, March 26, 1935.

153. Schumpeter, *Business Cycles*, 1:5.

154. Schumpeter, *History of Economic Analysis*, 183, 944, 1165. Schumpeter also believed that the chart was correct: "The fact is that the barometer curves indicated the approaching break in 1929 clearly enough—the trouble was that the interpreters of the curves either would not believe their own methods or else would not take what they believed to be a serious responsibility in predicting depression."

155. Morgan, *History of Econometric Ideas*, 60–61.

156. See Samuelson, "Paradise Lost & Refound," 11.

157. Garfield V. Cox, *An Appraisal of Business Forecasts* (Chicago: University of Chicago Press, 1929), 42–43.

158. Ibid.

159. Derek Bok, *Universities in the Marketplace: The Commercialization of Higher Education* (Princeton: Princeton University Press, 2003).

Chapter 5. Wesley Mitchell and Herbert Hoover: Forecasting as Policy

1. Mitchell quoted in Alchon, *The Invisible Hand of Planning*, 106. The quote is from "Meeting of the Economists with Members of the Committee on the Business Cycle," December 28, 1922, to discuss the tentative draft of the committee's report. Alchon's book remains the best source on Herbert Hoover's efforts at planning and the group he assembled to help him, including Mitchell. Important sources for this chapter were the Wesley Clair Mitchell Papers, 1898–1953, Archival Collections, Rare Book & Manuscript, Butler Library, Columbia University Libraries (hereafter Mitchell Papers); the Herbert Hoover Papers, Herbert Hoover Presidential Library-Museum, West Branch, IA (hereafter Hoover Papers); and the Franklin D. Roosevelt Presidential Library and Museums, Hyde Park, New York (hereafter FDR Papers). The three-volume set, *The Memoirs of Herbert Hoover*, vol. 2, *The Cabinet and the Presidency*, published by Macmillan in 1951, helped provide Hoover's reassessment of his years in office.

2. Quoted in Mark C. Smith, *Social Science in the Crucible: The American Debate over Objectivity and Purpose, 1918–1941* (Durham: Duke University Press, 1994), 50.

3. Joseph Schumpeter, "Wesley Clair Mitchell (1874–1948)," *Quarterly Journal of Economics* 64:1 (February 1950): 155.

4. Alchon, *The Invisible Hand of Planning*, chapter 6, "The Business Cycle Report and Its Aftermath, 1922–1923, 91–111, esp. p. 106. See also Evan B. Metcalf, "Secretary Hoover and the Emergence of Macroeconomic Management," *Business History Review* 49:1 (Spring 1975): 60–80.

5. See Pietruska, "Propheteering."

6. Patrick Hughes, *A Century of Weather Service: A History of the Birth and Growth of the National Weather Service, 1870–1970* (New York: Gordon and Breach, 1970).

7. *Yearbook of the United States Department of Agriculture, 1897* (Washington, DC: GPO, 1898), 265.

8. United States Dept. of Agriculture Statistical Reporting Service, *The Story of U.S. Agricultural Estimates* (Washington, DC: GPO, 1969), 56.

9. Committee of the President's Conference on Unemployment, *Business Cycles and Unemployment* (New York: McGraw-Hill, 1923), vi.

10. Quoted in Alchon, *The Invisible Hand of Planning*, 87.

11. Ibid., 91–111, esp. p. 107.

12. The dedication ceremony was held in October 1892, though the fair did not open to the public until May 1893.

13. Mitchell, *Two Lives*, 81.

14. John Maurice Clark, "Thorstein Bundy Veblen: 1857–1929," *American Economic Review* 19:4 (December 1929): 742–45.

15. Veblen's quantitative work included "The Price of Wheat since 1867," *Journal of Political Economy* 1:1 (December 1892): 68–103, which included charts of the ups and downs of prices in this commodity; and "The Food Supply and the Price of Wheat," *Journal of Political Economy* 1:3 (June 1893): 365–79, which included some statistics-based forecasts.

16. Mitchell, *Two Lives*, 305.

17. Ibid., 176. Mitchell's turn to statistics was also a way to defend Veblen's work. "This feeling has been growing upon me as I have realized how slight an impression Veblen's work has made upon other economists," Mitchell wrote to his wife in 1909. "To me he seems straight and clear; but when others contest his conclusions I often find that the only real answer lies in doing a lot of work with statistics—work which Veblen has not performed."

18. Wesley C. Mitchell, *A History of Greenbacks, with Special Reference to the Economic Consequences of Their Issue, 1862–1865* (Chicago: University of Chicago Press, 1903).

19. Mitchell, *Two Lives*, 95.

20. Ibid., 98; also on p. 98: In a later letter to Edwin F. Gay, Mitchell explained the origins of his interest in economic fluctuations: "What happened as nearly as I can recall is that I could not formulate a satisfactory account of the greenback phenomena without knowing a great deal more about oscillations in business activity. Nor could I fall in with the practices of many writers upon the greenback period of accounting for the oscillations of activity in terms of changes in the purchasing power of greenback dollars. It seemed to me that the changes in greenback prices were due, in part at least, to alterations in trade conditions which had a non-monetary origin."

21. See Wesley C. Mitchell, *Business Cycles* (Berkeley: University of California Press, 1913).

22. Ibid., 17–18. Mitchell also wrote approvingly of some of Fisher's efforts to determine the money supply (300–309).

23. Daniel Breslau, "Economics Invents the Economy: Mathematics, Statistics, and Models in the Work of Irving Fisher and Wesley Mitchell," *Theory and Society* 32:3 (June 2003): 379–411, discusses the use of the word "economy" by Mitchell and Fisher.

24. Smith, *Social Science in the Crucible*, 124.

25. Mitchell, *Business Cycles*, 587.

26. Mitchell in 1943, quoted by Dorfman, *The Economic Mind in American Civilization*, 4:361.

27. Mitchell, *Two Lives*, quoting Burns's review in 1949, p. 291.

28. Warren Persons, review of Wesley C. Mitchell, *Business Cycles*, in *Quarterly Journal of Economics* 28:4 (August 1914): 796. For another significant review, see A. C. Pigou, review of Wesley C. Mitchell, *Business Cycles*, in *Economic Journal* 24:93 (March 1914): 78–81. Pigou wrote, the "great value of [the work] lies in its realism and concreteness" (81).

29. Mitchell's articles during this time include "The British Board of Trade's Investigations into Cost of Living," *Quarterly Journal of Economics* 23:2 (February 1909): 345–50; "The Decline in the Ratio of Banking Capital to Liabilities," *Quarterly Journal of Economics* 23:4 (August 1909): 697–713; "The Rationality of Economic Activity: I," *Journal of Political Economy* 18:2 (February 1910): 97–113; "The Rationality of Economic Activity," *Journal of Political Economy* 18:3 (March 1910): 197–216; and "The Prices of American Stocks: 1890–1909," *Journal of Political Economy* 18:5 (May 1910): 345–80.

30. Mitchell, *Two Lives*, 174, 170. In 1910, when yet another offer was made through economist Frank W. Taussig, Mitchell declined it on the grounds of this cultural conflict. When President Lowell was told about Mitchell's reply, he wrote: "I think he is perfectly right in what he says about the atmosphere of Cambridge, and I have been grieved at it for many years. Our tendency, unconsciously, has been to value erudition above production; and this has been fostered." Mitchell, *Two Lives*, 175.

31. Mitchell, *Two Lives*, 241–42.

32. The two speeches are Wesley C. Mitchell, "Statistics and Government," *Publications of the American Statistical Association* 16:125 (March 1919): 223–35; and Irving Fisher, "Economists in the Public Service," *American Economic Review* 9:1 (March 1919): 5–21. Mitchell's talk was about the wartime growth of statistical agencies and his plea that the Central Bureau of Planning and Statistics be continued. Fisher's was about using economics to solve the world's problems. "[T]he world is far more open-minded, more expectant, and more desirous of getting at the real truth of things today than ever before," he wrote (21).

33. Mitchell, "Statistics and Government," 228, 234.

34. F. Y. Edgeworth remarked on Fisher's use of these terms in his review of Fisher's "Mathematical Investigations in the Theory of Value and Prices," 109.

35. Breslau, "Economics Invents the Economy," 379–411. See also Howard Sherman, "The Business Cycle Theory of Wesley Mitchell," *Journal of Economic Issues* 35:1 (March 2001): 85–97. Sherman wrote: "Whereas all neoclassical theory is stated in terms of eternally true laws, Mitchell stated an evolutionary theory. Whereas all neoclassical business-cycle theories are exogenous, relying on external shocks to the economy, Mitchell stated an endogenous theory, based on the internal dynamics of capitalism. Whereas neoclassical theories are deduced from unproven psychological axioms, Mitchell builds his theory from inductive generalities gained from empirical research" (85).

36. Mitchell, *Two Lives*, 240.

37. On the early history of NBER, see Solomon Fabricant, "Toward a Firmer Basis of Economic Policy: The Founding of the National Bureau of Economic Research" (working paper, National Bureau of Economic Research, 1984). On Rorty, see Malcolm C. Rorty, *Some Problems in Current Economics* (Chicago: A. W. Shaw Company, 1922), which contains some biographical information.

38. *Income in the United States, Its Amount, and Distribution, 1909–1919* (New York: National Bureau of Economic Research, 1921).

39. Fabricant, "Towards a Firmer Basis of Economic Policy," 3, on NBER's mission. The broader transition to quantitative methods is discussed in Roy E. Weintraub, *How Economics Became a Quantitative Science* (Durham: Duke University Press, 2002); Bernstein, *A Perilous Progress*; and McCraw, *Prophet of Innovation*, 217–22, on one economist's embrace of mathematical methods.

40. Fabricant, "Towards a Firmer Basis of Economic Policy," 6–7, describes the aims of NBER in terms of distributing data. Breslau, "Economics Invents the Economy," 399–403.

41. See *New York Evening Post*, October 17, 1921, p. 1.

42. Hoover, *Memoirs*, vol. 2, *The Cabinet and the Presidency*, vi.

43. Jeremy Mouat and Ian Phimister, "The Engineering of Herbert Hoover," *Pacific Historical Review* 77:4 (November 2008): 553–84, an overview of Hoover's early business career.

44. Joseph Brandes, *Herbert Hoover and Economic Diplomacy: Department of Commerce Policy, 1921–1928* (Pittsburgh: University of Pittsburgh Press, 1962), 22, on Hoover as a national figure.

45. Hoover, *Memoirs*, vol. 2, *The Cabinet and the Presidency*, 4.

46. Ibid., 30–31, on the industrial conference of 1920.

47. George Soule, *Prosperity Decade: From War to Depression, 1917–1929* (New York: Rinehart, 1947), 96–100.

48. Hoover, *Memoirs*, vol. 2, *The Cabinet and the Presidency*, 42.

49. Historian Joseph Brandes wrote, "An examination of the Hoover program in the 1920's necessarily reflects on the decade's economic optimism and business-orientation" (*Herbert Hoover and Economic Diplomacy*, x).

50. John M. Barry, *Rising Tide: The Great Mississippi Flood of 1927 and How It Changed America* (New York: Simon and Schuster, 1997).

51. Hoover, *Memoirs*, vol. 2, *The Cabinet and the Presidency*, 44.

52. See Dorfman, *The Economic Mind in American Civilization*, 4:368. "The basis of the problem was no longer considered a matter for the affected individual but rather a subject for social (including government) action," wrote Dorfman.

53. Brandes, *Herbert Hoover and Economic Diplomacy*, 20, provides a list of publications. For some contemporary sources, see "American Industry Acknowledges Its Debt to Herbert Hoover," *Industrial Management* 71 (April 1926): 199; and *How to Use Current Business Statistics* (Washington, DC: GPO, 1928), which was put together by Mortimer B. Lane.

54. Hoover, *Memoirs*, vol. 2, *The Cabinet and the Presidency*, 176.

55. Herbert Hoover, *American Individualism* (Garden City, NY: Doubleday, 1922), 1; Alchon, *The Invisible Hand of Planning*, 80. In this view, proper forecasting could lessen class conflict: Hoover's argument that both labor and management should receive recognition as actors who can stabilize the economy, and who should be equipped with a rational organizational and informational apparatus to do so, pointed to a different balance between manager-led and worker-led reform than that promoted by (some of) the private forecasters, who were as a body less interested in questions of class conflict. See also Robert Zeigler, "Labor, Progressivism, and Herbert Hoover in the 1920s," *Wisconsin Magazine of History* 58:3 (Spring 1975): 196–208.

56. See Alchon, *The Invisible Hand of Planning*, 80, who includes Mitchell's notes of Hoover's views expressed during a Business Cycle Committee meeting.

57. Herbert Hoover, foreword to *Business Cycles and Unemployment*, v. Hoover's initial experience in trying to mitigate unemployment came when Warren Harding called for a conference on the subject when four to five million people were unemployed. The President's Conference on Unemployment met in September 1921. It was a combination of businessmen, labor leaders, economists, and statisticians. It proposed an "exhaustive investigation" be made of the causes of unemployment and "methods of stabilizing business and industry so as to prevent the vast waves of suffering which result from the valleys in the so-called business cycle."

58. Dennison, "Management and the Business Cycle," 20–31.

59. Mitchell, *Two Lives*, 365.

60. Report quoted in Alchon, *The Invisible Hand of Planning*, 107.

61. The report was sent to Hoover as an enclosure with a letter from Babson to Hoover dated February 4, 1922, box "1921–27 & undated," folder "Commerce Papers—Babson, Roger W.," Hoover Papers. Babson's seventeen-page report (typed, unpublished, dated January 21, 1922), was coauthored with Clarence N. Stone. Its full title is "The Growing Demand for Organization of Government Statistics."

62. Oswald W. Knauth, "Statistical Indexes of Business Conditions and Their Uses," in Committee of the President's Conference on Unemployment, *Business Cycles and Unemployment*, 376.

63. One of Mitchell's former colleagues from the University of Chicago, Garfield Cox, published a study that attempted a systematic analysis of accuracy the forecasting industry as

it stood in the 1920s. As discussed later in this book, Cox's report concluded that forecasts, done by Babson, Moody, the Harvard Economic Service, and others, had often been helpful to customers. But Cox did find that forecasters generally had far less success predicting downturns than upturns and hence tended to be overly optimistic in their forecasts. Cox, *An Appraisal of American Business Forecasts* (1929).

64. Cox, *An Appraisal of American Business Forecasts* (1929), 42–43.

65. Wesley C. Mitchell, "Accountants and Economics with Reference to the Business Cycle," *Journal of Accountancy* 25:3 (March 1923): 167.

66. See, in the *New York Evening Post*, "The Outlook of 1921 as Seen by Bankers, Business Men and Economists," December 31, 1920, section 3, part I, p. 2; "Present Facts and Past Experience Indicate Revival Is Now at Hand," October 17, 1921, pp. 1, 13; "Business Revival Expected to Gather Momentum in Immediate Future," October 18, 1921, pp. 1, 10; "Business Making Progress in Positive Phase of Cycle," December 31, 1921, section 2, part I, p. 1; "Business Revival Shows Signs of Developing into Prosperity," December 30, 1922, section 2, part I, pp. 1, 9; and "Business during 1924 Likely to Be Generally Satisfactory," December 31, 1923, section 2, part I, pp. 1–2. Mitchell also wrote on the subject in "How You Can Use 'The Business Cycle,'" *System* 5:40 (1921): 683–85, 767–68.

67. Abraham Hirsch, "Reconstruction in Economics: The Work of Wesley Clair Mitchell" (Ph.D. diss., Columbia University, 1958), 121–24. The original source is "Unemployment and Business Fluctuation," *American Economic Review* 5:8 (1923): supplement, p. 47.

68. See Dorfman, *The Economic Mind in American Civilization*, 4:552. See Hirsch, "Reconstruction in Economics," 121–24, for a discussion of Mitchell's forecasts. See, in the *New York Evening Post*, "The Outlook of 1921"; "Present Facts and Past Experience"; "Business Revival Expected to Gather Momentum in Immediate Future"; "Business Making Progress in Positive Phase of Cycle"; "Business Revival Shows Signs of Developing into Prosperity"; and "Business during 1924 Likely to be Generally Satisfactory."

69. Hirsch, "Reconstruction in Economics," 126.

70. Ibid., 126; original source: "Unemployment and Business Fluctuations," 17–18.

71. Ibid., 127.

72. Alchon, *The Invisible Hand of Planning*, 108–9.

73. Ibid., 94. Historian Guy Alchon noted, "Donham ... was upset with what he may have regarded as the NBER's arrogance in taking on such a large subject in a six-month study and with Mitchell's insistence that the research had broken new ground" (95).

74. Donham to Crocker, October 27, 1922, B11 F18, Dean's Office, Harvard Business School, Donham Papers.

75. Alchon, *The Invisible Hand of Planning*, 6–7.

76. Ibid., 129, 132.

77. *How to Use Current Business Statistics*, vi.

78. It included Hoover, as chairman; the University of Chicago economist Adolph C. Miller; General Electric's chairman Owen Young; General Motor's John J. Raskob; Clarence M. Woolley; and Arch W. Shaw, publisher of *System* and professor at Harvard Business School; and others. The names are listed in U.S. Department of Commerce, *Recent Economic Changes in the United States* (Washington, DC: GPO, 1929), xxii.

79. Alchon, *The Invisible Hand of Planning*, 139.

80. Hoover describes his campaign and election in Hoover, *Memoirs*, vol. 2, *The Cabinet and the Presidency*, 210–15, and gives the election results on p. 210.

81. U.S. Department of Commerce, *Recent Economic Changes in the United States*; William F. Ogburn, review of *Recent Economic Changes*, *American Journal of Sociology* 35:2 (September 1929): 311–13.

82. Anthony J. Badger, *The New Deal: The Depression Years, 1933–1940* (Chicago: Ivan R. Dee, 1989), on Hoover's ideology, 42–43, and public works, 44–45.

83. Galbraith, *The Great Crash, 1929*, 143, for a mocking account of Hoover's meeting.

84. Allen, *Only Yesterday*, 299.

85. Romer, "The Great Crash and the Onset of the Great Depression," 617.

86. See Galbraith, *The Great Crash, 1929*, 147–49.

87. On Hoover's later years, see William E. Leuchtenburg, *Herbert Hoover* (New York: Times Books, 2009); and Richard Norton Smith, *An Uncommon Man: The Triumph of Herbert Hoover* (New York: Simon and Schuster, 1987).

88. Hoover, *The Memoirs of Herbert Hoover*, vol. 3, *The Great Depression, 1929–1941*, 5.

89. Alchon, *The Invisible Hand of Planning*, 151.

90. Hoover, *The Memoirs of Herbert Hoover*, vol. 3, *The Great Depression, 1929–1941*, 4n5.

91. Telegraph, Hoover to Mitchell Dinner Committee, December 15, 1934, box "Post-Presidential Individual Correspondence," folder "Mitchell, Wesley, 1933–1952," Hoover Papers.

92. Simon Kuznets, *National Income and Capital Formation, 1919–1935* (New York: National Bureau of Economic Research, 1937). On the history of GNP, see also Thomas A. Stapleford, *The Cost of Living in America: A Political History of Economic Statistics, 1800–2000* (Cambridge: Cambridge University Press, 2009), 319–24. See also Colin G. Clark, *National Income 1924–31* (London: Macmillan, 1932).

Chapter 6. Visions of the Future

1. On this, see Jeffrey Sklansky, "William Leggett and the Melodrama of the Market," in Michael Zakim and Gary J. Kornblith, *Capitalism Takes Command: The Social Transformation of Nineteenth-Century America* (Chicago: University of Chicago Press, 2012), 199. Sklansky writes of the "invention" of the market and calls it "born of the union of classical economics and popular culture, of Adam Smith and Frankenstein."

2. On this point, and others, I benefited from the advice of David Moss in discussing my case, "Forecasting the Great Depression," Harvard Business School Case (2008), number 9-708-046.

3. Cox, who graduated from Beloit College in Wisconsin, had a long interest in forecasting. In his early thirties, he published a survey of the field with Charles Hardy, *Forecasting Business Conditions* (1927), which provided detailed descriptions of individual agencies. But Cox became obsessed with the question of whether or not the forecasts made by these firms were accurate and returned, rather late in life, to write a dissertation at the University of Chicago on the subject.

4. Cox, *An Appraisal of American Business Forecasts*, 2–3.

5. Givens, "Roger Babson," 266.

6. Cox, *An Appraisal of American Business Forecasts*, 75–93. Cox's method ascribed to each individual forecast two numerical grades. One grade was given for how "correctly" it approximated the direction of anticipated change (whether things were getting better or worse),

as measured against the *New York Times* Annalist Index of Business. A second grade was given for the "boldness" of the forecast, or whether the forecaster correctly predicted the degree of upcoming change rather than just the direction. The two scores were then multiplied to yield an overall "accuracy" score. In total, Cox assigned a total of 4,389 grades for his six forecasters.

7. Cox, *An Appraisal of American Business Forecasts*, 267–68.

8. Cox scored Babson's ability to predict major turning points as "slightly helpful." Babson was graded as follows: 1919 upturn: slightly helpful; 1920 downturn: helpful; 1921 upturn: slightly helpful; 1923 downturn: slightly helpful; 1924 upturn: slightly helpful; 1927 downturn: slightly helpful; and 1927–28 upturn: slightly helpful. Cox rated the Harvard Economic Service's ability to predict turning points as follows: 1920 downturn: helpful; 1921 upturn: helpful; 1923 downturn: misleading; 1924 upturn: slightly helpful; 1927 downturn: neutral; and 1927–28 upturn: slightly helpful. Cox scored Moody's ability to predict major turning points as follows: 1919 upturn: slightly misleading; 1920 downturn: slightly helpful; 1921 upturn: helpful; 1923 downturn: helpful; 1924 upturn: helpful; 1927 downturn: slightly helpful; and 1927–28 upturn: neutral.

9. Cox, *An Appraisal of American Business Forecasts*, 28.

10. Ibid., 42–43.

11. Ibid.

12. These statistics are from N. Gregory Mankiw, "But Have We Learned Enough," *New York Times*, October 26, 2008.

13. McCraw, *American Business since 1920*, 34–35, provides statistics on declines in consumption and investment; Romer, "The Great Crash and the Onset of the Great Depression," 597–624, discusses the decline in purchases of durable goods.

14. Harvard Economic Society, *Weekly Letter*, November 30, 1929, p. 281.

15. Dominguez, Fair, and Shapiro, "Forecasting the Depression," 607.

16. Knight, *Risk, Uncertainty, and Profit*.

17. Letter to Babson from salesman, DLB, April 17, 1940, Special Collections, Papers of Roger W. Babson, Correspondence, box 2, RWB Misc.-Coleman, folder "Babson, Roger W. Miscellaneous Correspondence (iii)," Babson Archives.

18. Cowles, "Can Stock Market Forecasters Forecast?" On Cowles, also see Brown, Goetzmann, and Kumar, "The Dow Theory." He did not reveal the names of the publications he investigated.

19. Cowles's general method was to design hypothetical investments based on forecasts and to track their performance relative to some control variable. In an attempt to assess whether accurate forecasts are possible, he considered four groups of forecasts: financial services forecasts that give specific stock advice, insurance company choices for their own portfolios, stock advice of a popular columnist, and general business condition forecasts. He concluded that forecaster successes cannot be attributed to skill—they were equally likely to be due to luck. Failures, on the other hand, can be attributed to a lack of skill since "the least successful records are worse than what could reasonably be attributed to chance." On average, general forecasters underperformed randomly issued forecasts by 4 percent.

20. *New York Times*, January 1, 1933, p. 7.

21. Cowles, "Can Stock Market Forecasters Forecast?"

22. "Call Lady Luck as Good as Any Stock 'Expert,'" *Chicago Tribune*, January 1, 1933, p. A7; "Forecasters of Market Trend Given Black Eye," *Los Angeles Times*, January 1, 1933, p. 9; "Rates Luck Above Wall St. Experts: Alfred Cowles 3d Asserts That Turn of Card Is Preferable to Following Forecasters," *New York Times*, January 1, 1933, p. 7.

23. "Forecasting Business," *Fortune* 18 (October 1938): 66.

24. Alfred D. Chandler, *Strategy and Structure* (Cambridge, MA: MIT Press, 1962), 232.

25. Peter Passell, "The Model Was Too Rough: Why Economic Forecasting Became a Sideshow," *New York Times*, February 1, 1996, p. D1.

26. Rebecca Hourwich, "Forecasters of the Future Who Flourish in New York," *New York Times*, September 6, 1931, p. 106.

27. *Wall Street Journal*, February 2, 1933.

28. "By-the-Bye," *Wall Street Journal*, September 19, 1933, p. 6.

29. *Wall Street Journal*, August 1, 1938.

30. Benjamin Graham and David L. Dodd, *Security Analysis* (New York: McGraw Hill, 1934) and a more accessible discussion of his ideas, Benjamin Graham, *The Intelligent Investor: A Book of Practical Counsel* (New York: Harper, 1949). For a biography of Graham, see Irving Kehn, *Benjamin Graham: The Father of Financial Analysis* (Charlottesville, VA: Financial Analysts Research Foundation, 1977). Graham also told his own story in *Benjamin Graham: The Memoirs of a Dean of Wall Street* (New York: McGraw-Hill, 1996). See also Ryan Shayan Sepassi, "Intelligent Investing: Investing Practice in the Early Twentieth Century, Benjamin Graham and the Birth of Value Investing" (Harvard University Honors Thesis, 2010).

31. Ralph Nelson Elliott, *Nature's Law—The Secret of the Universe* (New York: R. N. Elliott, 1946); Robert R. Prechter Jr., *The Elliott Wave Theory* (1978; Gainesville, GA: New Classics Library, 1985). See also Eisenstadt, "The Origins and Development of Technical Market Analysis," 335–51. Eisenstadt helpfully summarizes the growth of both technical and fundamental approaches to market analysis.

32. The best guides to Keynes's thinking are Robert Skidelsky's several biographies, including *John Maynard Keynes, 1883–1946: Economist, Philosopher, Statesmen* (New York: Penguin Books, 2005); and *Keynes: Return of the Master* (New York: Public Affairs, 2009). For a brief discussion of Keynes, see Moss, *A Concise Guide to Macroeconomics*, 76.

33. Keynes was an active investor and managed the King's College, Cambridge endowment. See David Chambers and Elroy Dimson, "Keynes the Stock Market Investor" (working paper available through SSRN, 2012), no. 2023011.

34. This book has largely focused on efforts to predict the real economy rather than the stock market. But Fisher's work on the nature of capital and interest was also essential for the development of the Efficient Market Hypothesis by University of Chicago professor Eugene Fama and his colleagues. Fama studied stock prices and found them to be random in sequence; they did not follow past patterns. He and other Efficient Market Hypothesis pioneers believed that markets could not be predicted and asserted that share prices held all relevant information about a stock's value. Stock prices immediately embodied all available information because they reflected the collective wisdom at any given moment of thousands of buyers and sellers. The Efficient Market Hypothesis has had tremendous consequences. Some of the most prominent economists of the twentieth century, most notably Paul Samuelson, have developed this thesis. Burton G. Malkiel popularized the idea in *A Random Walk down Wall Street*, a book so popular it has now gone through ten editions. Though behavioral economists and others have attacked the hypothesis, it remains the dominant approach of investment advisory services, including large mutual fund investment houses. This story is told in Fox, *The Myth of the Rational Market*.

35. On the history of statistics and econometrics in this period, see Morgan, *History of Econometric Ideas*, and David F. Hendry and Mary S. Morgan, eds., *The Foundations of*

Econometric Analysis (Cambridge: Cambridge University Press, 1995). See also Klein, *Statistical Visions in Time*; Theodore M. Porter, *The Rise of Statistical Thinking, 1820–1900* (Princeton: Princeton University Press, 1986); and S. M. Stigler, *The History of Statistics: The Measurement of Uncertainty before 1900* (Cambridge, MA: Harvard University Press, 1986). See Morgan, *History of Econometric Ideas*, 115, for a discussion of Tinbergen's model.

36. Morgan, *History of Econometric Ideas*, 124.

37. Alfred Cowles maintained his interest in forecasting, however. See, for instance, Alfred Cowles III and Associates, *Common-Stock Indexes* (Bloomington, IN: Principia Press, 1938).

38. Hendry and Morgan, *The Foundations of Econometric Analysis*, 1–5. Hendry and Morgan provide a collection of articles on the formative years of econometrics. These highlight some of the people discussed in the book, including Warren Persons, Irving Fisher, and Wesley Mitchell, as well as George Udny Yule, Eugen Slutsky, and Henry L. Moore, who were also essential to the rise of the field of econometrics.

39. One of the few to advance an econometric approach to forecasting prior to this was the agricultural economist Bradford B. Smith. See Terence C. Mills, "Bradford Smith: An Econometrician Decades Ahead of His Time," *Oxford Bulletin of Economics and Statistics* 73 (2010): 276–85; and Bradford B. Smith, "Judging the Forecast for 1929," *Journal of the American Statistical Association* 24 (1929): 94–98.

40. On Klein, see William Breit and Barry T. Hirsch, *Lives of the Laureates*, 4th ed. (Cambridge, MA: 2004), 17–35.

Postscript

1. Nassim Nicholas Taleb, *The Black Swan: The Impact of the Highly Improbable* (New York: Random House, 2007); Nouriel Roubini and Stephen Mihm, *Crisis Economics: A Crash Course in the Future of Finance* (New York: Penguin, 2010); and Andrew Ross Sorkin, *Too Big to Fail: The Inside Story of How Wall Street and Washington Fought to Save the Financial System from Crisis—and Themselves* (New York: Viking, 2009).

2. See Charles R. Geisst, *Wall Street: A History* (Oxford: Oxford University Press, 1999) for information on changes to the Dow Jones Industrial Average.

3. Nathaniel Popper, "Runaway Trades Spread Turmoil across Wall St.," *New York Times*, August 1, 2012, p. A1.

4. "Blame It on Harvard," *Financial Times*, October 21, 2008, p. 1.

5. Charles D. Kirkpatrick and Julie R. Dahlquist, *Technical Analysis: The Complete Resource for Financial Market Technicians* (Upper Saddle River, NJ: Financial Times Press, 2007).

6. "Derivatives," *New York Times* "Times Topics" section online, updated April 18, 2012.

7. Carmen M. Reinhart and Kenneth S. Rogoff, *This Time Is Different: Eight Centuries of Financial Folly* (Princeton: Princeton University Press, 2009).

8. Testimony of Alan Greenspan before the House Committee on Oversight and Government Reform, as quoted in Edmund L. Andrews, "Greenspan Concedes Error on Regulation," *New York Times*, October 24, 2008, p. B1.

9. Gillian Tett, "Lost through Destructive Creation," FT Series: Future of Capitalism, *Financial Times*, March 10, 2009, p. 9.

INDEX

|||||||||||||||||||||||||||||||

Note: Page numbers in italic type indicate figures or illustrations.

ABC chart and curves, 129, 135, 138–41, *139*, 144, 152, 153, 160–62, *161*, 164, 187, 199, 246n41, 250n130, 251n154

academia. *See* universities, economic research in

accuracy, of forecasting, x, 5, 47, 53, 184, 197–98, 201–2, 255n63, 257n6, 258n8, 258n19

Adams, Evangeline, 1–3, 5, 20, 217n1, 217n2

agriculture, 168

Allen, Frederick Lewis, 190

American Baptist Education Society, 170

American Economic Association, 174–75

American Economic Review (journal), 52, 73, 135

American Eugenics Society, 67

American Magazine, 33, 107

American Public Welfare Company (A.P.W. Products Company), 46, 48

American Railway Association, 7

American Relief Administration, 178

American Rolling Mill, 65

American Statistical Association, 174–75

American Telephone and Telegraph, 112, 122, 142

Analyses of Railroad Investments (Moody), 101–2

Analyses Publishing, 100

Anderson, Sherwood, *Winesburg, Ohio*, 10–11

Annals of the American Academy of Political and Social Science (journal), 151

anxiety about the future, 1–2

applied economics, 206

A.P.W. Products Company. *See* American Public Welfare Company

Area Theory, 28–30, 46

Armour, Philip, 26

astrology, 1

atmosphere, as metaphor for economy, 119–20, *121*, 195. *See also* meteorology and weather forecasting

audiences for forecasting, 7–8; Babson's, 31; Fisher's, 52, 74, 79; Harvard Economic Service's, 141–44; Moody's, 95, 109

Auspitz, Rudolf, 56

Austria, 149

Ayres, Leonard, 34, 36

Babson, David L., 38

Babson, Edith, 14, 49

Babson, Grace Knight, 17–20

Babson, Nona Margaret Dougherty, 20

Babson, Paul T., 38, 227n147

Babson, Roger, ix, 3, 9–10, 12–50, *19*, *41*, 150; accuracy and effectiveness of, 197, 258n8; *Actions and Reactions*, 116; audience for, 31; autobiography of, 116; Babsonchart of, 27–32, 39, 43, *47*, 50, 118, 120, 200; in bond industry, 15–16; business and entrepreneurial activities of, 12, 13, 31–32, 37–39, 45–46, 99, 103, 144, 227n147; and business cycles, 22–23, 30, 39, 50; and business information and statistics, 16–20, 22, 31, 34–36, 38–39; character and personality of, 12; childhood and education of, 14–15, 51; and concept of business activity, 22, 193; death of, 50; economic maps of, 122; educational contributions of, 20, 30–31, 37, 39–40, 49; finances of, 33, 35, 48, 50; Fisher compared to, 51–52; and Fisher's Equation of Exchange, 73; and Florida land boom, 40–42; forecasting activities of, 32–33, 36–39, 45, 52, 100, 104; and the Great Crash (1929), 43–48, 53, 80–81, 159, 200; and Harvard Economic Service, 151, 159; Hoover and Mitchell shun, 169, 184; influences on, 6, 15, 23–27; marriages of, 17, 20; Moody and, 99–100, 103, 108, 110, 239n42; moralizing of, 30, 33, 42–43, 48–49, 99; and Newton, 12, 15, 28, 30, 49–50, 220n11; noneconomic interests of, 12, 15, 50, 52, 66;